OUT OF THE ITALIAN NIGHT

OUT OF THE ITALIAN NIGHT

Wellington Bomber Operations 1944−45

MAURICE G. LIHOU

Airlife
CLASSIC

Copyright © 2000 Maurice G. Lihou

First published in the UK in 1992 by Air Research Publications as *It's Dicey Flying Wimpys*
Re-published in 2000 by the Pentland Press Ltd

This edition published 2003
by Airlife Publishing Ltd

British Cataloguing-in-Publication Data
 A catalogue record for this book
 is available from the British Library

ISBN 1 84037 405 5

Typeset by Phoenix Typesetting, Burley-in-Wharfedale, West Yorkshire
Printed in England by St Edmundsbury Press Ltd, Bury St Edmunds, Suffolk.

Distributed in North America by
STACKPOLE BOOKS
5067 Ritter Road, Mechanicsburg, PA 17055
www.stackpolebooks.com

For a complete catalogue of all Airlife titles please contact:

Airlife Publishing Ltd
101 Longden Road, Shrewsbury, SY3 9EB, England
E-mail: sales@airlifebooks.com
Website: www.airlifebooks.com

Dedication

To
CONNIE, who else?

our children Maureen and Peter, our grandchildren
Naomi, Geoffrey, Natalie, Georgina, Ben, Sam and Josh

And the aircrews of 205 Group based in Italy from 1943 to 1945

Now here's Sergeant Lihou, he's on ops tonight,
Swinging down the runway in someone else's kite.
He'll shoot the shit when he gets back,
Of how he bombed through ten tenths flak.
It's dicey flying Wimpys around Italian skies.

CONTENTS

ACKNOWLEDGEMENTS

Without the skill, efficiency and companionship of my two crews, the ground crews and other friends in the RAF, I would not have been able to write this story. They made it possible. Without the support of family and friends I would have given up when trying to get it published. Without the help of people in the world of research and publishing, I would not have been able to experience a marvellous and fascinating new phase in my life: a phase of life I would have missed, one that has been crammed with discovery, revelation, interest, goodwill, unselfish help and personal enjoyment.

Among such people are Flying Officer D.A. Riggs, Sergeant P. Griffiths, Sergeant C.L. Ardiel, Sergeant G.N. Blyth, Sergeant J. McCabe, Flight Sergeant G. Blackstone, Flight Sergeant F. Edwards, Sergeant A. Oakes, Sergeant Bobby Budgett, Sergeant Ken Fairclough, Sergeant J. Seddon. If I have attributed to them things, sayings or happenings which may not be correct, I apologise – forty-eight years is a long time to remember everything and to get the facts right. My nephew Raymond (Mike) Conroy who showed me how to use the word processor on his computer, to get started. His mother Pauline Conroy who with my daughter Maureen Moss helped with the early editing. The staff of the Imperial War Museum, RAF Museum Hendon and the Photo Library at Keele University. Local researchers Mick Peters and John Goodwin. Tony Sebire (who spent hours photocopying my manuscript), photographer Brian Green who did an excellent job in copying my forty-eight-year-old snaps and Ralph le Page for his help in preparing the map. A thank you to my former publisher, Simon Parry, and to John Foreman for the excellent research into the 205 Group details.

Another man whom I have never met, but whose words spoken on the telephone continually encouraged me to 'write it – even if it is never published – it is something for your grandchildren' is Roy Conyers Nesbit. It is he who did the research at the Public Record Office, Kew, on my operations and who sent me the copies of documents with my own name on them – documents which I never knew existed. He has never failed to be unselfishly helpful and encouraging.

There are many more, not least airmen who are no longer with us, to whom I think the following says it all:

'To live in the hearts of those left behind is not to die.'

The Author

When Maurice Lihou joined aircrew he, like many others, did not know what he was letting himself in for. He tells his story as 'Lee', a young, newly married pilot, who found himself flying into battle in the much revered Wellington bomber known within the RAF as the 'Wimpy'. They were operating in 205 Group from the captured air bases around Foggia in Italy during 1944/45.

The conditions in which the air and ground crews lived were appalling. They lived in rotting desert tents – known as canvas-covered holes in the ground – through the cold, snow, ice, rain, mud and floods in the winter and the heat, dust, and flies of the summer. Their diet of dehydrated oily-tasting food, hard tack and heavily chlorinated tea and water did nothing to enhance their living standards or improve their often acquired stomach upsets.

With little or no navigational aids, the aircrew attacked targets in support of the armies advancing through Italy. They bombed communication centres and oil refineries in the Balkans and laid mines in the River Danube. They attacked airfields near Vienna and staggered over the Alps to Munich. Often they were sent to attack these targets in the most atrocious weather conditions or, in contrast, on brilliant moonlit nights. Unescorted, they were an enemy nightfighter's dream, being clearly visible in almost daylight conditions.

The storyline is unique and makes a refreshing change from umpteen other accounts of the air war in World War Two.

Lee tells his story in such a way that it has often been described as fascinating, enthralling, well written and very readable. Nevertheless, in doing so, he has been able to combine a historical record of events – that hitherto seems to have been passed over – in a very human and personal manner, with a compelling story that, according to historians and reviewers, had to be told.

Like all good stories it ends with a twist in the tail when, having survived forty-nine dangerous missions, getting lost, being struck by lightning, combating searchlights, fighters and flak, his flying career is brought to an abrupt and unexpected end.

Since the first edition came out in 1992, Maurice Lihou has received many letters and comments, congratulating and thanking him for writing his story.

Here are some of them.

'Besides the adventure, I did enjoy the touches of humour and romance running through it.'

'One of the best war stories I have read and I have thirty such books in my library.'

'Have read it twice already and will probably read it again and again.'

'It is absolutely fascinating and I strongly recommend it.'

'I started reading it at Heathrow and couldn't put it down until I reached the West Coast of America.'

'A candid and moving account.'

'Maurice Lihou is to be congratulated on producing such factual and nostalgic reading.'

Foreword

It is all a very long time ago now, but the demand for a reprint of this book is but one small reminder of how overwhelming is the fascination of a later generation for the firsthand accounts of a world at war.

Maurice Lihou is a little greyer now, and his boyish curls are a little less distinctive, but the twinkling eyes are still as vivid as his spellbinding recollections as a wartime bomber pilot.

They were clearly a remarkable breed of men, with a tenacious and enduring courage at which we can only marvel. Night in, night out, week after week, year after year, they thundered into the night sky with no lights, no beacons, no radio navigation aids, in fact nothing but their own cool reckoning of where hours of difficult flying, bad weather, enemy attack and unreliable instruments had taken them. Bombing runs had to be steady, accurate and unflinching, all in a blaze of flak and against heavy fighter defence, and then somehow they had to find their way many hundreds of miles back to base. Very many never made it.

Maurice was clearly a giant amongst giants. He seems never to have allowed his extraordinary patience and calm to have been rattled one iota (he hasn't changed) and he and his crew made it home to the very end. His book is a great tribute to his own courage and to that of a magnificent breed of men.

John Coward

His Excellency Vice-Admiral Sir John Coward KCB DSO
Lieutenant-Governor of The Bailiwick of Guernsey October 1994–April 2000

CHAPTER ONE

ON THE WAY

I**T was a cold night, the night of 21 February 1944, when the crew of
Wellington Bomber, Mark X, V for Victor, LP146, left Portreath in
Cornwall, bound for Rabat Sale in North Africa.

The pilot, whose name was Lee, was a young Royal Air Force sergeant
aged twenty-three who had just completed his Operational Flying
Training on 'Wimpys', as the Wellington bombers were so fondly called.
This was a brand-new Wimpy with which he had been entrusted, to take,
as far as he knew, to North Africa. He had no idea of what was to happen
after that. It was capable of flying at 255 mph at 14,500 feet, with a service
ceiling of 18,250 feet. It was armed with six .303 Browning guns, and had
a range of 1,325 miles with a bomb load of 4,500 pounds.

Sitting beside him in the co-pilot's seat was the bomb aimer in his role
of second pilot. They had exhausted their conversation and sat there in
silence, each with his own thoughts, neither wishing to start talking again
because of the lateness of the hour. It was early morning, just after
midnight – far too early for polite chit chat!

They had left Portreath a couple of hours ago and, after thundering
down the runway with their extra load of fuel on board, had climbed
quickly through dense cloud to 10,000 feet, the height given at their
briefing as the most economical at which to cruise in order to conserve
fuel. Levelling out, Lee felt his inexperience very keenly, and began to
be concerned about the task that lay ahead; ferrying a brand-new aircraft
to North Africa seemed to be an awesome responsibility. The only long
journey they had made previously was during operational training: a
cross-country trip from Lossiemouth in Scotland to the Humber in
Lincolnshire. That had been on a lovely starlit night, with clear visibility.
Not like tonight with 10/10ths cloud below and the occasional break
above!

The lateness of the hour, and worrying if he would be able to cope with
such a long journey, made him feel apprehensive. If he wandered off
course by as little as half a degree to the west they would miss Africa
altogether. God knows where they would end up – in the middle of
the Atlantic, he supposed. One thing was for sure – he must keep awake,
since they would be flying all night, due to arrive about half-past six in
the morning.

He wished he had remembered to look at the aircraft log to see how many flying hours this new plane had flown. He hoped now that it had been well air-tested; he didn't relish the thought of engine failure. What else had he forgotten? Thank goodness he had remembered to switch on his oxygen and had given the rest of the crew instructions to switch on theirs. He felt a brief glow of satisfaction for having remembered to do this, because they had not often flown at that height during their training, and switching on oxygen was something he had not been accustomed to doing. It was only a small thing to remember, but it was important, because, having remembered it, he could do with that little boost to his confidence. He would have hated it if one of the crew had cause to remind him, trying so hard as he was to establish his position as captain of the aircraft.

His mind started to wander over the lectures they had received during training about the importance of switching on the oxygen – how it had been very firmly stressed and emphasised to all the crew that failure at 10,000 feet and above to have an adequate supply of oxygen would give them a false sense of wellbeing. This, he remembered, was owing to the air at that height being less dense than the air at ground level, with a subsequent decrease in the total barometric pressure with higher altitudes. Thus the higher they went, the more harmful the lack of oxygen (and, of course, other gases) became. He recalled being told that it was so serious that, above 20,000, feet, most people lost consciousness within a short time and death followed shortly thereafter. It was unlikely, he mused, that the Wimpy would get to that height, but it did have a ceiling of 18,250 feet, and at 15,000 to 18,000 feet the first effects on the brain became marked.

He reflected upon how the Flight Sergeant from the medical section, who had been their first aid instructor at Advanced Flying Training in Canada, had strongly impressed upon them these effects: that it would make them light-headed, resulting in a lessening of their judgement and their ability to think clearly. This, in turn, would make them prone to making errors, thus fouling up their chances of survival. He had taken a great delight in telling them that lack of oxygen would also have the effect of decreasing their vision and hearing, particularly at night. It would make them clumsy and sluggish and, more importantly, lack any realisation of danger. In other words, it could make them feel drunk! But not 'happy drunk', he had added fiendishly when they had all burst out laughing at the thought, not if a fighter was on their tail!

That Flight Sergeant had been a bit of a pervert in his first aid lectures, with all his talk about VD, crashed aircraft and the gory details of blood, broken bones and bodies with limbs hanging off. No wonder some of the blokes had fainted during his so-called lectures. But it did have its lighter moments, like the time they were told about the expansion of body gases in the stomach and intestines occurring as the atmospheric pressure decreased, and the way to get rid of the stomach pain which would occur was to belch and fart. He smiled at the thought. Funny how talk of farting always raised a laugh amongst some of the chaps. But never mind all that now. Thank goodness he had remembered. The golden rule was: Always judge your need for oxygen by the altimeter. *Never* wait for the symptoms. He had better keep that in mind. Meanwhile he should just check that they have got their masks on OK.

After checking by intercom that all the crew had their oxygen masks on and they were all working satisfactorily, Lee switched in 'George', the automatic pilot, and sat back quietly listening to the synchronised drone of the twin engines. Now, although feeling reasonably satisfied at the way things were going, he kept looking anxiously through the cockpit window at the clouds ahead for any sign of them thickening. The flight was smooth except for the very occasional bumpy passage when they flew through the tops of mountain-high cumulus cloud. Above them the stars were blotted out by another layer of stratus cloud. Earlier, however, through a break in the stratus, the navigator had gone into the astrodome with his sextant and had managed to obtain a fix from the stars, enabling him to check their position and confirm they were flying on course.

His crew consisted of himself and four other men. His navigator was a Flying Officer in the Royal Canadian Air Force nicknamed Riggy. He was a small, slight man, with a very young face belying his twenty-five years. He had been a lecturer in mathematics before joining up, and this had helped him considerably when doing his navigation course, enabling him to graduate with excellent grades. By nature a fun man, he was the last person in the world one would have thought of being an officer. He had a very limited respect for service discipline, in spite of his rank, and was always looking for a way to show his contempt for it. His favourite expression of anything which came anywhere near service discipline, was 'Bullshit'.

Len, the bomb aimer, was another Canadian. A sergeant in the RCAF, he had been a storeman in a grain elevator in Vancouver before volunteering. Len had only just got married before he left Canada, and was waiting for news of his first baby. Sparks, the wireless operator, was a sergeant in the RAF. He had been out of work when the war started. A Yorkshireman who kept things close to his chest, he didn't seem to want to make new friends and was very reluctant to break up or lose old friendships. Since they had met, he seemed to prefer the company of his old wireless operator friends. Very interested in weight lifting and keeping himself fit, he had a very good physique.

Jock, the youngest member, was also a sergeant in the RAF. Not yet nineteen he was small in stature but not in heart. He, as his nickname implied, came from the highlands of Scotland. Extremely shy, he had worked with a farmer in civilian life. He felt his age difference very much, and seemed to be in awe of the other members of the crew.

After the usual initial tension of take-off, Riggy had reported that the Very light pistol had been loaded with the colours of the day, the navigation lights had been switched off and that the IFF (Identification Friend or Foe) system, had been switched on. The latter, an essential part of the radar defence system, was an electronic instrument which sent back to the ground forces a signal indicating the Wimpy as a friendly aircraft. The preparation for emergency and defence flying now completed, Riggy had settled down at his navigation desk revising wind speeds and direction, working out a new course to steer by, the estimated time of arrival (ETA), and filling out his log.

Sparks was in his wireless operator's cabin and, after carrying out his routine of in-flight checks, was probably listening to music between listening out on the flight frequency. He would be trying to obtain a bearing on broadcasting stations if he could find them, and more importantly, identify them, observing at the same time the strict W/T silence imposed upon all operational crews. When not at his radio his other job was to be 'lookout', looking out through the astrodome which was situated halfway along the top of the fuselage, quite near to his wireless cabin.

Jock was cramped up in his rear gunner's 'office' (turret), watching the clouds vanishing in the distance. The slipstream was roaring past his office, which was situated in the rear of the fuselage, below the high tail fin, and as usual wobbled about like a puppet on a string whenever they hit a bumpy patch. This effect of responding to the bumps was a recognised feature of the flexible construction of the Wimpy. It had been affectionately described as the Wimpy 'wagging its tail', because it was so pleased with its unique geodetic construction, the brainchild of its inventor Barnes Wallis. Jock's was a lonely life which did not merit the name 'Tail End' or 'Arse End Charlie', an unflattering description imposed on all rear gunners. He also had completed his in-flight checks, and as soon as they had levelled out and he had put on his oxygen mask, he had asked Lee if he could test his four Browning guns. They had worked satisfactorily, which pleased him immensely. He had not relished the thought of having to sort out any problems and probably having to strip down the guns while cramped up in his turret!

Whilst everything behind the cockpit was being checked, Lee and Len had been going through their in-flight cockpit checks. Finally Lee suggested to Len that he should go into the front turret and test those Browning guns also. This test completed, Len had now returned to the cockpit and was sitting beside him. And so it was that with their immediate duties completed, the crew had now settled down and were at action stations on the alert, looking out for long-range German fighters.

The crew had met for the first time in October 1943, at the Operational

Training Unit (OTU) based at Lossiemouth in Scotland. Here, shortly after they had arrived from their individual training units, they had been documented, received yet another medical and allocated billets. A few days later they had been assembled in a hangar, with all of the other newly arrived aircrews to form up into individual crew units in order for the whole of the new intake to commence operational training. This was to be very comprehensive and highly intensive, attending classes and lectures on specially designed courses, both theory and practical, on how to fly an aircraft and to operate under battle conditions in wartime. Lee and his friends, Bobby and Ken, from the pilots' conversion course they had just completed, had looked forward in eager anticipation to meeting their individual crew members, wondering how they were going to be allocated and on what basis members would be chosen to team up with each other.

The intake had come from many areas, having been trained in different parts of the Commonwealth and the United States. They consisted of many different nationalities – British, Canadian, Australian, South African – all with a varying degree of skills and backgrounds. Half were commissioned officers and half were sergeants. All, however, had one thing in common: they had reached a proficiency that had entitled them to wear a brevet, the wings of their trade, as either a pilot, navigator, wireless operator, bomb aimer or gunner.

Now had come the time for them to be grouped together as separate bomber crews, to be trained and moulded into an effective and efficient fighting unit. How, thought Lee as he stood half-listening to the speech of welcome from the Stationmaster (the RAF slang for the Commanding Officer), are they going to sort this lot out?

He was soon to find out. 'And now will you break off into groups and sort yourselves out into crews,' came the pronouncement from the CO. Lee didn't know what he had expected, but it had never occurred to him it would be like that. He and his pals looked at each other in astonishment. He thought to himself, 'What a bloody stupid way to go about an important job like crewing up.'

Turning to Bobby and Ken he said, 'What do you think of that?'

'Not much,' replied Bobby, a young, fair, almost blond-haired sergeant from Berkshire, normally a quiet spoken, serious, non-argumentative sort of a chap. 'How the hell do they expect us to know who would be suitable to fly together?'

'Looks like another bloody Fred Carno's to me,' said Ken, a tall dark-haired Yorkshireman. 'How can we possibly know who's who . . . and who to choose . . . or if they will get on with each other?' This question voicing something which they were all concerned about. 'Fancy going on ops with someone you didn't get along with.'

Lee felt let down. What a way to start a training course; this wasn't a very scientific or professional way to allocate crews. It certainly did not fit in with the standard of training that he had so far received. And so with his two friends he had just stood there wondering what to do and how to go about it. It was when a group of three commissioned RCAF officers, all navigators, had come over to their group and introduced themselves that things finally got under way for them. Riggy and Lee had started talking to each other – they seemed to get on well and decided they would team up. Together they started to look out for other members to make up their crew. His friends did the same.

They walked over to a group of wireless operators, where some were actively trying to get organised whilst others were not anxious to push themselves forward. Sparks was one of them; they teamed up and the procedure started all over again looking for a bomb aimer and rear gunner.

Len seemed to fit in naturally, but Jock was standing there on his own. His apparent shyness had excluded him from being offered a place in a crew. Lee and the others looked at each other and, without a word being spoken, nodded in agreement. Lee asked Jock if he would like to join them. Lee had his crew.

Having at last sorted themselves out, the crews broke off and went for a cup of tea or a pint to try to establish some sort of *esprit de corps* amongst themselves. It was much later, at the end of their training, in fact, whilst waiting to find out to what squadrons they were going to be posted, that this happened. Lee, Ken and Bobby were in the mess discussing over a pint the way the crew selection had been done.

'It was amazing that the hit and miss method worked out!'

'Well, these boffin RAF psychologists ought to know what they are doing.'

'Yeah, they know from experience that the majority of crews stay together.'

'They certainly know how to build up a team with a spirit of comradeship.'

'Got to give them credit, bloody marvellous how they got the crews all working together from scratch.'

'Bet a lot of them will stay mates when this is all over.'

Sinking another pint, Ken calmly remarked, 'I know bloody well that was the only way they could go about it.' He ducked as, amidst howls of derision, the others jumped on him.

Their intensive training had kept them busy until the end of December. They had all gone off on either Christmas or New Year's leave. A couple of weeks after their return, their posting had been announced: some of the intake, including Lee's crew and those of his two pals Bobby and Ken, had been posted to Moreton-in-Marsh on a special job. They were delighted that they were staying together. This special job had turned out to be flying over the Atlantic on fuel consumption exercises as training for a forthcoming flight to North Africa to ferry aircraft and be replacement crews for the Mediterranean and Far Eastern theatres of war.

The war in the Mediterranean area had escalated with the victorious Eighth Army and the American Fifth Army's invasion of Sicily in July, and the overthrow of Mussolini. This was followed by the invasion of the Italian mainland in September, and in October Naples had fallen. The Eighth Army, under Montgomery, had swept up the Adriatic Coast and had captured the airfields at Foggia. The Americans, under General Mark Clark, had found the German army under Kesselring determined to hold their positions after the fall of Naples, and the battle on the East Coast had become bogged down in the mud over the last five months. Cassino was a stumbling block and proving extremely difficult to get past.

Last month the landings at Anzio had not moved forward as quickly as had been hoped, and the Americans were trapped there like, as Churchill had put it, a stranded whale. The *Wehrmacht* were fighting a stubborn battle on every inch of Italian soil. If the Allies were to pursue the enemy up the boot of Italy and into Germany itself, aircraft were desperately needed there to destroy the German supply lines and lines of communication. These lines had to be broken and the forces holding them destroyed. Action was not moving quite so fast in the Far East, but forces out there were also being built up considerably.

The night of 21 February, being so dark with heavy cloud, was, in the opinion of the briefing officer in the preflight briefing, a good omen. It meant that the long-range German fighters, Junkers Ju 88Cs based in France, which had a reputation for shooting down the individual unescorted Wimpys, would have difficulty in finding them as they flew past the French coast.

The route they were to follow was the infamous 'Biscay Route' nicknamed 'Junkers Alley', which had proved so hazardous for many earlier Wellington crews ferrying aircraft to Gibraltar, the refuelling stopover for the African Desert.

Bomb-bays filled with extra fuel tanks, they had taken off into that dark unknown just before midnight, each wondering if they would ever see England again. Flying at 10,000 feet, the cloud tops became higher and more numerous. Lee took off the autopilot as the cloud became denser, and it wasn't very long before he noticed that ice was starting to appear on the leading edge of the wings; this was in spite of the fact that the leading edges had been smothered with the brown anti-icing gunge before they had left Portreath. Seeing this, he had a slight feeling of panic. He recalled stories he had heard of Wimpys at Lossie icing up, stalling and crashing into the sea.

Seeking respite, he took the aircraft down to 5,000 feet and was fortunate to find a slot between two layers of cloud. Skimming over the tops

Lee with his brand-new wings in Toronto after the 'Wings Parade'.

of the base clouds and flying just under the bottoms of the upper ones made it a very bumpy flight, so much so that it was impossible to bring in George, the autopilot, again. It was freezing in the cockpit. The Wellington Mark Xs which were being flown out as replacements were supposedly reputed to have a very good heating system, but either Lee couldn't work it properly or this one wasn't as good as it was cracked up to be. He was freezing. He felt his concentration turning to anxiety as he kept an eagle eye on the ice still forming and slowly building up on the wings. He was beginning to get frightened and his mind started to wander back to the momentous events that had happened to him a few months earlier.

In October of the previous year he had joined the OTU from the Advanced Flying Unit, which also incorporated a Blind Approach Training School. Here he had had to convert, much to his annoyance, from being a pilot on single-engined aircraft, Harvards, to becoming a pilot on multi-engined aircraft, Oxfords, having successfully obtained his 'wings' to become a fighter pilot in Canada that May. He would never forget that day when they had marched through a howling blizzard to the hangar at Camp Borden in Ontario, where the Wings Parade was being held for the presentation ceremony. Eyes smarting, ears and cheeks raw with the wind, the bottoms of their trousers wet with snow, they had marched, or rather sloshed, through about two feet of snow to reach the hangar. The band had struck up the Royal Air Force March as the British contingent marched in. He had lifted his head in pride and had promptly got a neck-full of snow which had accumulated on his bent head and was suddenly released down his back. He smiled to himself at the thought.

After removing their greatcoats, drying their faces (and, in his case, his neck, with handkerchiefs), shaking the snow off their boots and trousers, they had lined up in alphabetical order in front of a platform to receive the coveted wings – wings which he, like so many others, had worked so hard for over the previous two years. The official speeches over, the name of each successful cadet was called out. Each man, buttons shining and white belts Blancoed, had smartly turned, marched up on to the platform, saluted and, amidst applause from the assembly, received his hard-won brevet. His relatives had been there, distant cousins on his mother's side, coming all the way up from Hamilton to Camp Borden to share with him the magical moment. Then, after his name was called, he had marched up on to the platform, his heart bursting with pride, to have the pilot's brevet pinned on his chest by the Air Chief Marshal, Flying Training Command.

What a moment to treasure that had been. He remembered the time he had first gone solo. The thrill of taking off on his own, and the noise of the wind rushing past him in the open cockpit of the Tiger Moth trainer. How he had ground-looped on landing and thought that he had cocked up his chances. How he had got lost during a sudden blizzard on

Pilot training in Harvards at Camp Borden in Canada.

Lee's final destination: a Wimpy.

a solo cross-country in a Harvard. He had only just managed to get back safely by following the railway lines, the only things that had stood out in the snow on the ground. Otherwise, he mused to himself, he could have been harvested by the Great Reaper at that time and he wouldn't be here now. How he had struggled with the delicate controls of the Link Trainer; God, he had only just managed to scrape through that exercise on his test. But he could fly: his take-offs and landings were good, so were his aerobatics, and he was reasonably sound on radio, airframes, navigation, aero engines, meteorology, astronavigation, signalling and instrument flying.

And to think that that event had nearly not taken place because a group of Aussies the night before made a bloody great snowball and had rolled it into the hangar right in the middle of the parade section. It must have measured at least six feet across and had frozen on the concrete floor. Fortunately, it had been noticed in time for it to be removed, causing much grumbling among the poor ground crew whose job it had been to remove it. That day had been bitterly cold. When they had got up in the morning the sun was shining, but when he had poked his nose outside the door for a breath of fresh air, the wind was biting, almost taking his breath away; his eyebrows, the corners of his eyes, mouth and his nostrils had iced up.

He snapped out of his thoughts. What about the ice outside? He looked out of his cockpit window. There it was again, ice still slowly forming on the wings. Good grief. Ice, snow, blizzards, what a bastard of a night. How he longed for sunny days. But now the aircraft's wings were icing up and it looked as if he was going to end up in that dark, sodden, cold, wet fore-boding sea below, taking his poor bloody crew with him. He refused to think about it any more; he would just fly on and hope for the best and pray that it didn't get any worse. He was cold and fed up with the bloody stuff. He switched his thoughts back.

His thoughts then wandered to the day he had met Connie. He had met her shortly after the crewing-up exercise when the crew, as a whole, had been instructed to go to the stores to be kitted up for their operational flying kits. Feeling good, they had had a reasonably successful day and had now to go to another section to receive their oxygen masks. Behind the counter was a very attractive WAAF sergeant, the first senior NCO in the WAAFs that Lee had ever had dealings with.

'What do you boys want?' asked the very attractive brunette sergeant.

'Oxygen masks, Sarge,' nudge, nudge, chuckle, chuckle, they replied in unison with broad grins over their faces.

'Have you got your forms FC674b?' she replied, not at all amused.

'What forms?' said Lee. 'That's the first we've heard of them, and we've got the rest of our kit without them.'

'Nothing to do with me. You should have forms signed by your officer before we can give out your kit.'

'What a load of bullshit. We have to report for flying duty in a few moments and we can't go without our masks,' argued Lee.

'Too bad,' said the attractive woman who was fast becoming an officious bitch. 'Get your forms and you can have them, but be quick, as we are running out of stock.'

The now very much subdued crew had gone back, grumbling about the bullshit, bloody WAAFs and wondering if they would ever win a war with that sort of attitude.

The following Sunday the Sergeants' Mess put on a regular dance with the other ranks of the WAAF invited. Lee and another pilot called Ian, with whom he had been billeted when they had arrived at Lossiemouth, decided to go together and to meet up with their new crews there. After polishing the buttons on their tunics, spit and polishing their non-regulation shoes and Brylcreaming their hair, they had donned their best blues and had set off smiling and confident to explore the local WAAF talent. The attractive WAAF sergeant from the stores was there with a WAAF corporal. Having blotted his copybook over the oxygen masks affair, Lee had said to Ian, 'Bet you a pint I'll get the WAAF sergeant to dance with me.'

'You're on,' said Ian. 'You don't stand a cat in hell's chance after the fuss you made over the oxygen masks.'

Lee went over to the bar to buy a couple of pints for himself and Ian.

On the way over he stopped at the table where the two girls were sitting. 'By God she's pretty,' Lee thought to himself as he spoke to the sergeant. 'Any chance of the next dance, Sarge?' he said.

'Sorry, it's booked,' came the almost curt, automatic reply, and the sergeant carried on talking to her friend.

Lee was shaken but, not to be outdone, he started to walk towards the bar. 'Can I get you a drink?' he called to the girls, looking over his shoulder. A stony stare was the only reply he received. Undaunted, Lee flashed a smile and asked, 'Later, maybe?'

Pushing his way back from the crowded bar he made his way to the table where Ian was sitting, he placed the two pints of beer on the table and sat down in the chair which Ian had saved for him.

It was some moments before Ian spoke. 'How did you get on?' he asked.

'All right,' replied Lee. 'She's a smasher.'

'Is that my free pint?' queried Ian.

'Is it hell as like! Give me a chance, the night is still young,' replied Lee. 'You're still on for the next shout.'

They were sitting a few tables away, but Lee could not keep his eyes off the WAAF sergeant. By goodness, she was pretty, and so attractive, her dark hair rolled up above her forehead and flowing down, gently rolling just above her shoulders. Her make-up was flawless. She reminded him of the lady who came on at the beginning of the Gainsborough Pictures, not a bit unlike Margaret Lockwood. He was longing to get to know her better to find out who she was. She was looking over. He tried another smile, and she laughed, turning her head away and started talking to her friend. Then she looked up again.

Did he notice they were both looking at him now and talking? And did he notice a slight smile of encouragement? By this time other aircrew had joined his table and attention was drawn to a French airman who was standing at the bar; it looked as if he was eating a pint glass. 'Look at that Free French bloke, Ian, he's eating a pint glass.'

'So he is, swallowing it too! God only knows what that is going to do to his guts. Must be bloody mad.'

The noise in the mess was getting louder and louder as the drinks began to take effect. They were fascinated by the Frenchman who appeared to be on his own. Suddenly, without a word to anyone, the Frenchman took off his jacket and shirt and started swinging monkey-fashion across the beams supporting the roof, banging his chest with a free hand and giving Tarzan-like shouts. 'Now we've seen it all,' said Lee.

'Guess he's trying to work his ticket,' commented Ian.

Lee looked back across the room to where the two girls had been sitting, but they had gone. He guessed that they had gone into the dance. 'Coming into the dance, Ian?'

'No, you go in. I'll get in another pint.' Lee sauntered across to the dance room.

The dance room was an extension to the mess, opened up by large concertina-type folding doors. The band was playing an excuse-me quickstep and he spotted the WAAF sergeant dancing with an Army Regimental sergeant-major.

Lee butted in. 'Excuse me,' and took her in his arms. She was as light as a feather and her body was firm and supple. He tried the line that had never failed him in the past.

'Gee, you're pretty. Do you know you're the prettiest girl in the room?'

'I know,' came the quick and smiling retort.

The reply came as a shock. Usually it was met with a blush of demure silence, which left him in control to carry on with another flattering remark, but now he didn't know what to say. He was floored. They continued to dance in silence. Then Lee asked, 'Did you see the Frenchman?'

'Yes, he does that every week,' had come the 'You're new here' no-nonsense reply.

'Can I have the next dance?' asked Lee when the music stopped, fully expecting a refusal. But no, she nodded in consent. He could hardly contain himself. He dared not give himself away by speaking. They stayed arm in arm on the floor together. Lee was thrilled at the nearness of her. He pressed as close as he dared. He touched her hand. She smiled up at him. He was captivated.

The next dance was a tango. A WAAF who had removed her jacket got up on the stage and started to sing 'Jealousy'. Lee and Connie joined in singing it together as they danced and, as they danced, they laughed in pleasure, ostensibly at the efforts of the WAAF up on the stage. They stayed together dancing and laughing, relaxed in the company of each other, and as the last waltz was being played they clung tightly to each other, Connie resting her head on his shoulder. He could smell the perfume in her hair; it felt like there was no one else in the room.

Just as the dance was ending, Lee quickly asked her if he could see her again and, to his great joy, the answer was – Yes! They agreed to meet the next evening. Chatting and laughing they made their way back to where her friend was waiting. The ice had been broken.

Lee's thoughts were interrupted; the plane was becoming sluggish. He looked at the wings, and saw that the icing was getting worse. He realised it was the continual 'drum drum' of the ice flying off the prop tips and banging against the fuselage that had interrupted his thoughts; his own built-in danger alert system had brought him back to reality.

He had better do something pretty damn quickly. He had two choices: get above the clouds or below them. He opted for going down where the air should be warmer, particularly as they were flying south. 'I'm taking her down, Riggy,' he said over the intercom. 'This icing is getting bad.'

There was no comment from Riggy. Slowly he started to descend in the pitch black unfriendly cloud. Luckily they were over the sea. He levelled off at 2,000 feet, but still the icing persisted. Lee was longing to get back to the comfort of his thoughts, but the nagging fear of that bloody ice took over. 'Sorry, Riggy, but it's still there,' he called over the intercom. 'I'm going down again.'

'OK, Skipper,' came the reply. 'I'll give you a new course to steer when we are out of it.' If we ever get out of it, thought Lee.

Down he went and he broke cloud at 800 feet. It was pouring with rain and sleet, something he hadn't bargained for, and the aircraft was bouncing about like a cork on the open sea, but still the ice persisted. There was only one other option left now: he would have to climb through it and try to get above the clouds. What a bloody mess up!

Lee had previously made up his mind, if ever a decision had to be made which would effect their well-being, he would always bring the crew into that decision-making, but as captain he would have the final say. He explained the position over the intercom. 'I am going to try to climb above this mess, lads,' said Lee. 'Any idea of the height of the clouds, Riggy?'

'No, Lee,' came the reply. 'Met didn't mention this lot at all.'

'Christ, that's just what we need,' exclaimed Lee. 'Go up into the astrodome, Sparks, and keep an eye on the tail plane and wings from there.'

He had no idea of what good that would do, but it sounded reassuring and as if he was in control of the situation. 'Better put your oxygen masks back on if you have taken them off, and keep them on,' he commanded. 'How are you back there, Jock?' he asked the rear gunner.

'Cold,' came the brief and complete answer.

'What about some coffee, Len?' he asked his bomb aimer.

'Good idea,' came a shout from all.

Opening up both throttles as far as he dared, he started to climb. How he wished he knew more about carburettor icing; anyway, no time to think about that now. Better keep his eyes on the artificial horizon to make sure he was keeping straight and level as they were climbing. The power of the engines as they responded to his hand on the throttles made him feel more confident. His fear was ebbing; the decisions had been made and now it was in the lap of the Gods. Fate was being challenged. If they were lucky they might have time to climb out of it before the extra weight caused the Wimpy to stall and plunge them into the sea below. But better to try that than to sit there and let it happen anyway.

He felt pleased with himself. This must have been the most important decision he had made in his life. The lives of the crew and the fate of this very valuable aircraft and the job it was being sent out to do now hung on his ability, and more importantly his luck, to get out of the trouble they were in. Little did he realise it at the time, but that was to be a moment that was to influence him for the rest of his life. He had discovered the fact that fear feeds on indecision and it helps a hell of a lot if you are positive and know what you are doing.

Keeping a watchful eye on his altimeter, he noted the steady rate of climb as slowly but surely the aircraft began to climb. I hope we are not climbing into more trouble, he thought to himself. Would he be able to climb out of this ghastly weather, before it stalled? Anxiously he watched his airspeed and engine revs as his eyes darted across the instrument panel. It was pitch black outside, and after that temporary feeling of confidence he felt his eyes getting tired through watching the dimmed green lights of the panel in front of him, and through peering out into the unremitting blackness. God, how he wished it was over.

They reached eleven thousand feet and – good – the icing was getting no worse. He carried on climbing, and he noted that the engines didn't feel so powerful now. Fourteen thousand feet and – were they through it?

Conditions outside seemed to be much more settled now. Was it possible that there in the blackness he could discern the horizon? The Wimpy V for Victor was wallowing, twitching and rattling as if to say 'you are pushing me too far.' He decided to level out and give it a try. 'Levelling out at fourteen and a half thousand, Riggy,' he called down the intercom to his navigator.

'OK, Lee, new course to steer coming up in a moment.'

Lee sat there, relieved. Stars, those lovely friendly stars, were beginning to faintly peep through. The ice was slowly dispersing, and it was getting warmer outside. They had made it. How pleased all those people who had made V for Victor would be if they knew that their aeroplane was safe. There would be no 'reported missing' letters from this trip so far, after all.

A quarter of an hour later a shout came from Sparks in the astrodome. 'Red light on the port side, Skipper.'

'What the hell is it?' asked Lee.

'No idea,' came the reply.

'Is it another aircraft?'

'Don't think so. It seems to be getting larger.'

Lee saw it. 'Looks like something on fire,' he said.

'It is,' said Sparks. 'It's the glow of a bloody great fire!'

'Where are we, Riggy?' asked Lee.

'We should be nearing Cape St Vincent,' replied Riggy.

As they flew on, keeping an eye on the mysterious red glow, Lee suddenly shouted, 'It's the bloody sun rising!' Sure enough, the most beautiful red hue of a glorious sunrise filled the horizon, settling softly on the clouds above and below. Daylight had arrived! The agony was over. It was another moment to treasure. Never before had any of them had such an experience. Another quarter of an hour went by when the cloud below, uneven and like an enormous fluffed-up cotton wool blanket, came to an abrupt end. It was as if they had walked to the edge of a cliff, and there below, in glorious sunshine, was the sea, calm and tranquil, and far over to the port side, the coast line.

'Recognise it, Len?' asked Lee to the bomb aimer who was sitting next to him. Len reached for his maps.

'Yes, it looks like Cape St Vincent.'

'Bloody good show!' exclaimed Lee. 'We are spot on course. Wonders will never cease! Well done Riggy, that was a bloody good bit of navigating.'

Lee woke up after a sound and restful sleep. The sun, the glorious sun, was blazing through the window into the huts in which they had been billeted when they arrived. And it was hot. Overnight they had been transported back to those lovely hot summer days in pre-war England. He felt refreshed and safe. The rest of the crew had got up and must have gone out. He was alone in the billet. It had been an uneventful arrival. No one had known they were coming or to where they were going, but apparently this was normal with aircraft arriving unexpectedly at all times. Formalities over, they had breakfasted, been allocated a billet and left to their own devices. Lee had been treated like a fully experienced, responsible pilot when he had checked in. He realised that now other people recognised that he was the captain in charge, with complete responsibility for getting his crew and aircraft into a theatre of war.

His training was now over. He was on his own. But, nevertheless, how thankful he had been for his training last night. Last night he had been frightened. Now he would have to find out how he would react over a target. He decided to let that take care of itself – he would soon find out. Just now all he wanted to do was have a shower and a shave and relax for a bit. The other members of the crew returned with some of their pals. They had familiarised themselves with the camp and if they weren't needed, were now going into the local town to have a look around and possibly take in a meal. They asked if he wanted to go with them.

'No, but I'd better go to the operations room and see what's what before you go,' said Lee.

In the ops room he was told, 'You can move on when you're ready.' He decided to have the aircraft serviced and made plans to move on the following day. The next move was to take the aircraft to Maison Blanche in Algiers, but that was tomorrow, so the crew went into town. Lee stayed behind as he didn't feel like socialising.

*   *   *

Connie and he had been married at Moreton-in-Marsh on 10 February. His crew had done what they could to make it a day to remember for them both. They had organised a reception at the White Hart Hotel and, in spite of all the red tape, Lee had eventually managed to get a day off to have the wedding in St David's Church. Because they were on battle orders his best blue had been handed in and all he had was his battle dress. However, someone had organised the loan of a best blue from one of the permanent members of staff on the station.

They had been married at half-past five in the evening when the station padre was free. Nan, Connie's corporal WAAF friend, had come down from Lossiemouth with her and had been her maid of honour. Riggy was the best man. The bridal suite contained the bed that King Charles I had slept in and that was their honeymoon treat.

When he had been posted to Moreton, Lee had not known that it was an overseas posting. There had not been any embarkation leave. Such was the secrecy of war. From hurried phone calls to Connie, with whom he had fallen in love from that very first meeting, they had decided to get married before he went overseas. The moment when they both realised

During the often difficult and extremely dangerous operations, one person was never far from Lee's thoughts: Connie.

they were in love was the evening they had gone to the cinema in Elgin to see a film in which Alice Faye starred. In this she had sung the song 'You'll never know'. They had sat close to each other on the bus on the way back to camp. The bus was filled with smoke and smelt of cigarettes and stale beer. The windows were all misted up and airmen and airwomen were singing RAF versions of well known songs.

Lee and Connie were in a different world, locked in each other's arms, gently kissing and caressing each other. He could still feel the warmth of her gentle kiss upon his lips.

After they left the bus they walked slowly back to the hotel in which Connie was billeted, singing 'You'll never know' together in a dream world. They were in love, but it was unspoken as yet. It was a lovely night as they strolled along. Those friendly stars were out and Lee had taken a great deal of trouble pointing out to her which stars were which. The constellation of Orion was theirs. They promised that every time they saw it they would think of each other and every night they would look for it and say a little prayer.

When the moment came it had been magical, particularly as it could have gone disastrously wrong because, a few minutes later, when stopping to kiss, Connie's peaked WAAF cap had fallen to the ground. Lee stooped to pick it up and laughingly teased her, running off with it, saying she wouldn't get it back until she promised to marry him.

Connie panicked. There she was, a WAAF sergeant outside of her billet improperly dressed without her hat. She would be in trouble if she was seen by an officer, or humiliated if seen by other WAAFs. She pleaded with Lee to stop fooling around and give it back to her.

'You will only get it back if you promise to marry me,' he retorted. She had stamped her foot and angrily stalked off, away from the billet towards the golf course which was nearby, leaving Lee standing there holding the offending hat.

He chased after her. Now it had been his turn to plead with her, begging her to come back, but Connie was mad at being humiliated like that and had run on. Lee gave up and stood wondering what to do next.

A few moments later, Connie came back towards him. 'I've come bach for ma haat,' she said in her delightful Scottish accent. Lee ran towards her, catching her and hugging her closely to him. They showered kisses upon each other.

'I love you, I love you, I thought I was going to lose you,' Lee murmured softly and tenderly to her.

'So do I, I love you too, my darling,' she whispered.

'I think about you all the time. I have never felt this way about anyone else. I am sure we are meant for each other. I certainly don't want to wait for the war to end or for us to drift apart. Do you love me enough to marry me?'

'Oh my darling. Do you really want us to marry? You mustn't joke about such things.'

'I have never been more serious in my life.'

They kissed. The world was another place for them both and, locked in each other's arms, they again walked slowly back towards the hotel. Reluctant to part, they had dawdled towards the rear of the hotel and, leaning against the wall, fondly embraced. He could feel the warmth of her cheeks and the sweetness of her lips. Connie was now very late, but no matter – she knew of another door at the rear of the hotel by which she could get to her room unnoticed. Another long lingering goodnight kiss and she slipped furtively away. Lee returned to his quarters walking on air. They were in love.

Having declared their love for each other, it was natural to make plans to get married. With no money and in war time, they subsequently had fits of laughter choosing where to hold the reception. The favourite place was the 'Sally Ann', a canteen in Lossiemouth run by the Salvation Army. A meal of fish and chips was to be the fare, followed by tea and a wad.

If he couldn't be with Connie he did not want to be with anyone else, thought Lee as the rest of the crew went off. Later in the afternoon he sat on his bed and wrote the first of his daily letters to Connie. He tried desperately not to show how miserable he felt without her, but thoughts of her dominated every moment of his waking hours. He was hopelessly in love. He stayed in the camp, met up with Bobby and Ken, and together they went for a meal and a drink in the mess.

Early next morning they were airborne, on their way to Algiers. It was a lovely morning with not a cloud in the sky. Below, the Atlas Mountains cast patterns of light and dark as the sun threw alternate shadows over the peaks and valleys. Except for the steady drone of the engines, there was neither sight nor sound of anything around for miles, and Lee reflected on the briefing they had had: that should they come down in that area, they were to destroy everything, because of the bands of marauding tribesmen that frequented the hills.

With the warm sun on the Perspex, the steady drone of the engines, and George, the automatic pilot, flying the aircraft for him, Lee was soon daydreaming. He conjured up pictures in his mind of the engines failing and having to make an emergency landing in one of the valleys below. Then, in his daydream, from nowhere, hordes of tribesmen came thundering along the valley on horseback, flashing scimitars and shouting obscene calls as they came racing towards him and the crew. They tried desperately to destroy their crashed aircraft. And as it caught fire, they stood there, their backs to the aeroplane, firing their service revolvers as the bearded leering faces rushed towards them. He snapped out of his dream in a cold sweat.

He looked down; it was a truly magnificent and peaceful picture below, with the sun shining on the desolate, barren, rocky mountain tops. Nevertheless, he still cast a quick glance at his instrument panel. Thank God, everything was in order! He could continue to admire the sheer majestic, desolate beauty of the scene below, and think about Connie.

They arrived at Maison Blanche three and a quarter hours after setting off. Here, a completely different sight from anything he had experienced welcomed him. The airport was a hive of activity. There were fighters, bombers and huge transport planes all around, most of them belonging to the American Air Force. They were ushered to the British section of the airport, debriefed and told to wait until someone found out what to do with them. What a cock-up! Other crews began to arrive and to meet up with those who were already there.

The following evening a group decided to go to the Casbah in Algiers which was out of bounds to all ranks. Lee and most of his crew stayed in camp, but the following morning the stories that came back were horrific of girls with donkeys and dogs, pimps and pickpockets.

For three days they hung about at the airport, then captains were called to the ops room and told they could either go on to Italy or India. Lee was told that there was a much better chance of getting back to the UK if you did two tours and a rest period in Italy, whereas India was a definite three-year posting. Lee opted for Italy; he wanted to get it over and get back to his beloved Connie as quickly as possible. The die was cast. And because Bobby and Ken also opted for Italy, it made it easier for his crew to accept.

Lying on his bunk that night, Lee thought about how supportive his crew were to him. He thought about the wedding, the flight out and the fun they had the night of the WAAF's own dance at Lossiemouth. Connie had told him the dance was on just after they had first met, but she had already asked the RSM to take her. Lee and his crew had gate-crashed the dance using Connie's name to get past the WAAF on duty at the door. Seeing the RSM at the bar they had offered to buy him a pint, which he had accepted. Whilst he was drinking, Lee had asked his crew to carry on entertaining him whilst he and Connie danced together. This they had most readily agreed to do and Lee and Connie danced together for the rest of the evening. They had had a wonderful time, enjoying themselves so much that she hardly gave a thought to her companion. When she did, Lee assured her that the crew were looking after him. They did such a good job on keeping him 'entertained' that when the band played 'God save the King' the RSM was so sloshed he couldn't stand up for it!

Connie had been furious with this ploy, particularly as she had had to see him home! They had followed, helping her to get him out past the guardhouse, but keeping a respectable distance behind until his pals had come along. That was the end of the RSM in Connie's book! How Lee longed for her now.

Flight plans were prepared for the next stage of the journey, which was to be to Tunis, El Aouina airport. This was uneventful and, after an overnight stop, they moved on to Catania in Sicily.

The sight that greeted them there was amazing, with wrecked Italian aircraft on either side of the runway. 'What the hell's going on?' Lee asked one of the ground crew as soon as he stepped out of the cockpit at the marshalling point.

'It's these wops,' came the reply, 'surrendering their air force. Either they can't fly, or they're deliberately wrecking them so that the Allies can't use them.'

A truck came to take them to the ops room in the control tower. As they waited, two more Italian bombers came in to land. Both skidded off the runway on landing and ended nose up on the grass verge. 'What a bloody air force; no wonder they surrendered,' Lee said to Riggy.

The following day they again reported to the ops room. Here, at last, they received definite orders: they were to fly with all haste to 205 Group based at Foggia Main in Italy, where the Group were waiting for them.

The weather had clouded up when they set off. Mount Etna was covered in cloud and the sea below was choppy and uninviting. 'A definite change in the weather, Riggy,' Lee commented.

'Yes, the weather in Italy is either rain or sleet,' replied Riggy.

They landed at Foggia Main in the pouring rain. Touching down on a metal runway, it could be seen that the area was one of desolation and off-runway mud. Bombed buildings pointed their agony to the sky and a feeling of hopelessness came over the crew. Lee wondered what the hell they had let themselves into.

However, the welcome from the Duty Officer was warm and friendly. 'Thank God you've got here,' he said. 'We could do with some fresh blood and new aircraft.'

After giving news about how things were back home, there followed a brief résumé of what had taken place following the invasion of Italy. The squadrons had come from the North African Desert Campaign and were very much just settling down to their new role of being a support force in the Italian campaign.

Packed into a lorry, the crews were taken to their billets in Foggia town. The scene that greeted them was appalling: bombed-out buildings, desolation and debris everywhere; squalid streets with ragged children shouting while playing and others begging. They saw dirty women in torn and fragmented clothes, some with bundles of rags in their arms from which peered out the thin faces of undernourished babies.

But what had most indelibly stuck in their minds was the look on the faces of the population. The men were nearly all very old, thin, bent and wrinkled, and the women were of mixed ages. They moved about hopelessly, bedraggled, dispirited, and they all seemed to be dressed in black. It was quite a cultural shock to the young spirited airmen to observe this spirit of defeat which was everywhere, and to witness the dejection written upon all of the sad and doleful faces.

Meanwhile, victorious troops were busying themselves trying to bring order into the chaos. American Jeeps were rushing around the town. American and British servicemen were on traffic duty. Hastily erected road signs were in English with such slogans as Piccadilly Circus and Old Kent Road written on them, but devastation was everywhere.

They were taken to an old school building in the centre of town where they received their second cultural shock. They were to be billeted on a second storey floor with dozens of other airmen. Each was given a palliasse (a mattress filled with straw) and they were to sleep on the floor with just about enough bed space to enable them to get out of bed. Some of the windows had been boarded up but others were without glass and were open to the elements. Everyone therefore huddled against the inside wall. There was no furniture whatsoever in the long, narrow, high-ceilinged room, neither were there any doors, which meant that the chill icy wind whistled around the room to add to the discomfort. There were battle scars everywhere, bullet holes pockmarked the inner walls and many of the outside walls had shell holes in them. The latrines had chipped wash handbasins with no plugs in them and the lavatories were without doors, openly displaying broken and chipped toilet basins with no seats. Some were already occupied and smelt. This and the smell of stale urine mixed with the overpowering smell of disinfectant was revolting.

The Mess was little better. This was filled with the smell of the kitchens which had oil burning stoves and were situated at one end of the so-called dining area. Meal times were spread out as there was insufficient room for everyone to sit down together on the makeshift tables and benches. Quite often one had to stand up to eat the hard rations which were the normal daily fare. The tea was ghastly, and about the only decent meal was the cup of greasy cocoa and the hard tack biscuit that was saved from the daily rations and dunked into it at night time. Everywhere there was the overbearing smell of the very powerful disinfectant; it was over-whelming, initially making Lee feel sick.

There were notices everywhere one looked – large red notices with the word DANGER written above them warning about VD. Notices with large skull and crossbones printed on them in black, warning about cholera and lice and not to drink the water in the taps. There were areas marked off with 'Danger' and 'Forbidden to Enter' signs. Many of the walls bore notices in German which meant that the German troops had also been

22

billeted there at some time. They had most certainly arrived in a war zone!

A very powerful rumour was going round that the retreating Germans had infected the local girls with VD as a means of putting our troops out of action. Whether or not that was HQ-inspired, they never did find out. Sufficient to say, nobody took the chance. They were also advised that if they did go out they were to go in groups of three or four, never alone. Many of the bars were out of bounds, as were certain areas of the town. When they did venture out it was a waste of time because there was nothing in the shops that they wanted. The only advantage to going out was the exercise from walking.

And then it snowed. It came billowing into the room through the open windows one night as if it was the most natural thing in the world. There was nothing to stop it, and everyone became absolutely fed up. It formed a carpet on the floor and it piled up in corners of the room and against their bed spaces. Just as when it rained, they had to immediately turn to and mop-up, angrily slipping on their flying boots and putting their great-coats on over their pyjamas. It was about three o'clock in the morning, and they were to spend the rest of the night trying to keep the room clear of the snow.

Morale sank to an all-time low. They were cold, frustrated and not a little scared of what their stark exposure to the elements meant for their future. Operations were already going on; surely they were not expected to fly on ops and live like this?

The news that there were to be camps at the airfields with the men sleeping under canvas came as a blessing from Heaven. Anything was better than the dump they were in now!

CHAPTER TWO

INTO BATTLE

MEANWHILE, on 2 March, Lee had been on his first operation over enemy territory. He had been taken in a gharry, a small pick-up truck, to the airfield to be second pilot and to obtain experience with an Australian flight sergeant pilot who was coming to the end of his tour. He had been posted to 37 Squadron, part of 231 Wing, which in turn was part of 205 Group. As far as Lee was concerned, the trip was a non-starter. He was very disappointed. There was very little activity over the target which they were to illuminate with flares before doing their own bombing run. Apart from the few moments in which they approached the target and his own expectation and anticipation of waiting for something to happen over the target itself, the trip was uneventful.

They had been detailed to attack marshalling yards at Orbetello, a small town on the Tyrrhenian Sea on the west coast of Italy. Arriving on time, they did a first run to illuminate the target and a second to bomb it. They had dropped their bombs in two sticks, a stick being a succession of bombs dropped onto the target one after the other as they left the aircraft. The first stick went across the centre of the yards, scoring direct hits on some buildings west of the yards. The second stick was dropped in the same area.

Eight Wellingtons from the squadron had taken part in the raid. The weather was good and all aircraft identified the target and attacked it under good illumination from the flares which they had dropped on their first run. The raid lasted some twenty-two minutes; the time over the target was from 2102 to 2124 hours, and the bombs were dropped at varying heights from 6,000 to 8,500 feet. Many sticks were seen to straddle the yards and bombing was reported as 'well concentrated in the target area'. Many direct hits were scored on railway lines and buildings, and three fires were left burning. There was only slight heavy anti-aircraft fire concentrated in the target area. All aircraft returned safely to base. If this was what it was all about, he told his crew later, then they should have no problems. So far, the accommodation itself was far worse than ops!

Lee's second op, again as second pilot, was to Genoa, on 11 March. The crew with whom he had been detailed to fly had been given the job once again to illuminate the target – the marshalling yards – with flares before carrying out their bombing run. However, flying northwards they ran into 10/10ths cloud at Leghorn, which continued right into the target area, covering it completely. So their attack was aborted and the flares dropped over Elba on the way home. Seventeen Wimpys from the squadron had taken off for the attack, but owing to the poor weather conditions one aircraft returned early, and two others, which included the second illuminator, also abandoned the task. Two aircraft bombed other targets. One bombed Orbetello, observing bursts across the railway lines, and the other the port of San Stefano, starting a large fire at the base of the main north-west mole. The remaining aircraft bombed what they believed to be the target from 4,500 to 12,000 feet, encountering moderate to light and heavy flak and enemy fighter flares in the target areas. All the aircraft returned safely to base.

As far as Lee was concerned, so far he had not seen a shot fired in anger and was quite frustrated. The weather continued to be poor. The next night five Wimpys took off from the squadron, but none found the target. Four jettisoned their bombs and the other attacked a secondary target without observing any results. Seven more nights were to go by without further attacks because of bad weather.

On 15 March he went on his final flight as second pilot. The target was the marshalling yards at Sofia, in Bulgaria. Landfall was Mount Cherni,

Sofia, Lee's last operation as second pilot.

25

about fifteen miles to the south-west of Sofia. Flying over the Adriatic, the navigator wanted to check his course. One of the ways of doing this was by using the flare chute inside the fuselage to drop a flame float into the sea in order for the rear gunner to train his guns on them. Either Sparks or Len would have to be responsible for dropping out the flame float, thought Lee. As the aircraft flew on, the gunner would keep the float in his gunsight and, in so doing, the turret would turn automatically. He would read off the angle of drift on the special scale marked on the base of the turret and inform the navigator. The navigator used the information to check the wind speed and direction he was using to plot the course for the pilot to fly on. Over the Dinaric Alps in Yugoslavia incendiaries were dropped for the same purpose.

Eventually they made landfall at Mount Cherni and there, unexpectedly, in the valley below, out of the darkness of the mountain range lay Sofia, completely unprepared and with no apparent blackout. The city was lit up in all its glory. The scene that greeted them, for which they also were completely unprepared, was that of a fairy city aglow with a thousand and one lights set in a backcloth of snow. It reminded Lee of a scene on a Christmas card, or of a giant birthday cake lit by a thousand candles. It was as if the whole city was on a night out enjoying the music of Strauss. It looked enchanted. Furthermore, to add to its enchantment, the snow reflected the shimmering lights up on to the dark, black clouds above. It was like a chandelier in the sky; the whole picture laid out in front of them was beautifully serene, wonderfully calm and peaceful.

They gazed at the sight ahead in wonderment, but the drone of the engines and the black shapes of the bombers around them served to remind them of the awesome task that lay before them. Their job would be to shatter that peaceful scene. Below, the ground defences were obviously taken by surprise because, all of a sudden, the lights went out. They must be in a panic down there, thought Lee. That must have thrown everyone into confusion. Searchlights came on, lighting up the sky in place of the city's lights, and they saw fingering beams of light in all directions. These were augmented by one or two bursts of light flak, splattering and crackling orange bursts of fire, like rockets in the sky on firework night. Then there was the odd burst of red tracer coming straight up from the ground and curving away harmlessly.

'They know we are around,' said Lee.

'But they don't seem to know where we are,' replied the Skipper. 'They probably think we are Russians.'

Then, astonishingly, as quickly as the lights of the city had gone out, they came on again. They stayed on for a few minutes, then off they went again. They really must be in a panic, thought Lee as they flew on relentlessly. He could imagine the people below running away in all directions, like a scene out of the H.G. Wells' film, *Things to Come*.

The beams from the searchlights wandered aimlessly about the sky. Flares from the attacking bombing force lit up the target area and at 11,000 feet the bombing run commenced onto the marshalling yards. Flak was bursting below, light in intensity and not very accurate. Lee was fascinated. He could clearly see the target ahead: railway lines running into it then intersecting and crisscrossing each other, with engine sheds and numerous other buildings dotted around. There were long straight roads leading into the yards, with blocks of buildings intersected by streets fanning out from them. He could clearly see what he thought looked like a river or canal running close by, with boats or barges on it. It appeared to be about five or six blocks away.

Whatever it was, it had long, clear boulevards running either side of it with bridges going across it. It was the first major target he had ever seen and he was enthralled. The bomb aimer steered the skipper towards it. 'Steady, left, left, right a bit, hold it there,' came the instructions over the intercom. 'Bombs gone.'

The bombs were dropped in one stick and bursts were seen in the target area. The pilot broke off his attack, but stayed on course for thirteen seconds to take the photographs.

Turning for home, Lee felt a little disappointed. He would have loved to have gone around again to see more. That had been a real target compared to the other two ops he had been on, and he had thoroughly enjoyed the experience. It was 1.30 in the morning and they had a three-hour flight back to base in front of them. Of the thirteen Wimpys that took off, two abandoned the task owing to faulty airspeed indicators and the remainder, including the illuminator, bombed the target from 0122 to 0137 hours from between 10,500 to 13,000 feet under good illumination. Two 4,000-pound bombs and seventy-two 500-pound bombs were dropped.

Bombing was reported to have covered the target area, several sticks being seen to burst across the yards and buildings to the south. Two fires were reported burning in the area. Nearly 18,000 leaflets were dropped, telling the inhabitants that they were no longer safe from attack and to overthrow their leaders. The weather had been bad *en route* and, on the return journey, was so bad that the crew of the aircraft captained by the Commanding Officer baled out and one aircraft landed away from base. Fortunately, all crews returned safely to the squadron. The weather closed in and it was a further six days before the squadron was able to operate again.

That was his last op as second pilot; the next he would be with his own crew, thought Lee as he lay on his bed. The bacon and dried scrambled egg they had received for breakfast when they got back had tasted oily again and the tea had been like dishwater. Furthermore, the meparcrine tablet they were issued with at meal times to ward off malaria had

27

dissolved in his mouth before he had had time to swallow it and it had left a bitter taste. Nevertheless, Lee felt unnaturally elated. It was 5.30 in the morning. Better get some sleep, he thought.

The following morning, joy of joys, he received his first letter from Connie. He read and reread it all day. Apparently there had been some trouble with the families over the wedding arrangements, because their parents hadn't been there. But she loved him and that was all that mattered.

A week went past before the crew were to go off on ops together. The target was Padua in northern Italy, and once again the marshalling yards were chosen. The Allies were desperately trying to stop the Germans from supplying their troops at the front. The Americans were attacking the supply routes by day with their Flying Fortresses and the RAF were bombing by night. The Wimpy was proving itself to be an ideal weapon for the work it was being called upon to do.

After briefing, sitting in the back of the truck that was to take them to dispersal to collect their aircraft, Lee wondered how his crew would work together on a raid. The whole sequence at dispersal prior to take-off had become a regular pattern, so much so that it was now almost a superstition. Before getting into the aircraft, Sparks and Jock would go to the rear of the aircraft to have a last smoke and to relieve themselves. Len and Lee would walk around the aircraft together to carry out the aircraft check, and finally Riggy and Lee relieved themselves against the port wheel.

Getting into the aircraft. Well, that procedure was a thing unto itself. It had started at OTU and had now become a habit which was hard to break. Jock went in first, followed by Sparks, followed by Riggy, followed by Len and finally Lee. It was funny to see the great lengths they would go to stop anyone inadvertently getting out of sequence. If this did happen, they would get into a flap trying to put it right. Sparks would even pull the ladder down from underneath the nose for them to get into the aircraft. That had become his job; if the ground crew had left it down he would push it up again and pull it down himself!

Taxiing out from dispersal, they had joined up with the other aircraft and had taken their place in the queue to taxi slowly up to the end of the runway and await the green Aldis lamp signal for them to take off. That was a thrilling moment. With the cockpit window open, he could hear the noise of the aircraft engine idling over as they all moved slowly forward, and then came the bursts of flame from the exhausts of the engines and the wait at the end of the runway whilst the previous aircraft thundered on its way.

Then it had been their turn to be airborne, gathering speed as they sped down the metal runway. With its full bomb load and fuel aboard this was the heaviest aircraft that Lee had been called upon to take off.

As it thundered down the runway he wondered if it would ever become airborne. The liftoff came barely feet above the airfield boundary and, as they climbed away, he heard the thud as the wheels came up and locked into place. He made a gentle turn as they slowly climbed away on to the course set by Riggy.

'OK to test the guns?' asked Jock after they had levelled out and had been flying on course over the Adriatic for about ten minutes.

'Sure is,' replied Lee. 'Make sure you don't shoot the arse off another Wimpy. There are plenty of them around.'

A couple of quick bursts soon followed.

'What about the front turret, Len?' asked Lee.

'OK, Skip,' came the reply. The aircraft swung violently as the turrets were turned, firing the guns.

'What the hell's going on!' shouted Riggy into the intercom from the depths of his navigation section. 'Watch your course Lee, it's all over the place!'

'Oh, for Christ's sake, they've got to test their guns, haven't they?' replied Lee.

They flew on in silence whilst Riggy worked away at his log.

'We need to drop a flame float,' said Riggy later, 'to check our course.'

Len moved out of the front turret and went towards the flare chute situated in the middle of the aircraft. As he passed he grimaced at Lee.

'Flame float away,' he called a few moments later, and returned to his seat. Lee held the aircraft on a straight and level course whilst Jock checked the drift.

'Five degrees starboard, Riggy,' he called.

'Can't be,' came the reply. 'Check it again.'

'The flame float is out of sight,' called Jock.

'Well, drop another bastard!'

Back into the body of the aircraft went Len. In future Len will have to stay there until that little exercise is over, thought Lee.

'Five degrees starboard, Riggy,' called Jock.

'Christ, it can't be, Lee,' complained Riggy.

'Are you sure you're reading it right, Jock?' asked Lee.

There was a pause.

'Sorry Skip. Five degrees port, Riggy,' called Jock.

The crew were learning fast.

Spot on time they reached the target area. Len's job was now to move out of the second pilot's seat next to Lee and go down into the bomb aimer's position. Lee watched as he went down. To his surprise, Len reached up and took off his tin helmet which he had just put on and placed it on the floor beside him. Next he took from his breast pocket a rabbit's foot and a baby's pink bootee and carefully placed them inside his helmet.

Because Len had not yet plugged his intercom back in, Lee could not resist telling the rest of the crew over the intercom what he was doing. Next, instead of putting the tin hat back on his head, Len strategically placed it in position on the floor of the bomb aimer's position, before laying down on top of it, to cover his private parts.

He then plugged in his intercom, not knowing that Lee had been watching him or that the rest of the crew knew.

'What's that for?' asked Lee.

'What's what for?' queried Len.

'Putting your tin hat there.'

'If I'm going to get shot, I want to keep that part of me in one piece. That's one part I want to save. My wife would hate it if I lost that!'

The crew burst out laughing.

Len, who had only been married a few months before he was posted overseas, had only just received the news of his daughter being born. The letter package had contained a pink sample of the baby's bootee. The tension was broken.

'You can come up now, Riggy,' called Lee.

After getting the aircraft to the target area, it was the navigator's job to occupy the seat vacated by the bomb aimer and to keep a look out for night fighters on the starboard side of the aircraft. Meanwhile, the bomb aimer took over and guided the pilot on to the actual target visually. The target below was covered with flares and incendiary bombs. Fires had already been started, flak was bursting around and the scene was one of intense action and excitement.

Riggy opened the door behind the second pilot's seat and took one look at what was going on outside. 'Christ!' he exclaimed, and went scurrying back to his navigator's desk.

Lee was too busy to handle the situation at that moment. Len had the target in his bombsight and was giving instructions.

'Left, left, right, right, steady, steady, left again.'

The aircraft was edging slowly into position right over the target area. Sparks and Jock were giving a commentary of what they could see going on outside.

'Be quiet, you two,' called Lee. 'I can't hear Len.'

'Bomb doors open,' called Len. There was a shudder as the doors below swung open.

'Steady, Lee. Steady, right a bit – hold it there – got it! Bombs gone!' called Len.

The aircraft rose slowly as the bombs fell away lightening the load. Then came the thirteen-second count flying straight and level over the target for the photograph. It felt like thirteen hours.

On the way back to base Lee asked Riggy what happened over the target.

'I can't face that,' said Riggy, 'I don't want to sit there. I would rather not see what was going on.'

Realising how much more work was going to be placed on him, having to watch both sides of the battle area when over the target, Lee reluctantly agreed that in future Riggy could stay at his desk.

Twelve Wimpys had taken off from the squadron and all successfully bombed the target from heights of between 3,000 and 9,000 feet under good illumination. Bombing was reported to be well concentrated in the yards; many bombs, including two 4,000-pounders, were seen to burst in the yards and at the junction. Fourteen fires were seen in the target area, visible from seventy to eighty miles away on the return journey, and some excellent photographs of the target area were taken during the raid. It was unfortunate that, because of the smoke and fires that had been started, Lee's crew and some of the others were unable to see any visible results from their attacks. The weather was good and only light flak was encountered. All aircraft returned safely to base.

One night off and they were on duty again. This time the target was Sofia once again. 'Communications and domestic installations' was the official definition of the target area, but at the briefing it was more than that. They were also to drop leaflets to the civilian population. The Allies were hoping that continual bombing would encourage the Bulgarian leaders to withdraw their support for Hitler and the German war effort.

This time the scene over the target was completely different from his previous visit. The target area was covered by 10/10ths cloud. However, the flares had been dropped and the light from them was clearly visible in the clouds. What is more, by their own dead reckoning navigation, they had been dropped over the target area, but they could not identify it for sure. As instructed they carried out their bombing run on the flares.

On their return to base the weather closed in immediately they left the target area and in no time at all it worsened. Very soon, visibility was so poor that they were unable to see any land below, or stars above, for a 'fix' on their position; neither could Sparks get a fix through his radio.

They were in heavy cloud once again and were being bumped about unmercifully as they flew back over the hills and mountains of Yugoslavia. On reaching the estimated time of arrival for the Italian coast, it was nowhere to be seen; they were flying in cloud which was completely covering the area. Lee turned and went back out to sea, reducing height to 5,000 feet on the way out and back in again. He was reluctant to go too far inland or below 4,000 feet because he knew there was a range of hills just north of base.

He flew in and out several times, with the eyes of Len, Sparks and himself searching for that break in the cloud which they hoped would reveal land below that they could identify. Eventually Len, who had gone

31

down to the bomb aimer's position to try to pinpoint their position, could just make out the Italian coastline between breaks in the cloud. But without sufficient sightings to fix their position they had no idea where they were.

He turned and went up and down the seaward side of the coastline trying to give Len and Sparks, who was in the astrodome, a chance to identify and pinpoint their position. Without any checks on course since they had left base nearly eight hours ago, they had obviously been blown quite a bit off course. They weren't even 100 per cent sure that it was the target they had bombed, having bombed on the flares without actually identifying it. It could have been someone else releasing flares trying to find the target. If that was the case their starting point back could have been wrong. They could be anywhere. By now, normally in reasonable weather and with reasonable visibility, it should have been very easy to see the three crisscrossed searchlights that were put up to guide crews back to base. Under ideal conditions they could be seen from miles away, but now they were nowhere in sight. They were completely lost.

Suddenly a fighter passed close by and vanished quickly into the clouds again, but Lee was able first to identify it as a Beaufighter. Lee asked Len to switch to his reserve fuel tanks. Worrying about the amount of fuel he had left, he was beginning to give up hope they would ever recognise any of the coast below. Furthermore, a bigger worry was that they could even be above a base, in German occupied territory. Then there was a shout from Sparks in the astrodome.

'Flarepath on the starboard side, Skipper.'

Lee turned his head. Yes, sure enough there was a flarepath. Why hadn't he seen it before? They had been up and down the coast three or four times. It looked very small. Could it be a trap? He turned out to sea and flew back, losing height at the same time and discussing the situation over the intercom.

'Look lads, there's this flarepath below, but it could be a German fighter 'drome. It seems to be too small for a bomber 'drome. On the other hand it could be where that Beaufighter came from.'

'Could you land there, Lee?'

'Looks as if I will have to; there's nowhere else to go.'

By now there was no alternative but to try and land there, so without any more ado Lee decided to go in to land. He circled it once to have a closer look whilst he was losing height, dropping down to 500 feet. Approaching the flarepath Lee could see that the lights were oil lamps spaced along a grass strip. He made a perfect landing, bringing the tail down as soon as he crossed the boundary and shut off the engines just as he reached the end of the flarepath. Funny, but there was no perimeter track to taxi back to the control tower. He became very suspicious.

'Put on your revolvers,' said Lee. 'We don't know who the hell these people are running towards us.'

They could just make out a group of men running towards the aircraft from a small covered-in truck parked near the end of the flarepath.

'Put all your papers together, and Riggy, maybe you should stand by with the Very pistol to destroy them and the aircraft if it comes to it. I will go out first followed by Jock, then Sparks. Len, will you wait at the top of the ladder to give Riggy the signal to fire? As soon as he has done that, let him run out past you, and as he jumps to the ground, you fire another into the cockpit and jump out after him.'

Lee opened the hatch and dropped out the ladder. He was the first one out of the Wimpy and, with one hand on his revolver, was relieved to see an RAF squadron leader holding a torch standing before him with a group of airmen.

'It's OK, lads,' Lee called back quietly to Jock.

'Where are we?' asked Lee of the squadron leader.

'Crotone,' replied the squadron leader. 'The last airstrip on the toe of Italy. Welcome. That was a first-class landing you did.'

Back in the hut that served as a mess, a meal was provided with hot cocoa. The squadron leader, who was a regular officer and looked as if he had gone past the age of retirement, explained that this was an emergency landing strip for just such an occasion, and Lee's crew were the first to use it. The Beaufighter had been sent up to identify them and once they had been identified, the groundstaff had quickly lit the oil lamps and put them out for them to land by. He said that he would get in touch with 205 Group HQ and tell them they were safe.

It was an extremely friendly atmosphere. A bottle of whisky soon appeared; warm and well fed they spent some time chatting before turning in. A small number of men of other ranks made up the airstrip staff, and they were delighted that they had been able to be of some use, it being a very boring and lonely existence in that part of Italy. The crew in turn were grateful and very relieved that they had landed there, otherwise they could have ended up in the drink, somewhere in the middle of the Mediterranean.

The following morning, after breakfast and warm thanks, they set off for base at Torterello, arriving there some two hours later. Lee reflected that Crotone was nearly two hundred miles from Foggia. They had been extremely lucky. What on earth had gone wrong to have been blown or steered that much off course? The wind speed and direction from the target given to Riggy at briefing must have been a hell of a way out! They had missed the heel of Italy altogether, or had flown over it, through the bad visibility. But, good grief, that was a hell of a long way to be off course.

Then they heard the rumour sweeping round the camp that many other aircraft had been lost through the bad weather that night. So that was that. The preflight winds and the weather forecast given by Met. to Riggy and the rest of the navigators had been hopelessly wrong.

News was that the Allies were having a difficult time at Anzio. The crew were on duty again the following night, 26 March, attacking the marshalling yards at Vicenza in north-east Italy. The weather forecast was good. The frontal system that had caused so much havoc on the last sortie had moved right over the Balkans, and to all intents and purposes they should have no problem with the weather. They could expect opposition from the ground, as the target was heavily defended. This time, instead of carrying the usual nine 500-pound bombs, they had been entrusted with one 4,000-pound bomb, a cookie.

The journey up the Italian coast of the Adriatic was uneventful and they turned inland over the Po estuary, flying up the Po valley and passing Padua on their starboard side. The target was alight with incendiaries and flares when they arrived, but not with the main illuminators – they arrived five minutes late. Nevertheless, as they commenced their bombing run, they had no difficulty in identifying the yards as they were clearly distinguished by the railway lines running into them. They released their cookie at 5,000 feet, aimed at the eastern end of the yards.

The target was defended with up to twelve heavy and some light anti-aircraft guns. A few enemy aircraft were seen, but they did not intercept any of the squadron's aircraft. Twelve aircraft had been detailed from the squadron for this attack, but one failed to operate. The remainder identified the target and bombed in good weather from heights of 4,500 to 8,000 feet, dropping two 4,000-pound and fifty-one 500-pound high explosive bombs with 2,670 four-pound incendiary bombs. The attack lasted ten minutes between 2118 and 2128 hours. The yards were well covered with bombs and the fires which the bombs had started were visible from fifty or sixty miles away.

Leaving the target after taking the photograph, Jock and Sparks reported an almighty explosion as what must have been a 4,000-pound bomb landed amidst the chaos below, Jock reporting a huge fire that had started as they flew away. All of the squadron's aircraft returned safely.

CHAPTER THREE

DOUBTS SET IN

THAT night as he lay on his bed, Lee was unable to get off to sleep immediately. His thoughts went from Connie and the comfort of her lying close beside him, to the events that had now completely changed his way of life. There was no getting away from it – the thrill and excitement of being over a target was a tremendous and most exhilarating experience. Lee was grateful and thanked God that he was not afraid when he was in action like that. But as he lay there he became more concerned about his own character, of what was happening to him as a person. Why at the time, amidst all the thrill and exhilaration, didn't he have any feeling of guilt or of being ashamed of what was happening to the poor people down below? Why was it that it was only at moments like this, when he was safely back, that he felt any concern or compassion?

He had been in several raids himself in England and he knew how the people on the receiving end of a raid felt. He remembered the time that he was caught in a raid in Exeter. Returning from leave after visiting his parents in Gosport, he was on his way back by train to Torquay, where as an aircrew cadet he was on his Initial Training Course. As the train drew into the station at Exeter, the air raid sirens had gone off and the train and station were evacuated. Left to his own devices he had walked towards the city centre, but didn't have any idea at all of what direction to take. He recalled walking down a tree-lined road with a very high wall running alongside the pavement. Guns were going off and bombs were dropping; searchlights lit up the street around him. He felt very afraid and very lonely, but as he hurried along, not knowing where he was going, the thought which concerned him most of all was that if anything happened to him, his parents would not know anything about it, he being on his own in this unfamiliar city. Nobody knew he was in Exeter and if he was blown to bits nobody would know. Furthermore, when he didn't report for duty in Torquay after his leave, the RAF would start looking for him. His parents would be informed he was missing, and they would evermore have the worry of wondering what had happened to him. It might even be thought that he had deserted! Heaven forbid. As he walked along he had sought protection from the shrapnel dropping around him by walking as close as possible to the wall. Suddenly, out of the darkness, the wall came to an abrupt end, and from what had been a wall of about six to seven feet high it had dropped to a small garden wall of about two to three feet. As his eyes got used to the gloom he could make out that the small wall now made up the front garden walls of a row of terraced houses. He hadn't walked on very far when in the window of one of the houses he saw the familiar sign of the Toc H lamp shining very faintly through some red paper. He had walked up the garden path and knocked on the door. It was opened by a very friendly gentleman who ushered him into the front room through a small hall. After establishing who he was, the man had offered him a hot drink of cocoa and some sandwiches. These Lee had accepted gratefully and ate them sitting down with the company who were gathered there. Some were on duty as air raid wardens. The raid outside continued and eventually it was decided to offer him a bed in a room which had a number of bunk beds in it and which were occupied by other members of the services. He must have been very tired because, in spite of the air raid going on around him, he had soon dropped off to sleep.

The next morning, after a hearty breakfast and thanking his host, he had walked to the railway station and was shocked to see how very badly damaged it was from the raid the night before. He had been lucky to have got out of it. But now, in contrast, his complete lack of concern for the people on the ground, when the thrill and excitement took over, worried him. On the ground, when the shoe was on the other foot, he had called the German bombers murdering bastards – is that what the people below thought of him when he was over the target? He tried to reconcile his thinking with the fact that his crew always attacked the target and went to great lengths to ensure that they did just that. He would never knowingly drop his bombs at random on crowded cities, but he knew in his heart of hearts that it was inevitable that some of the bombs missed and fell on the civilian population. He further tried to console and to explain it away to himself that this was total war and they, the enemy, had cheered when their aircraft were bombing other cities. He thought about Exeter in particular and also Coventry, and he pictured the attack on Poland. But the nagging feeling of conscience was there, particularly when he thought about the women and kids they had seen when they first went to Foggia. What sort of person was he turning into? The thoughts going through his mind worried him, and he became even more fearful when he thought that, perhaps on the other hand, they were in fact doubts setting in. Was this the build-up to him flunking his job, and would he use the doubts to become a coward? He lay there continually wrestling with these thoughts, always coming back to the same question. Was he becoming a coward? Why was it only when they got back from a raid or when they knew they were going on one that the doubts set in?

Once airborne, all doubts of survival, people below, what they were doing and more importantly being a coward, vanished. Up there when he wasn't concentrating on flying and getting to the target, he was thinking about Connie. The RAF had a terrible stigma for airmen who failed to carry out their duty on ops. It was called LMF – Lack of Moral Fibre. Apparently this was marked on your personal documents and stayed with you for the rest of your career. Aircrew by and large were more afraid of this stigma than they were of going into action. Later he was to find out that this was a deliberate policy to deter aircrew who wanted to quit. He felt this was pretty harsh because aircrew were all volunteers in the first place.

Another night off and they were on duty again on 28 March 1944. This time the marshalling yards at Milan Lambrate were the target, where 5,000 heavily laden railway trucks were reported to be waiting to move off. The usual complement of twelve Wimpys from the squadron were detailed for the attack, and all set off in good weather conditions. Lee was experienced enough now to have a new pilot to the squadron with him as second pilot, to be shown the ropes as he had been when he had first joined the squadron. They flew up the east coast of Italy, but could not identify their landfall to turn in to the mainland and along the Po valley because of low cloud. Above the cloud the weather was lovely with perfect visibility.

'Mountains ahead, Riggy,' called Lee.

'They are a long way off. I'm surprised you can see them, Lee,' he replied.

'Oh, they're not that far off. As a matter of fact they're getting nearer.'

'Can't be,' said Riggy.

'Bullshit,' said Lee. 'We're now almost right in amongst them.'

Outside both on his port and starboard side loomed the snowcapped peaks of the mountain range.

'I'm increasing height, Riggy,' called Lee.

'Oh Christ, Lee, you mustn't do that. You'll upset my calculations,' replied the navigator in Riggy.

'Bugger your calculations, Riggy. I'm climbing fast. We've got these bloody mountains all around us and I know damn well we should not be here. Tell him, someone. Come up front and see for yourself if you don't believe us.'

The door behind them opened. 'Christ!' exclaimed Riggy when he saw the peaks. He quickly disappeared again.

'We must have been given duff winds again, Lee,' said Riggy when he had arrived back at his table. 'But don't worry. I think I know where we are. I'll give you a new course in a moment.'

A new course was quickly forthcoming and they arrived over the target which was clearly visible below, the earlier cloud having disappeared. They arrived late in the target area as did the aircraft sent to illuminate it.

The target was therefore well illuminated for them, and they attacked it with one stick of nine 500-pound high-explosive bombs. Bursts were seen towards the west end of the yards, where later it was reported that a direct hit had been made on the roundhouses, starting a fire. Bombing was well concentrated in the area and four large explosions were seen in the centre of the yards. A number of good red fires were seen, three probably oil, and many smaller ones. Subsequent reconnaissance proved that the raid was very successful.

After they had attacked it with the usual excitement of fires, flares, flak and tracer, they had just finished the thirteen-second straight and level run to take the photograph when the cockpit suddenly lit up! They were bathed in a brilliant white light. The strength of the light completely dazzled and blinded Lee. Good God, we are in a search-light! he thought. For one horrible moment he panicked, shouts came from the rest of the crew, and he could just make out someone shouting 'Tracer! tracer!'

Pulling himself together, he called out, 'Hang on!' and he flung the aircraft into a dive, zig-zagging as they dived. He levelled out then zig-zagged again, first left, then right. He opened the throttles and, pulling back on the stick, began to climb, trying to get out of it, but it was too slow. Putting the nose down, he started a dive again. Quickly he pulled out of the dive and once again started to climb with full power. The engines were screaming.

He weaved left to right, right to left. It seemed incredibly slow. He couldn't go any faster. Still the searchlight held him. He stall-turned. Down he went again, zig-zagging as the aircraft sped downwards. Flak shells with their orange spurts of flame were bursting all around them. The smell of cordite made him feel sick. Slowly he pulled the stick right back – nose up and they started to climb again. He could feel the strain on the aircraft as he pulled out of the dive, twisting first right and then left. How that aircraft never broke up was a miracle.

'Fire down the beam, Jock!' But he needn't have bothered because just at that moment they flew out of the entangling beam leaving it and the others searching and probing the sky anxiously trying to find them again.

Lee broke out into a cold sweat. God, that was a narrow escape. He turned out of the target area and, putting the nose down, headed quickly in the general direction of home.

'Well done, Lee,' came the shouts from the crew.

'I'll have to change my underpants,' someone yelled.

With the target behind them, Riggy gave him a course to steer for base.

On their way home his racing pulse and the hubbub of excited chatter amongst the crew having settled down, Lee's thoughts turned to his darling Connie and, through them, to his pal Ken. Ken's navigator and Riggy were also great pals. His rear gunner was a Canadian called

Smithy. Smithy was a terrific character, full of fun, extremely witty and very popular. A good six feet tall, one wondered how he fitted into the tiny rear gunner's turret. He had a dry, laconic sense of humour, always ready for a practical joke, but could take it as well as give it. When in Lossiemouth he was always trying to find a Scottish ancestor; he was very proud of this and wore, with a great sense of fun, the tartan braces which they had given to him at Christmas. Connie and Lee thought the world of him.

Lee thought back to the time when, with Smithy, they had all gone to a dance one Sunday evening in the Sergeants' Mess at Lossiemouth. Smithy had poured a pint of beer in the Group Captain's hat. The Group Captain loved to come to the dance to do the Highland fling and had left his hat on the hall table when he went in to dance with his lady. The crews had gone in just afterwards. Smithy, seeing the hat lying there in all its glory with the 'scrambled eggs' – gold braid – on its peak, could not resist the temptation of putting it on. With shouts of horror from the rest of the lads, he took it off again and, as calmly as you like, picked up a pint of beer which someone had left nearby and poured it into the hat. The crews were horrified and scooted off, taking Smithy with them into the bar as quick as lightning.

Meanwhile the Group Captain's party had gone on in to the dance, where they thoroughly enjoyed doing the Scottish dances. Unfortunately for them, a WAAF had been sick on the dance floor just as the Group Captain and his party had started on an eightsome reel. They landed on the sick and slipped down onto the floor, right in the middle of it. There was a dreadful hush. The band stopped playing. The Station Warrant Officer had the presence of mind to turn out the lights. When they were turned on again, he was seen to be trying to clean the sick off the Group Captain's wife with his handkerchief. Brushing him aside, the Group Captain and his wife stalked out in high dudgeon. When they got to the hall where he had left his hat, he snatched it up and put it on his head, and the pint of beer that Smithy had put in it soaked him! He was furious. The Mess dance was put out of bounds to WAAFs and other ranks for a month. Lee chuckled to himself as he thought of that night.

They arrived back at base tired and thankful to be in one piece and delighted to hear that all of the squadron's aircraft had returned safely. Little did he realise at the time that a few months later, Ken would be shot down over that very target, Milan, and that the bodies of Ken and his crew would be buried at Bergamo in Italy by partisans.

It was the end of March when they were told to move to the tented camp that had been prepared for them. Delighted to leave the old school building, they clambered into lorries that had been borrowed from an army unit – these were in addition to the squadron's own transport. By so doing the move of all aircrew personnel from the old school to the camp was carried out quickly and smoothly.

By 1400 hours on 1 April, the move was virtually complete and all the personnel concerned, many of whom were under canvas for the first time, proceeded to make themselves comfortable. Lee and his pals were split up and posted to different camps, Lee to 37 Squadron's camp based at Torterello, a satellite of Foggia Main, and Bobby and other friends, who had come out with him, went to the camps of other squadrons nearby. This was the first time since OTU that Lee found himself without a pilot friend he could discuss problems with, and he felt the separation very keenly.

A battered and dilapidated old farmhouse, set in a field of mud, was the headquarters of the Squadron. From there they were taken to the tents that had been erected in the nearby olive grove. However, because Riggy was an officer, he had to go to a section of the grove reserved for the officers' quarters; this meant that the remaining four crew members could all be together. Riggy was quite annoyed at this form of segregation, but was much happier when he realised how cramped up they would have been in the one tent.

As it turned out they could not have all slept in the one tent anyway, the tents only being large enough to sleep four. The tents were the bivouac type, about twelve feet long, six feet wide and about four and a half feet high. In order to obtain more headroom, the first job was to dig out a hole of about eighteen inches under the tent itself, being careful to ensure the walls of the hole they had dug did not collapse into it. It was very difficult work, particularly as the roots of the olive trees had to be cut away as they came across them. The floor was covered with a rubber groundsheet, supplied with the tent.

There were no beds or palliasses, everyone had to find what material they could to construct their own beds or sleep on the ground. Lee was able to scrounge four very strong round cardboard containers with metal bottoms that the tail fins of the bombs came in. Putting these in his bed space, which was in the front half of the tent, he placed one in each corner with the metal bottoms uppermost. Each was about a foot across, and this gave a strong base upon which to place an old closed up Venetian blind that he had previously found lying around on a scrap heap. The result was a bench, off the ground, on which to lie. Finally, he used his kapok-lined inner flying suit to act as a mattress, and with the two army blankets that were issued to them, plus his RAF greatcoat over the top of them, that became his bed.

His pillow was his kitbag, rolled up, in which he also stored his spare clothing – primitive, to say the least, particularly as the bed had to be far enough away from the sides of the hole to prevent grass snakes and other unwanted creatures getting into it, spiders and beetles being the chief offenders. The tops of the beds came level with the ground outside, and if they were placed too near the sides, it was a simple matter for these creatures to slip in under the canvas and into the bed! It wasn't a happy thought, knowing that you could wake up with something like that crawling over you. Each night before he turned in he had to shake the so-called bed clothes to remove these unwanted visitors.

Len slept opposite him. He had managed to find an old door which he placed on old ammunition boxes and he had made up his bed on that. There was a gap of about two feet between them. Sparks and Jock had similar positions behind them at the rear of the tent. They had made up beds by making wooden and metal frames with strong twine laced criss-cross fashion over them. These were also propped up on tail-fin containers and old wooden ammunition boxes to keep them off the ground.

Having got themselves reasonably comfortable, the next job was to dig a small ditch around the outside of the tent so that rain dripping off the sides would be carried away and not seep into the interior. Finally, sacks and cardboard were placed outside of the front of the tent in an effort to stop the mud being carried off their feet into the inside – not easy to prevent when it was pouring with rain. Lighting was by shaded candles or by homemade oil lamps, but because of the blackout they were very rarely used.

Heating came from a drip stove which the crew had made them-selves. A small jerrycan formed the base plate of the stove, upon which dripped used oil, taken from the sumps of the aircraft engines. The oil dripped from a small oil drum, located outside the front end of the tent, through a narrow metal pipe controlled by a little tap, onto the metal base plate. Next to this, water from another similar sized drum, also housed outside and also controlled by a small tap, dripped alongside that of the oil. To initiate the process, a small fire was lit under the base plate. As soon as it became hot, the oil and water taps were turned on, allowing small quantities to drip on to the top of the stove. The heat ignited the oil and the dripping water caused it to splash over the surface of the base plate, causing the whole of the base plate to become red hot.

After the fire had gone out from under the base plate, the heat from the top of the stove continued to ignite the oil. They also used this heat to boil water for strip bathing, shaving, making cocoa and to cook what food they could buy when the food from the field kitchen became un-bearable. There were several snags to this heating arrangement: the risk of fire should the flap of the tent get too near to it; and the care needed when stepping in and out of the tent barefoot or in socks, particularly at night, when going outside the tent for a pee. But the most regular and unpleasant snag was when a large black beetle landed on the top of the

The changing faces of
Foggia – none of them
particularly pleasant!

stove. It frizzled and, as it burnt, it caused such a stench that evacuation of the tent became the number one priority. These beetles would be attracted by the glow of the stove, and before they could be chased away, would commit hara-kiri by doing three point landings on top of the hot plate!

The other essential piece of equipment was the jerrycan in which to hold their drinking water. This water was also used for such things as cooking, washing – both their bodies and their clothes – and as a fire extinguisher in case the tent caught fire. Water came into the camp in a bowser which was used to serve the whole camp, and each member of the crew took it in turns, whenever the jerrycan became empty, to go and collect the water. This was a chore most looked forward to because, whilst in the queue that gathered there, they were able to meet and chat to the other crew members. It was here that most of the rumours started, particularly early in the morning after a previous night's raid.

'I hear we lost so many last night.'

'So and so didn't come back.'

'The Yanks are going back today to finish it off.'

'I hear it's such and such a place tonight.'

And so on. At the back of the bowser there was a big heavy tap that was used to fill the jerrycans. Below it the ground was like a quagmire, where the water, during the filling of the cans, had overflowed. When it was cold, their feet became frozen stiff through standing around in their gumboots. This was in spite of wearing the special large white woollen socks issued for wear in their flying boots. These same socks were very useful and served another purpose: they used them inside their gumboots, which they wore instead of their flying boots to protect these from getting wet and muddy. If some idiot stamped his feet in an effort to warm them he was greeted with shouts of derision as the mud spattered everywhere.

Carrying the heavy jerrycan filled with water back to the tent was no easy matter either, and quite often another member of the crew would turn up to give a hand. The water tasted foul, being heavily chlorinated, therefore once back in the tent a further can was used in which to boil it and, when cool, each member filled his water bottle up with the stuff. Nevertheless, sometimes when they were not on duty, an evening in the tent together could be quite cosy. The stove gave off a comfortable heat and, sitting on the beds of Lee and Len, with a blanket wrapped around their shoulders, the crew would brew up a mug of cocoa, make toast and bacon and eggs, light up a fag and have a chat. Often they would save their candle ration by not lighting them and just sit around the warm red glow of the stove, telling stories of their lives in civvy street. Other times after they had received their beer and chocolate rations they would sit around the stove again in the dark, having a quiet drink and listening to the steady drip of the stove and the hiss of the water as it splashed across the hot plate, turning it to steam.

The weather closed in after the move and there was a three-day respite before they took off again. During that time they carried out dinghy and parachute drills. It was normal practice for the crews who were selected for ops that night to have their names posted on the operations board in the morning. They would then be on standby, carrying out the usual routine equipment checks, air tests and attending briefings until the operation was either confirmed or scrubbed. If scrubbed, it was then a rush to the Mess for a jolly good drink and a singsong.

The Mess and its bar was a homemade affair. The building was a Nissen hut, with the bar at one end. Tables and chairs were made from bomb carton cases. The large cookie bomb case was cut down to serve as a table, and the smaller bomb cartons were cut out in the shape of a chair. The atmosphere was laden with smoke, and the mood reflected the emotions of the airmen: celebrations when an op was cancelled; sadness when crews never returned; and celebrations when crews were 'tour-expired'. Lee kept away from the place when losses were high and, more particularly later, when the 'tour-expired' celebrations seemed to be getting less and less frequent.

The Australians on the Squadron were a wild bunch. It was not uncommon, after a rowdy drinking session, for them to pile the bomb cartons in the centre of the floor and set them on fire. On other occasions they would play 'Cowboys and Indians', whooping around the tents using their revolvers and firing them, using live ammunition. There were several tents with unexplained bullet holes in them! Or they would take a gharry and go pigsticking around the Italian farms. Needless to say, it didn't take much encouragement for others with too much *vino* inside them to take part. On one occasion they even upended the Squadron Commander's caravan with him in it. For that the Mess was put out of bounds for two weeks.

After about a month or two of this sort of camp life, nights like that seemed to Lee like a bad dream. It was all so unreal. Connie and home seemed so far away. He became fed up and wanted to get away, as far away as possible, from the bloody camp and all that it stood for. It was nothing but mud and slime. The food was gut rot. Even after boiling, the water was foul and still tasted of chlorine. No wonder you got the 'shits'.

The lavatories consisted of a tent, with a trench dug in the ground, and a plank with holes cut in for you and about a half a dozen other men to sit on. Underneath each hole were large buckets. They had to use what paper they could find. Letters from home were the favourite. Sometimes some wag would set fire to the paper in the bucket. The stench was horrible. If you had what was known as 'eyetie tummy' and had to use them under those circumstances, you wanted to be sick.

Lee felt trapped in the ugliness of the camp. Its barren trees, its bombed-out buildings, its greyness, its rows of dull canvas tents, its mud, its cold, its damp, its bugs, its dirt, its monotony.

The only true escape from it was to go on operations, even though that meant the same old routine with the same people. Sadly, they lacked other friends. The crews as crews, ate, slept, worked, and fought together. They went off camp together, they drank together, they went to the pictures together and to the showers together. As much as they got on well together, there were times when he cried out for something different. He was also trapped in their dependence upon each other. Living under canvas in primitive conditions was, to say the least, extremely restrictive, besides being very frustrating and emotionally draining if they should carelessly let their thoughts slip back to their home life.

Night-time bombing operations brought pressure enough, without the additional pressures of a sordid lifestyle. When they came back from an op they got fed up with 'trying to make the best of it'. They would give anything for an easy chair or a comfortable bed or even a decent meal. The main problem really wasn't the difficulty of making friends, but that everyone on flying duties held back. They didn't want to become too involved with other crews because of the fear that you might not see them again.

Rumours were always around. One of the most frightening was the one about aircraft crashing when approaching base. Apparently, by the time the rescue teams got to them, the Italians had stripped the aircraft and crew, leaving them naked on the ground after stealing everything. Sometimes they were embellished even worse. Dislike for the native population flourished, and this was further inflamed by the German radio propaganda. However, there was one opportunity for unity before some of the crews became too sloshed, and that was the singsongs in the Mess. Songs united the aircrew. They loved them and in the dingy smoke-filled bar they would sing their hearts out with gusto, particularly the RAF bawdy versions of 'Bless 'Em All', 'Old Fashioned Wimpy', 'Clementine', 'Little Angeline', to name but a few.

'Lili Marlene' with the English words and verses made up for the Desert Campaign was a very firm favourite.

The Italian version was also being made up for the crews now on ops. Lee didn't escape, his version was:

> 'Now here's Sergeant Lihou, he's on ops tonight,
> Swinging down the runway in someone else's kite.
> He'll shoot the shit when he gets back,
> Of how he bombed through ten tenths flak.
> It's dicey flying Wimpys around Italian skies.'

Later, when he was promoted to Flight Sergeant, the words were changed to: 'Flight Sergeant Lihou, he's on ops tonight'.

The favourite drink was the local *vino*, although they did receive a ration of beer and whisky.

And so the daily routine and squalor dragged on and on: eat, sleep, drink and ops.

CHAPTER FOUR

THE DANUBE AND NAPLES

THE weather cleared and on 1 April they were on duty again. Piombino, on the west coast of Italy, was the target. They were to attack shipping and dock installations to assist the Allied troops. The Americans were keeping the ports closed during the day, and the British had to keep them closed during the night. Sixteen Wimpys were airborne in waves of eight aircraft, with the additional object of harassing the unloading of the enemy's supplies at the port by arriving at five minute intervals. One aircraft dropped a 4,000-pound bomb on the area's roads at Orbetello, and the remainder bombed the target from 8,000 to 11,000 feet, between 2130 and 2155 hours, and from 0015 to 0033 hours in good weather conditions. Bombing was reported to be well concentrated in the target area, many bursts being observed on the jetties and moles extending to factories inland. One large fire was reported burning at the base of the south mole.

Lee's crew were circling the target area, changing height and varying their orbit. Sparks was throwing 'window' out through the flare shoot as quickly as possible in order to upset the German radar and locking-on devices of the German Ack-Ack guns. (Window was thin strips of silver paper which, as it fluttered down, played havoc with the enemy's electronics, jamming the effective use of the radar and tracking devices of the defences below.) It was uncannily quiet. They were to be over the target for five minutes before releasing their bomb load of nine 500-pound bombs. Below, the sea glistened in the darkness. The five minutes were up.

Immediately after starting the bomb run there was an almighty explosion just outside the port tail. The aircraft shuddered. Lee was convinced the aircraft had been hit.

'Heavy flak on the port side, Skip,' shouted Jock.

'Anyone hurt back there?' asked Lee.

But before he could get an answer, a call came from Len. 'Target in sight.'

'Steady as she goes.'

Lee concentrated on the job in hand. Jock was OK, but what about Sparks?

'You OK, Sparks?' he called.

He was relieved to hear Sparks' reply. 'OK, Skipper.'

Riggy's voice came on. 'What about me?'

'Shut up,' shouted Len.

'Bomb doors open,' a pause, 'Bombs gone.'

Lee thought quickly. Should he abort the photograph – the Ack-Ack had obviously got them in their sights – or should he carry on? But by now there were only a few more seconds to go. They carried on and broke off the attack with a split arse dive out of the target area.

'Christ, that was close,' observed Lee on the way home. 'Any damage back there?'

'Can't see anything, Skipper,' answered Sparks.

Opposition had consisted of intense heavy AA guns and one light gun. It must have been the heavy one which had nearly got them. Very little flak was encountered by the second wave, and all sixteen aircraft from the two waves returned safely to base. Lee was glad that he had pressed on with his photograph because he was one of the high percentage of the crews who obtained excellent photographs of the target area.

Upon arriving back at base, they had a look around the aircraft to see if they could find any damage. All they could see was a few very small flak holes in the fabric. They had been very lucky.

After a night's sleep they wandered down to the ops room. Much to their surprise they were on again that night, taking with them as second pilot the same one who had been with them the night before. The target was again the marshalling yards at Vicenza. Twelve aircraft were detailed to carry out the attack.

Arriving at Vicenza, all but one identified the target in good weather conditions. Together they dropped two 4,000- and eighty 500-pound bombs, together with seventy flares, from heights of 4,000 to 10,000 feet. Some of the illuminations were over a town to the north-east of the target and the one crew that did not identify the target dropped their bombs there. The remainder who bombed the marshalling yards at blitz time reported a good concentration of bombs at first, with many bombs being seen to straddle the yards causing one small explosion. As the raid progressed one large fire was seen to start amongst the rolling stock and several smaller ones were seen in the yards, together with three large explosions followed by flames. Opposition was negligible from the ground, but up to five unidentified aircraft were seen in the target area. However, there were no interceptions. All the aircraft returned safely to base.

Lee's crew had an uneventful trip. They had located the target with the main force and successfully attacked it, dropping their bombs in one stick aimed at the centre of the marshalling yards. The bombs were seen to burst in the northern end. The small amount of flak they encountered had been concentrated but, fortunately for them, not effective. Nearing base, Sparks reported that he had received a message that a German night fighter was prowling about the airfields attempting to shoot down aircraft as they were coming in to land. They were to be constantly on the alert even after landing and were to land without the benefit of navigation or landing lights. Getting into the landing circuit was a most uncanny experience. The dark shapes of aircraft would suddenly appear above, below and alongside them. With one eye watching his instruments and the other trying to identify the dark shapes, Lee tried to force himself not to become too concerned about the fighter. But fate being what it was, it was just their luck that they had to go round three times before getting the green signal from the Aldis lamp to land!

Each time they went around, the nagging fear that they could be in the sights of any enemy fighter added to the normal strain of getting down safely after an op. In addition, under those conditions, it was more imperative than ever that, in order to avoid collisions, they kept a careful look out for those other Wimpys who were also jostling for position and were anxious to come in to land at about the same time. It was nerve racking. However, they landed without incident.

The following night, much to their surprise, they were on ops again. God, three nights on the trot. This time it was a big one: Budapest, the capital of Hungary. The target was the Manfred Weiss Works in the city itself. It was a long way, about seven hours' flying time, and over enemy territory most of the way. Rumour had it that it was a raid to give moral support for the Russians because Churchill had promised we would do what we could to help them. Fifteen Wimpys were detailed and airborne, extra fuel tanks were put on and the bomb loads reduced to six 500-pounders. Later, one aircraft abandoned the task owing to engine trouble and returned to base.

They were to attack at midnight from 13,000 feet. Being one of the first night attacks on Budapest, Intelligence had limited knowledge of what the defences would be. Nevertheless, the crews were warned to take care and not to stray off course, and in particular to avoid the flak batteries situated at Zagreb on the way. They were to fly first on to the eastern end of Lake Balaton which was to be their landfall position, and from that point they were to commence their bombing run in to the target itself. Here they were to meet up with the other aircraft in a group at 15,000 feet and fly in together on the bombing run in order to blitz the target. Needless to say, the weather was foul over Yugoslavia. Lee's crew got into the target area early – so early, in fact, that they flew right past Budapest.

After they had arrived at Lake Balaton and had started their run in to Budapest, they realised that there was no sign of any other aircraft. Len went down into the bomb aimer's position to try and pinpoint their location, but was unable to identify anything below on the ground. Lee wondered if they had got the right lake. There was a smaller lake not far

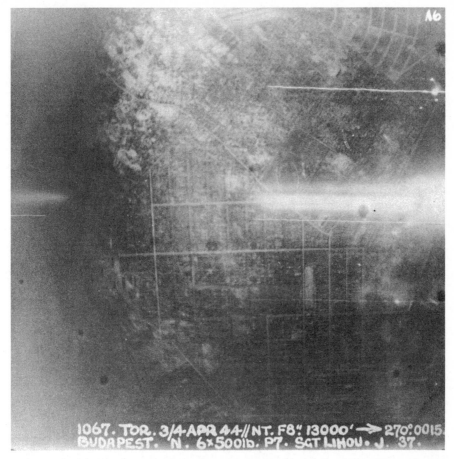

Budapest, 3/4 April 1944, was Lee's first long trip and first major target. They overshot and went back fifteen minutes late.

away and, with the ground mist, had they mistaken that for Balaton? But Riggy was sure they had the right lake.

Midnight came and there was still no sign of Budapest or flares on the target area, although the weather had cleared up and visibility over the plains below, except for a slight ground haze, was quite good. Lee was reminded of one of the verses of the desert version of 'Lili Marlene': 'Couldn't find the target, too much blooming sand'.

'Searchlights immediately behind us, Skipper,' called Jock from the rear gunner's turret.

'How many?' asked Lee.

'About twenty,' came the reply.

'Does it look like the target?' asked Lee.

51

'There's a hell of a lot of activity going on back there,' said Jock, not committing himself.

'How far behind us?' asked Lee.

'About thirty to forty miles,' replied Jock.

'It's easily that,' said Sparks from the astrodome.

'It can't be the target!' exclaimed Riggy. 'ETA is now. It should be below us right now.'

'It bloody well isn't,' replied Len from his bomb aimer's position. 'I can see no sign of it.'

'OK, I'm going to turn back,' said Lee. 'We were not told about that bad weather over Yugoslavia and maybe the winds have changed from those that they gave to you at briefing, Riggy.'

He turned the aircraft round and headed back to what was now obviously the target area. Searchlights were pointing in the direction from which the main attack was coming and the whole area was a hive of intense activity.

'Aircraft below,' called Len.

'Ours or theirs?' asked Lee.

'They are certainly not ours,' replied Len, 'and they don't look like theirs.'

Lee spotted them. 'Must be bloody Russian,' he quipped.

They were approaching the target. Len took over. They were a quarter of an hour late. The searchlights were pointing in the opposite direction, obviously searching for them in the same direction from which the main attack force had approached the target. It was a panoramic scene that greeted Lee as he flew in. Set in the middle of the plains below, lit up by the searchlights, was the city of Budapest. Rising from it and waving towards the west were the fingering beams of those same searchlights looking for them. As they approached, Lee could see the fires burning and the smoke rising from the attack of the main force. They were the straggler, approaching from the east and, in their ignorance, completely oblivious to the danger they were in. Riggy queried the fact they were approaching from the wrong direction and possibly heading into the main stream of aircraft coming out. Lee told the crew that, being fifteen minutes late, he assumed that they would not meet any of the main stream coming out as they flew in. They should be away by now – so they were going in.

'We can see the target,' he said, 'and we have not come all this way on a wasted journey. Anyway,' he said jokingly, 'it's on our way home.'

On to the target they went on a perfect bombing run. The flak was heavy as they flew through it. Bombs away, and a perfect photograph. To their utter amazement, as they were flying out of the target area towards the west, the searchlights swung right past them and started looking for them in the east! This was the direction in which all the other aircraft had left.

'They certainly didn't expect us to come in by the back door, and leave by the front,' said Lee.

'Thank God they don't know what they are doing, otherwise we would have got the lot.'

'And that was a good bombing run, Skipper,' added Len. As bomb aimer, he was delighted that he was able to carry out his job so effectively – a good and very conscientious man who took his job extremely seriously.

At debriefing, two of the squadron aircraft had failed to return, believed shot down by night fighters. The remaining aircraft had identified the target in good weather conditions and under good illumination, dropping their bombs from 10,500 to 13,000 feet. Bombing appeared to be well concentrated in the target area, particularly the incendiaries, and crews reported the target was well alight. Detailed observations of the results were difficult to assess because of the fires, smoke and dust from the many explosions caused by the bombing. Fires were seen for up to fifty miles away on the return journey. The target had been well defended both from the ground and in the air, with moderate to intense heavy anti-aircraft and intense light anti-aircraft guns with 'flaming onions'. Several enemy fighters were seen in the area. One enemy aircraft, a Focke-Wulf Fw190, was shot down by an attacking Wimpy over the target.

By the time they got to bed it was five o'clock in the morning. Christ, I hope we are not on again tomorrow, thought Lee as his head hit his kit bag which served as a pillow. He lay there, very happy and satisfied about the job they had done that night, but also thinking how lucky they had been, realising now, with the two aircraft being shot down, the danger they had been in, having been the one solitary aircraft over a target like that. Then quite unexpectedly he shuddered as a wave of fatigue came over him and, for the first time, he felt very, very tired and utterly weary. He dropped off to sleep exhausted. Later, Riggy told Lee that ops control were not very pleased with what had happened, but because no one said anything to Lee, he wasn't bothered. They had done their duty and bombed the target, and at least their photograph, which had been taken a little later than those of the main stream, showed the extent of the damage inflicted by the main wave.

It was as if the Gods had heard Lee's wish not to be on ops again so soon, because various combinations of bad weather, high winds and last minute cancellations due to target changes meant it was nine days before they were to take off on another mission. This time it was a most unusual op: they were to 'sow cucumbers in the River Danube'. What this really meant was that they were to lay mines in the Danube.

At briefing, a boffin explained that the mines were specially constructed to lie just below the surface of the river, so that when a barge passed over them they would rise and explode, sinking the barge. The

Germans were bringing oil from the Ploesti oilfields in Romania by barge because of the hammering that the American air forces were giving their railways in the Balkans by day. The Germans were also having to use the Danube to bring other supplies to their front lines, because the Russians had cut off the use of the railway in eastern Europe. The alternative route of the Danube which flowed through Germany, Austria, Hungary, Yugoslavia, Romania and Bulgaria was being used extensively because they could carry some 10,000 tons of supplies daily. It was a natural link between Germany and the Russian front, but above everything else it was a lifeline connecting the German forces with the Romanian oilfields.

So it was that No. 205 Group at the beginning of April 1944, working with naval boffins, commenced 'gardening' (the code-name for minelaying) in the River Danube. The job was to block the river by sinking barges, and to throw chaos among the hundreds of others that used the river. There were, of course, the usual snags to such a venture. It had to be carried out in moonlight, at 200 feet above the river and at low speed to prevent the mines exploding upon impact. The danger to the aircraft at that moment did not bear thinking about.

That night, 37 Squadron had been detailed to carry out three separate raids, two sowing cucumbers in the Danube, which involved seven aircraft. Four aircraft were detailed to 'sow their cucumbers' in one

Photo of Lee taken for forged documentation in case of being shot down.

section of the river and the three others to 'sow' in another. The third raid was to be three further aircraft ordered to take part in an attack on the marshalling yards at Budapest.

Lee and his crew were glad to have been given the new experience of mine-laying and, loaded with two 1,000-pound cucumbers, they set off. One good thing about this trip was that the Met. had to forecast good weather in order for the crews to find the 'cucumber beds' in the moonlight and to be able to fly at 200 feet between the banks of the river. On the other hand, it meant that it was going to be an almost daylight attack in the bright moonlight and they would be clearly visible to the enemy defences.

The squadron were to sow their cucumbers in a patch of the river between Novi-Sad and Belgrade. The crews were told not to destroy their parachutes if they had to bale out, because they could be bartered in exchange for their return home with the Yugoslavian partisans who wanted the silk. They were also told that bars of soap were another good bargaining source. Before they had completed their training at OTU the crew had had passport photographs taken in civilian jackets, shirts and ties to use on false documents if ever they were shot down over enemy territory. It was pointed out that this was a good time to make sure they had these with them, together with their silk handkerchiefs, which had maps of the area printed upon them, as these were also good bargaining items. They had also to make sure that they had their shirt studs, which had a small compass in the base, and the metal files cased in rubber which were supposed to be sown into the lining of their battledress jackets. But whatever else happened, if they were shot down, they stood a good chance of being picked up by the Partisans. Good God, thought Lee, they certainly know how to cheer you up!

This was also the fourth consecutive trip that Lee had a second pilot with him. Len was getting a bit fed up with it, because it meant that he had to stay in the bomb aimer's position for most of the journey.

In the brilliant moonlight they found their 'vegetable patch' (target area). Flying low along the Danube with the river banks rising on either side of them, they could clearly see motor traffic with dimmed headlights moving along; they must belong to an enemy convoy, they concluded. They laid their deadly traps and continued flying low at 200 feet over the river. To Lee, it was a tremendous thrill.

'Let's see if we can find some barges to shoot up,' suggested Lee. 'Want to go into the front turret, Len?'

'OK, Skipper.'

It wasn't long before the first barges came into sight, sitting low in the river, chugging along leaving a telltale wake of white foam behind them. They were much bigger than Lee had expected; he counted eight of them, four lots of two side by side.

'Got them in your sights, Len? Then go to it first. Are you ready at the back, Jock?'

Len needed no second bidding. The burst of machine-gun fire filled the aircraft and, as they flew on over the barges, it was Jock's turn in the rear gunner's turret to have a go. He also let rip.

'What about a second run, chaps?' asked Lee.

'OK by us, Skipper.'

They turned, flew alongside of the river bank, turned again and flew up on them from the rear. There seemed to be no one on board. They did a second run over them, both turrets in action, and then flew on for a few more miles, but no more were sighted.

'Better head for home now, Lee,' said Riggy.

On the way back, Lee reflected on how, at Advanced Flying School at Edenvale in Canada, the cadets used to low fly around a half sunken ship in Lake Simco, pretending to shoot it up, very much against orders as it was out of bounds. That 'exercise' had come to a tragic end when one of the lads, a young Canadian, crashed into it. Needless to say, no one was around when it happened!

Tonight had been great. Two aircraft returned with a mine each 'hung

An aerial reconnaissance photo of Leghorn, taken in May 1944, reveals a concentration of bomb craters in the dock area. *(© 1992 MoD reproduced with the permission of the Controller of HMSO)*

up' and landed at Foggia Main with them on board. All aircraft returned safely from the night's activity.

Then there was a night off, after which they were back on duty again, this time the target being harbour and dock installations at Leghorn on the west coast of Italy. They were to attack with nine 500-pounders at half past midnight from 10,000 feet.

The usual ceremony of checking, peeing and entering the aircraft took place, and the crew were in fine form. It was a lovely bright night with good visibility, and the weather forecast was promising. They were to head west and, when they reached the coast, fly down to Ischia and head north from there. Lee had a second pilot with him. They set off in high spirits.

'Coastline coming up, Riggy,' called Len.

'Can you see where we are?' asked Riggy, 'We are well ahead of ETA for the coast. It shouldn't be coming up yet,' he added.

'Difficult to see. It's very hazy down there,' came the reply.

Lee looked out of the window and opened it to get a clearer view. He was unable to recognise anything but it was certainly the coastline coming up. He asked the second dicky to assist Len.

'Crossing coast now,' said Len.

'OK, alter course for Ischia, Lee,' called Riggy, giving him his new course.

Lee promptly altered course slightly to the south-west. He was flying along quite happily when, a few moments later, the whole sky suddenly opened up around them with searchlights, tracer and flak.

'Jesus Christ!' shouted Lee, 'What the hell's happening? We should be over friendly territory. I'm altering course out of it.'

'You mustn't do that,' shouted Riggy.

'Bullshit,' replied Lee, 'I'm getting the hell out of here. There's a bloody raid going on and we are heading straight into it.'

'There can't be,' said Riggy.

'Come and see for yourself,' cried Lee.

Riggy opened the door behind where the second dicky was sitting.

'Christ! That's Naples,' he said.

A split-arse dive and they were out of it.

When sanity had been restored, the inquest started. That was Naples, a restricted area. When the Fleet anchored in the bay they took no chances, any unauthorised flight would have the lot and they had got it.

'We altered course too early,' said Riggy.

What Len had thought was the coastline was, in fact, a layer of very low cloud over the land, and from the air it looked just like a coastline. They continued the milk run, the name given to those raids which entailed flying up the coast to a port where one aircraft at a time flew over the port for fifteen minutes, dropped their bombs and pushed off for the next one to take over. Thus the port below was in a continual state of alert all night long.

Two nights later they went back to Budapest, with an Australian flight sergeant as second pilot. This time they were to drop leaflets as well as bombs informing the Hungarians that they were not safe from the Allies and to quit the war whilst they had the opportunity. Fourteen aircraft were detailed to attack the marshalling yards. Two aircraft carried out illumination which was good at the time of attack, particularly as the weather was very hazy over the target and visibility was poor. Some of the fires that were started in the marshalling yards early in the attack formed an aiming point for many crews and a large number of bursts were seen near these in and around the yards. Len commented on the

Lee's raid photo taken at San Stefano on 23/24 April 1944.

poor visibility to Lee as they were making their approach to commence the bombing run.

'Can't see much of the target below, Lee, but it looks as if there are quite a few fires in it. Shall we bomb on them?'

'Guess we should, Len,' he replied, hoping the excitement of the situation was not affecting his judgement.

Riggy was given the job of dispatching the leaflets through the flare chute. Having decided to bomb on the existing fires, they dropped their bombs in one stick across what appeared to be the yards, but were disappointed because they could not identify their results among the other bursts that were taking place in the smoke-filled haze below. All the aircraft, except the two that had returned early due to engine trouble, bombed from 8,000 to 12,000 feet. Opposition was reported as consisting of some scattered light flak from two or three heavy guns. There were about twenty searchlights operating. Window was used very effectively to counter and hamper this opposition. All the squadron's aircraft returned safely to base.

Two more milk runs on San Stefano, a port on the west coast of Italy, followed in quick succession. The first, with a nine 500-pound bomb load, was again to harass the enemy whilst unloading shipping. Considerable haze over the Italian west coast made visibility bad and greatly hampered the operation. Thirteen aircraft from the squadron took part, and bombing was carried out between 4,700 to 9,500 feet with opposition of slightly heavy flak coming from three or four guns, which was fairly accurate at most times. There was also light flak from one or two guns. Bombing was undoubtedly scattered, yet it appeared that the object was achieved in spite of the adverse weather conditions.

The next day Lee and his crew had been all prepared to go on a raid to Ploviay, but their aircraft was pulled out just as they were about to taxi out of dispersal, for no apparent reason. In the official records it was not required for operations. Meanwhile, 37 Squadron had a change of command with the old Squadron Commander going to No. 614 Target Finder Squadron.

On the next raid to San Stefano they carried a 4,000-pound bomb and 'Safe-Conduct' surrender leaflets. Twelve aircraft operated to attack the shipping and harbour installations and continue harassing unloading operations, designed to prevent the enemy unloading war material at the ports of Genoa, Leghorn, Piombino and San Stefano. Bombing was carried out from 8,000 to 10,000 feet in good weather, but poor visibility owing to haze. Slight heavy flak, fairly accurate, was encountered from the north-west and south-east of the target area, probably from two batteries only.

Bomb bursts were seen to be covering the area well, and the attack was spread out from 2300 hours until 0200 hours the next morning,

One of the 'Safe-Conduct' leaflets dropped over enemy troops.

successfully accomplishing the purpose of the mission. Lee's 4,000-pound bomb was seen to burst on the centre of the harbour installations. Once again they also had a second pilot with them which meant that, in between dropping window, Riggy was gainfully employed also dropping out the 'Safe-Conduct' surrender leaflets telling the German troops that if they surrendered with the leaflet they would be guaranteed safe conduct through the Allied lines. Lee often wondered whether or not the leaflets worked, but doubted it.

This brought them to the end of April 1944; in about eight weeks they had successfully carried out sixteen operations.

CHAPTER FIVE

DOUBTS GET WORSE

L ETTERS between Connie and Lee were erratic. Sometimes it would be two or three weeks before he heard from her, then several letters would come together. He wrote every day either by airmail, airletter, airgraph or sea mail. It was embarrassing because the officers censored all letters leaving the camp, and Lee knew that Riggy would be reading his letters to Connie. In fairness, Riggy did sign one or two blank air letters for Lee, but he was taking an awful risk.

It was getting near the halfway mark of their tour and as they went on, the pressure on them built up. Lee's crew were well aware that the more ops they did, the more the odds against them surviving were shortening. They couldn't be lucky all the time, and were very conscious of the fact that, so far, they had hardly had a scratch.

Aircrew relied on mail from home as a booster to their morale, to ease that pressure. It was a magic moment in camp when mail was received from wives, sweethearts, mums and dads. However, it was sad and disconcerting to see the disappointment on the faces of the men who, after waiting eagerly for news, came away empty-handed from the mail call. Poor Len suffered far worse than Lee; his letters had to come all the way from Canada and he was anxiously looking forward to hearing news of how his baby daughter was progressing. Aircrew, though, were a resilient bunch and after the initial disappointment of not receiving a letter, their sense of humour came to the fore by asking anyone who had received a letter from their wife or sweetheart if he would pass them the 'Sports page!'

It was nine days before they went on operational duty again. However, their names had been on the operations board and they had been on standby most of that time, which meant they had the anxiety of not knowing whether they were going or not at the back of their minds all day. Sometimes they were even sitting in the aircraft waiting to take off before the op was scrubbed at the last minute. Nevertheless, these cancellations, owing to a mixture of bad weather and the change of mind about the target, gave them a welcome break from flying.

On 2 May, when the conditions were right, twelve Wimpys were detailed to carry out another raid with a full bomb load on the docks at Genoa. The objective: to harass enemy shipping once again and so prevent them unloading supplies for the German army in Italy. It was to be a six-and-a-half hour trip. Bombing was to be from 8,000 to 9,500 feet, covering a three-hour period. It was to be carried out in two waves of six aircraft.

However, when they arrived over the target area they found it covered in a heavy layer of strato-cumulus cloud which unfortunately hampered the attack and prevented accurate observation of the results. One aircraft, unable to identify the target, moved off and attacked Leghorn instead. The remaining aircraft, including Lee's, attacked on dead reckoning navigation the estimated position of the target. They were fairly convinced they were on target because up to six heavy and about four or five light anti-aircraft guns could be seen firing, their gun flashes reflecting on the clouds below; they also saw the puffs of smoke from the shells bursting around them.

Lee had just started to head into the firing when he heard a cry from Len. 'Aircraft immediately below.' He raised the nose of the aircraft and started to weave out of harm's way. It was another Wimpy which had been spotted just in time. It was only slightly below them and Len had noticed it outlined by the light of the flares on the clouds below as he was about to commence their bombing run. It was so near, in fact, that they were caught up in its slipstream, their own aircraft bobbing up and down like a rowing boat being tossed about on the open sea. They were extremely lucky not to have collided with it. Having just missed it and having weaved back on course, they were able to follow in behind it, and Lee managed, in spite of a bumpy run from the tail end of the slipstream, to fly a reasonably straight and level course in order to release their bombs. Len said afterwards that it had just appeared out of the blue. All of the aircraft returned safely.

The following morning came the shock: they were to carry out another first. They were on again, but this time it was to Bucharest in Romania. Being such a long way away they could only carry three 500- and two 250-pound bombs. The rest of the load was extra fuel tanks. 'What the hell sort of damage can we do with such a small bomb load?' thought Lee. It was obviously another political attack. What was worse they were going on a moonlit night again, nearly 500 miles over enemy territory; and more, the flight was expected to take over seven hours there and back and, as they were to attack at 0130 hours, it meant not getting back to base (and so to bed) until early morning. However, as always, doubts were soon dispersed as they prepared for the flight.

As soon as they were airborne the nature of the target was forgotten as they went about their normal routines. Again the weather was good and, after skirting a few flak batteries on the way, it didn't seem to take so long to reach the borders of Romania and to see the River Danube glistening in the moonlight below.

As a precaution against fighters creeping up on them when over enemy territory, Lee was accustomed to weaving gently, scanning the skies above and below. He also made it a habit to keep to the dark side of the sky on the flight path in to the target. It was such a lovely moonlit night that Lee could not resist humming the tune of the Blue Danube Waltz, and the rest of the crew, hearing him over the intercom, joined in. Soon they were all singing away, nobody knowing the words. Len and Lee started swaying, sitting side by side in the cockpit keeping time to the rhythm, and as they swayed, Lee weaved the aircraft up and down, left and right, above the River Danube in time to the music. They were dancing in the sky!

All that was soon to change as they approached the target. There was 8/10ths cloud at 10,000 feet and considerable haze over the target area. It was very heavily defended, but in spite of the haze, the marshalling yards were clearly visible among the melee of flak, tracer, searchlights, flares, incendiaries, and bomb bursts. Once again the sheer intensity of the action gripped Lee. He felt himself being drawn into an excitement which was hard to comprehend. The crackle of flak above the roar of the engines, the ever-changing patterns of light and darkness, the peculiar smell of the cockpit, the strain on his eyes, the aches in his body, the monotonous voice of Len: 'Left, left, right, right. Steady, steady,' the eagerness, the anticipation, all felt as if it was going to explode about him. He felt sure his blood pressure must be up to a thousand over a thousand. It was intoxicating!

The rest of the crew were in position, Sparks in the astrodome and Jock in his turret. They were now disciplined to be silent during the bombing run; only in the gravest emergency were they to draw attention to what was going on around them. Calmly and deliberately he flew on, full of purpose, straight and level on his bombing run, knowing that Len would guide them faithfully onto the target to obtain the maximum results for their efforts. Good, reliable Len.

How he loved the experience, and how much he enjoyed the immense feeling of satisfaction and elation he felt when they left the target. He loved being in charge: being determined, being thorough and so much in control of the situation. To use a very, very hackneyed expression among aircrews: 'To press on regardless'. He could be called a creep any time rather than miss that thrilling experience. Bombs gone. Photograph taken. They altered course for home.

No sooner had they left the target area when Sparks' voice rattled in Lee's ears.

'Weave! for f— sake, Lee! A German fighter's locked on us.'

Lee's training of simulated fighter attacks at OTU came into play as an automatic reaction. He pulled back on the joystick and up went the nose of the aircraft as the throttles were pushed forward at the same time, then into a steep climb out of danger, almost on stalling point, a quick kick on the rudder and the faithful old Wimpy responded gallantly as over the top of the climb she went. The port wing dropped and they plunged downwards into a steep dive. The ground below rushed towards them as they went hurtling down. Papers, leaflets and other bits and pieces flew up in the air, the contents of the Elsan chemical lavatory splashed out, but they had escaped at least for the moment. As Lee levelled out, it was over as quickly as it started. The crew were shaken, but unhurt. Lee asked Len to go into the front turret and told Jock to keep his eyes open.

'Christ, Lee,' called Sparks, 'the inside looks as if a bomb has hit us.'

'Well done, Sparks,' called Lee. 'Where did it come from?'

'It came up from the rear port side, Skip, heading straight for us; that's why Jock couldn't see it.'

'Crafty bastard,' said Lee. He looked at his altimeter; they had bombed at 12,000 feet and they were now flying at 8,000 feet. They could see other aircraft being shot down.

Lee climbed quickly to 11,000 feet and then, putting the nose slightly down he raced for home, weaving all the time. Another German fighter (or was it the same one?) appeared and headed down slightly from the starboard side in front of them. Lee could see the flashes from its gun ports. But as quickly as it had appeared, it passed swiftly below and, because Lee was weaving, it missed them. As it passed, Len, who was now in the front turret, tried to give him a steady burst but he was gone before anything came of it.

'Did you see where that bugger went, Jock?' asked Lee excitedly. 'Wonder if it was the same bastard?'

'No sign of it, Skipper,' replied Jock calmly.

They eventually arrived safely back at base. After debriefing and a lousy breakfast they hit their beds, exhausted.

Twelve Wimpys from 37 Squadron had been detailed as part of 205 Group to carry out that attack and, in spite of the opposition, all the aircraft had attacked their objective. Many observed bomb bursts on or near the marshalling yards with several violent explosions and flashes following bombing. It was estimated that there were some twenty light and twenty heavy guns defending the target.

As well as Lee's encounter, several other enemy aircraft had been seen and air-to-air firing observed. In conjunction with the bomb load, eighty-six packets of leaflets were dropped to fall on the city, advising the citizens of the futility of fighting in the war and to get rid of their leaders. They never did get to know if there were any squadron or group losses that night.

After getting to bed, they woke later that morning in time for a spot of lunch and a beer in the Mess, followed by a walk down to the ops room. The board in the ops room showed that they were not on duty that night, which was a relief, as they were beginning to feel quite drained.

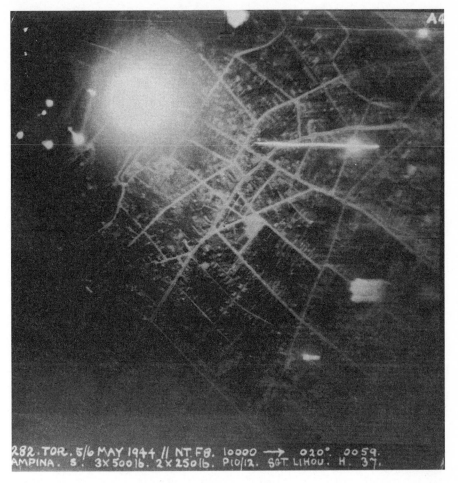

Lee's raid photo taken at Campina on 5/6 May 1944.

However, on the next day, to Lee's amazement he saw that they were on duty again. This time the target was Campina in the foothills of the Transylvanian Alps, ten miles north-west of the Ploesti oilfields above Bucharest, where they had been the night before.

Good grief! This was to be another long trip with another seven-hour journey over enemy territory. They were to attack the oil installations and marshalling yards where oil supplies were reported to be assembled for supporting the enemy front against the Russians, and again they were to carry a very limited bomb load. It was quite a switch from harassing shipping on the west coast of Italy to helping the Russians in the Balkans. Lee wondered if this was because things were slowing down on the Italian front. Mud was impeding the movement of the Allied tanks and it was getting to be like Flanders in the First World War.

The flight out was a repeat performance of their previous journey, except for one vital ingredient: the high-spirited attitude had gone. There was no singing or 'dancing in the sky' this trip. The crew were tired and more subdued. Tonight was a tough one and they all knew it. The USAF had been attacking the Ploesti oilfields by day for some time, with rumoured heavy losses. This was to be no picnic.

Reaching the target the defences were, as anticipated, very active. Searchlights were probing the skies, the flak was intense and seemed to be everywhere. The smell of cordite filled the cockpit and excitement was again at fever pitch. Once again Lee was in his element. This was superb, it really was something. All tiredness drained away as the adrenalin took over, stimulating his awareness of the dangerous situation they were in. He was on his toes, ready, anticipating, waiting for something to happen.

The attack proved to be most successful. Bombing heights were from 10,000 to 12,000 feet. Weather and visibility were good. Several strikes were seen as direct hits on the oil storage tanks in the north-east section of the target. The marshalling yards had formed the aiming point for the attack owing to their central position between the oil refinery plant in the south-west corner of the target and the storage tanks in the north-east corner.

Len dropped his bombs in one stick, scoring a direct hit in the middle of the target. Several other sticks were observed to straddle the marshalling yards. Three large fires were seen to be burning furiously after the attack and photographs taken with the bombing showed these quite clearly. Lee wanted more; he would have loved to have gone around again, but this was not allowed. As they flew away, the excitement abated and that funny feeling of pleasure mixed with self-satisfaction of knowing they had made it, took over. And how quickly it all changed to the routine task of getting home safely once it was over.

Leaving the target area, Lee put the nose of the aircraft down and sped for home along the valley of the Danube, flying as low as practicable. He didn't want night fighters coming up underneath them.

They arrived home at 4.30 in the morning, and at debriefing it was reported that several enemy aircraft were observed over the target area and air-to-air firing had been seen. One sergeant and his crew did not return from this operation. Another aircraft was also missing, but all of the crew except the wireless operator safely returned to the squadron a few days later, suffering minor injuries and shock after they had ditched in the Adriatic. The wireless operator was not saved from this crash, and was presumed lost due to the rapid sinking of the aircraft after hitting the water.

A follow-up attack was carried out the next day by the USAF in daylight and their crews reported that before their attack commenced, the fires which had been started the previous night were still burning. After the raid it was some time before Lee managed to get off to a very fitful sleep. He woke up startled, looking at his watch. It was 11.30 a.m. ... blimey, only four or five hours' sleep!

He knew he had had a bad dream, but he couldn't remember anything about it. Lying in the shade of the tent he felt cold, although outside the sun was shining and it must have been quite warm. Len was up trying to get the stove to light up. Sparks and Jock were still fast asleep. Lee felt dreadful, his eyes were tired and his left leg was sore with cramp where

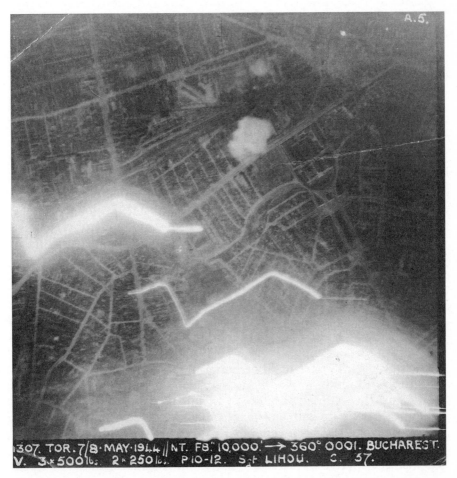

Bucharest. The raid on 7/8 May 1944 marked their 20th op and the half-way mark in the tour. Following this operation the crew went on leave to Sorrento.

he had been lying heavily on it just before he awoke. Maybe it was this that woke him up, he thought to himself. He sat up on his bed. He felt drained, irksome, still utterly exhausted.

'Morning Len. Sleep well?'

'So-so, Skip, and you?'

'Not bad,' he lied. 'I suppose we had better get these two up and get down to ops and see where the poor sods are going tonight. I don't suppose we will be on again.'

Whilst Len roused Sparks and Jock, he slowly got out of bed. Fully convinced that they would not be on operational duty, he washed and shaved, chatted to the rest of the crew and together they went down to the ops room.

As if three long journeys in four days were not enough, he couldn't believe it when he saw that they were on again. He had been wrong, they were among the poor sods. Back again to Bucharest, the target the industrial area of the city. Another seven-and-a-half hour trip . . . Shit!

There were ten other Wimpys from the squadron detailed to carry out this further attack on the industrial area. However, this time they had all been picked to carry out a precision attack, which was to be more accurately executed against a prescribed area than on the previous night.

Bombing was carried out from 10,000 to 11,500 feet in good weather and visibility, although there was some haze. Most of the sticks were aimed at the factory building which stood out particularly well in the prescribed area and without doubt nearly all the bombs found their mark on the target section of the city, Len's stick being one of them. It was seen to straddle the factory with bursts in the middle of it. They were getting good! Reports at debriefing later and the subsequent photographs confirmed this point.

The whole squadron had been able to carry out the attack successfully in spite of the heavy ground defences. These consisted of some ten light guns, hosepiping and apparently firing at flares, with up to twenty heavy gun batteries which seemed to be fairly accurate. Window was used with marked effect against the fifteen or so searchlights. Several enemy aircraft were seen in and around the target area, and air-to-air firing was observed by many of the attacking forces going into the target.

Lee's own flight there had been uneventful, although he had to fight hard to keep himself awake flying over the Adriatic and the Yugoslav mountains. He was mad at himself when he dozed off a couple of times and, after waking up with a start, was thankful he had put the autopilot on. The crew had all been very quiet and it wasn't until they got close to the target that the tempo increased. This time, however, Lee did not feel the usual elation over the target. His only reaction had been that he was satisfied that Len felt they'd had a good result; other than that there was nothing more. Such was his frame of mind. On any other occasion he would have been overjoyed that they had such a good result from a precision attack.

To add to his disenchantment with the night's effort and the low state of his morale, on the way back to base, some thirty to forty miles to the west of the target, they saw a Wimpy shot down only about a mile away from them. Lee had been gently weaving when he saw the Wimpy ahead on what had appeared to him to be a straight and level course back home. With Len, who was in the front turret, and Sparks in the astrodome, they watched in horror as they saw a Ju 88 creep up from the stern and fly underneath the Wimpy which was flying in the light part of the sky.

'Oh my God! Look what's going on over there on the port side,' exclaimed Lee in a slow hushed voice over the intercom.

'Is there anyway we can warn him, Sparks?' he asked.

'No, Skipper,' came the equally hushed reply.

'Shit! Christ, I hope they see him.'

But it was not to be. They saw the Ju 88 shoot the Wimpy down in flames, break off its attack, dive away and head straight for them. It was the last they saw of it. It was all over in a few seconds. Lee felt helpless and frustrated, aggravating the mood he was in. Although all the squadron's aircraft had returned safely there was no news regarding the group's losses.

Arriving back at base in the early hours of the morning, the only thing that Lee wanted to do was sleep. He was tired; he felt dull, and the enthusiasm had gone. He had felt as if all this was becoming routine, very hum-drum and matter of fact. He put it down to his tiredness and the fact that he was feeling irritable and out of sorts. After all, he had felt worn out before they started.

He couldn't get debriefing over quickly enough. Coming out, it started to rain, a heavy shower pelting down. With his parachute banging against his legs, and clinging to his helmet and mask, he ran as fast as he could in his flying gear with the rest of the crew to the gharry that was waiting to take them back to the tents. He got soaked. Once on board he tried to light a cigarette, but gave up as everything was dripping wet. Sitting on the wet benches of the field kitchen, they had the usual lousy oily-tasting breakfast of scrambled dehydrated dried egg, streaky bacon and fried bread.

The rain had stopped as they trudged back through the mud to their tent. In the half light of the dark they tried to remove the mud from their flying boots before they entered the tent using the tent pegs and the open bottom of the wooden box that Lee used as wash-hand table. With some difficulty in the cramped conditions of the tent they got out of their wet flying suits and lay them at the foot of their beds. The air in the tent was steamy and damp. They quietly got ready for bed. Lee struggled into his pyjamas and climbed into his bed, then with grunts of 'Goodnight' the candles were snuffed out.

Lee lay on his bed, wide awake although his body was aching with tiredness. His eyes were also aching behind his closed eyelids, which themselves felt heavy and were tender and sore around the rims. His ears felt blocked and he could still feel his flying helmet on his head although he had taken it off long ago. He was very aware that his neck ached also but he was too tired to do anything about it.

The rain started again, bucketing down on the roof of the tent like a drum. A drip fell on his face, then another. He reached up and, with his finger, traced the drip and carried it down a line on the canvas to the skirting of the tent; that kept it off him. He then realised his bed was slightly damp, but he was too tired to do anything about it. God, it was hard and uncomfortable. He was so tired, yet still he was unable to sleep.

And then it started in his thoughts again: Duty versus Conscience. Whenever he was alone or unable to sleep he found his thoughts turning to his attitude to the events which so dominated his life. He could not escape from this continual worry about his personal emotions. It worried him incessantly. He could not reconcile his duty with his conscience. The stark fact that he was dropping bombs on innocent people below bothered him immensely. Duty and conscience, the two seemed to be so incompatible. Even though he did not know for sure that it was his bombs that killed people, the chances must be that they did, for once they dropped out of the aircraft on their way to the city below he had no control of them no matter how careful he was. Nowadays, each night as soon as he got into bed to sleep, instead of dropping off right away as he used to do, he would start worrying about it. Furthermore, what made matters worse, much worse, was the nagging feeling that if his conscience bothered him so much, why did he enjoy being over the target so much?

The question of why he was so happy being over the target kept coming to the forefront of his mind, but he kept dispelling it. He wasn't going to admit to being happy about what he was doing. Other pilots he spoke to freely admitted they didn't like the flak, but he had no feelings about that one way or the other. Tonight had confirmed it; he wasn't bothered at all about flak over the target. On the contrary, he rather enjoyed it. The crackle, the puffs of smoke, the flame-like colours as the shells burst and scattered around them, the smell of cordite, all added to the excitement.

The rain poured down outside. He thought the roof of the tent was going to collapse. God, I hope we are not going to be flooded out. That's all we need. He searched in the darkness for his rubber cape. Feeling under his kitbag pillow, he touched the cold damp slimy surface of the cape, pulling it out and placing it over the top of his great coat which served as an eiderdown. That done, he felt under the venetian blind on which he was lying to make sure his wellies were still under the bed.

Satisfied that he was ready in case the tent flooded, he lay back. Even the exertion of doing that seemed to have put an additional strain on him. He wondered why even a little thing like that added to his tiredness. He tried to think about something else, but his thoughts wandered back to the problems he was having with his conscience. He realised he was starting to think again about his doubts about himself, instead of attaining the sleep he so desperately needed. He tried to blank out his mind, but the worries persisted. He had no control of the emotional wind-down that was taking place within him.

He was on the edge of sleep, but his thoughts raced away, worrying over and over again about his emotional reactions. Why on the one hand could he become so psyched up, so stimulated and so cocksure of himself when over a target and yet now, on the other hand, when in the safety of his bed, when he should be relaxing, was he frightened and unsure of himself? Just at this moment he felt like a miserable little coward who was so unhappy, he could quite easily cry himself off to sleep. It was unbelievable.

Was he becoming flak-happy to feel like that over the targets? What did flak-happy actually mean? The rear gunners' flight commander was said to be flak-happy because he didn't want to leave the squadron until he'd got a gong! A stupid bloody medal. As if that mattered. There were pilots who had the reputation of going in for the kill; was that what it was? Good God, he hoped not. Surely this bloody war hadn't done that to him?

His thoughts wandered back to the barrack room days and the discussions they used to have in the pubs. How he and his pals had often wondered if, coming face to face with a German, would they be able to kill him? That topic was usually left unresolved because no one had the guts to admit what they would do one way or the other. *No one had the guts.* Is that what this was all about? Guts to do your duty in spite of your conscience? But now, trying to get off to sleep, he wasn't so bloody brave. There was no bravado in him, now he wasn't over the target; as a matter of fact, his emotions were so mixed-up he wanted to be sick. He felt so tired, weak and helpless. He wondered if soldiers felt the same as they lay in their tents or dug-outs?

His thoughts went back to the Commando training they had received at Whitley Bay to toughen them up when they came back from Canada. The powers that be had obviously thought that the soft life they'd had over there needed to be knocked out of them, before they went into battle. He started to think about the various ways they had been taught to kill a man. A piece of wire around his neck, the edge of a tin helmet. How they had thought how ridiculous it was, running to shove bayonets into those hanging sacks, screaming and shouting abuse.

71

'Thou shalt not kill.' The words haunted him. Even so, this is what they were doing. God, he hated the thought, yet if he hated it, why at the time did he enjoy being over the targets so much? If that was duty, you didn't have to enjoy it. But I'm not like that, he thought to himself. How was it possible for anybody to become so mixed-up? How was it possible that they became so uncaring, so insensitive, with no thoughts of what was happening to the people below?

The questions and the reality of the situation confused him. Then there was tonight. What about his attitude tonight? What the hell was that all about? He couldn't blame excitement – he was bored stiff – his only re-action had been to feel pleased, mainly for Len's sake, for a good attack. Was complacency setting in?

At least before, he could blame the excitement of the occasion, but tonight it was so matter of fact, so bloody ruthless. Press on regardless. God, what bullshit!

All the same, what if he did become complacent; if he didn't keep on top of his job it could spell disaster for the rest of the crew. It was at that moment when he realised that he was only making excuses. Then the truth really hit him. He was frightened; more than that, he was scared stiff!

Lying there at this moment he had to admit to himself that he was afraid of the bloody targets. Only he knew how his stomach twisted up when he saw his crew's name on the board for ops, and more so when they found out where they were going and if it was going to be a tough one. Yet he was the one who had to pretend that it was OK to the rest of the crew. But wasn't he the one who had taken it upon himself to put on a brave face in front of them? Poor sod, if only they knew. He suddenly began to feel sorry for himself. A wave of self-pity surged over him.

Now as he lay there cold, tired, lonely and miserable, he felt he had finally discovered what it was all about. He was scared. Scared of getting hurt, of not knowing what was going to happen; scared of the unknown. But he reassured himself he wasn't scared of dying. No way. That didn't worry him at all. What he was scared of was of being scared, of how Connie would feel, of what his parents would tell the neighbours, friends and relations back home; scared of failing. In his mind's eye he saw his mother standing by the clock in the living room waiting for the two minutes silence at 11 o'clock. He remembered how his mother cried each Remembrance Day.

The rain stopped.

Christ, he didn't want to go on ops again. He had had enough. Now he was safely home and in his bed, he wanted to stay there. He was fright-ened, worried, scared and anxious for the future. What if he was maimed? Len always took his tin hat with him – they had all laughed. Maybe he had the right idea, after all. Would Lee let his crew down in a crisis? What if he panicked in an emergency? As much as he tried not to, he let his thoughts torture him.

Would he ever see his darling Connie again? His eyes filled with tears through the sadness of his self-pity. He felt thoroughly miserable. How he longed to hold her in his arms, caress and cuddle up to her as he did on those few nights they had had together in Moreton. The softness of her body, the warmth of the sheets and the pillows, the perfume of her long dark hair as it nestled against his chest, the tender words of their love-making. How he longed for her. What would she think of him in this state?

Full of self-doubt and self-pity, he continued to worry and torment himself. His thoughts raced endlessly and aimlessly around in his head. He tossed and turned, desperately seeking and longing for those precious hours of sleep. But no matter how he tried, he could not fall asleep. *If I don't get off to sleep soon, I'll be hopeless in the morning. I must stop thinking about myself, about everything. I must try to get off to sleep. Why the hell am I worrying about all this?*

He tried blanking out his mind again, counting sheep, deep breathing, but still he continued to worry and fret and now he realised, he was worrying about not being able to sleep. What a terrible state he was getting himself into. Lying there he felt as if his body was asleep, that it was only his mind that was active and on the brink of sleep. He became conscious of the discomfort of his bed. This bloody bed is damp. It was raining again, thundering down on the tent. Listen to it. It's pissing down outside again. I hope this bloody tent isn't going to collapse. What a dump!

What a scramble there had been climbing, soaked, into the gharry earlier on. He had given his knee a bang on the bolt holding the tailboard as he had tried to clamber in quickly, and it had hurt like hell, even through his flying suit, and it still hurt. He would have a bloody great bruise there tomorrow. His thoughts switched once more to what had happened when they had got back tonight. There had been glum faces in the debriefing room when they had returned and an air of despondency. Those poor devils in that Wimpy that had been shot down. They had never stood a chance. He wondered what squadron they had come from. They had been taken completely by surprise; they must have all bought it as Lee and his crew never saw any parachutes leaving the burning aircraft. He felt sure that losses that night had been high. In any case, the powers that be never did tell them the results of a raid with regard to the number of losses. They only got to know through rumour. Maybe if losses were high 'they' were afraid that it might affect the morale of the crews. What the hell! It didn't bother him one way or the other right now; all that he wanted was sleep.

What, then, if they were on again tonight and he had had no sleep? He was exhausted last night, and he would be bloody useless tonight. Serve him right. After all that was the real truth of the matter. He was shit-scared. He hated himself for thinking that way. He could find no solace, happiness or contentment in his thoughts. It never dawned on him, as he lay there so wrapped up in his own emotions, what the real answer to his problem was. If only he could have stepped outside his guilt complex, he would have been able to realise that the powers that be were pushing them too hard. They were not being given the chance to recharge their batteries. Day in, day out, seven days a week they were on duty, on call all of the time; they were only allowed out of camp for a few hours at a time. They were flying at night, and returning in the early hours of the morning when most people were in bed, fast asleep. Later that same morning, once they were up and dressed, they were reporting for duty. It was this constant pressure that was getting to them, sixteen hours a day on duty! Even when they were not flying, owing to a mission being cancelled, they nevertheless had to go through all of the pre-op routines until such time as the op was scrubbed. Pre-flight checks, aircraft and equipment testing, target briefing, weather reports, route planning and crew briefing – quite often it was just prior to take-off that they were advised that the op was cancelled. It was nothing to do with being scared. It was inexperience, not yet being fully blooded to the rigours of war.

As he lay there, he could sense that day was breaking. He shivered in his home-made bed . . . his feet were cold. He reached up and threw his battledress jacket over them. Len, Sparks and Jock were sleeping the sleep of the innocent.

Daylight coming was no friend. It was beginning to creep over the ridges of the tents as they flapped noisily in the early morning breeze. The early morning, watery sun with its silver shimmering rays empha-sised the puddles of dirty water lying in the mud of the ground outside the tent entrance. What a bloody mess! Mud would be everywhere tomorrow: on their boots, on their clothes, in the tent, every-sodding-where. Oh my God . . . he sighed in desperation.

Slowly, those same rays started to slip furtively through the flaps of their tent, passing over the rusty dilapidated eyesore of their home-made stove, seemingly to highlight deliberately the squalor in which they lived, and so compound his utter dejection and misery. His eyes were full of tears as he finally dropped off to sleep, utterly exhausted and emotion-ally drained.

Chapter Six

A Welcome Break

LEN woke him. 'Lee, what do you know? We're going to a rest camp,' he said.

'Where to?' asked Lee.

'Don't know,' came the reply, 'but I was told by Riggy in ops control a few minutes ago, and he is on his way over to see you now.'

'Where's Sparks and Jock?' asked Lee.

'They have both gone down to their sections, to see what's cooking.'

'What time is it?'

'Twelve.'

'Good God.'

'We let you sleep on, Lee. You looked knackered. You OK?'

'Yes, I'm OK now, thanks. It took me hours to get off to sleep. That bloody rain kept me awake. It poured down after we'd gone to bed. What's it like now?'

'Not bad.'

The tent flap was open. Lee looked outside. It was sunny with intermittent cloud, and the small white cumulus clouds, with their fluffy tops, skidded across the pale blue background of the sky as if in haste to depart and leave the sun to dry out the soggy mess below. Whispy ribbons of steam were rising off the sloping sides of the nearby tents, and formed shimmering columns of mist, slowly evaporating as they travelled skywards. Around the camp men from the other tents were busying themselves mopping up or repairing the ravages of the previous night's downpour. Lee looked about him; the inside of their tent looked deserted, as all the damp bedding and clothes of the others had been taken outside. Even so, there was still a musty smell of dampness. Len and the others had let in a flow of chilly air by opening both the front flaps and lifting up the skirting at the rear in an effort to give it an airing.

The only damage they had suffered was the drip stove which had got wet and was already starting to go rusty. Len was waiting for it to dry out before he could light it. It was very warm outside in the sunshine, considering it was early May, and Lee, once fully awake, decided that outside was the best place to be away from the draught which whistled around his legs when he stepped out of bed. Slipping on his battledress trousers, warm socks, wellies, shirt and pullover he stripped his bed. Seeing that the others had put their blankets and damp clothes out to dry on the branches of the olive trees or on a makeshift clothes line hung between two others, he did the same. After a quick wash and shave with cold water in the upturned tin hat that he used for a wash bowl, balanced on an old wooden box outside the tent, he was ready to greet the day.

They were halfway through their tour and they could do with a break. Sparks and Jock returned, complaining that the camp was waterlogged, mud and mire everywhere. Jock had slipped up in it; his trousers and battledress jacket were in an awful mess, covered in wet, soggy mud. He only had his denims to change into. Feeling fed up, he went into the tent to change. Riggy arrived and confirmed that there were to be no more ops for a while. They were off tomorrow to an aircrew rest camp at Sorrento. The relief was enormous, and the muck and mud were all forgotten as they chatted excitedly about the forthcoming break.

At last, Len and Sparks had managed to light the stove. They were sitting on the two front beds, waiting for some water to boil to make mugs of cocoa when a sudden shout came from Jock at the rear of the tent,

'I've been robbed! Some bastard has whipped my shaving kit.'

Sure enough, whilst they had been chatting at the front of the tent, someone – mostly likely an Italian worker on the camp – had put his hand through the rear of the tent which had had the skirting raised and stolen his leather shaving kit, which had been a present from his parents when he joined up. Jock was furious.

'Christ, you've got to have eyes at the back of your head with these Italian bastards,' he said. It wasn't Jock's day.

That evening, after a few beers in the Mess, they packed up the belongings they were not taking with them, getting them ready to put into the stores the next morning before they left.

The following morning they soon packed their remaining few possessions into their haversacks and set off to the waiting truck that was to take them to the railway station at Foggia. Their train puffed into the station about an hour late; it consisted of an old, decrepit Italian engine which looked incapable of pulling anything. It had old-fashioned wooden carriages with wooden bench-like seats, some of which had been reserved for the local population. There were also a considerable number of goods wagons, some of the closed ones also being used for carrying the locals, but to all intents and purposes it was a troop train. British and American Military Police were everywhere. The whole set-up looked as if it was going to be a most uncomfortable journey, and interminably slow, but the crew had managed to get into one carriage and sit together and were in high spirits.

As the train puffed and panted its way out of the station, the full devastation of what war was all about greeted them. It was obvious that the marshalling yards at Foggia had been the subject of several raids before it was captured by the Allies. There was virtually nothing left of the station itself. The engine sheds and warehouses were in ruins, and damaged railway trucks lined the route.

Later, sitting in the railway carriage as the train twisted and turned on its tortuous journey across the hills and through the valleys on its way to Naples, Lee became very aware of the desolation and poverty of southern Italy. He could well understand how a man like Mussolini could whip up enthusiasm among the peasants, promising them a better way of life. He mentioned his thoughts to his colleagues and this started the usual round of political discussions. Very few of them had any ideas at all about Fascism or what it was all about. They only knew that Mussolini was a dictator and was supported in power by the Blackshirts, a fascist militia ruled from Mussolini's headquarters, an organisation separate from the army or police. Some blamed religion for its rise to power, for no matter what else, everywhere there were small well-kept shrines built into the rock-face or at the sides of the roads and railway track.

The rugged and barren nature of the landscape as they passed through the hills and valleys, together with the ramshackle farms and derelict cottages, seemed to confirm that, in the hot, dry, arid climate of the south of Italy, nothing would grow. There was virtually nothing for the native population to scrape a living from. The far distant prosperous population of the industrial north of the country seemed to have forsaken this barren area. What cattle and livestock they saw were thin, undernourished and looked uncared for. Chickens, goats and pigs scratched and sniffed around the vineyards or olive groves of the small forlorn homesteads searching for morsels of food. Dirty children in ragged vests, barely covering their dark-skinned, underfed, pot-bellied little bodies, wandered aimlessly around or squatted huddled pathetically together on the hard uncompromising stony soil. The sun beating down on them provoked the thought, 'what must it be like for them in the middle of summer?' The men concluded that the whole area would need more than promises; drastic changes would be needed before it could ever be prosperous.

Arriving in Naples, they were billeted in a transit camp and, after the first decent wash and shower for weeks, decided to take a look at this city with its 'see Naples and die' reputation. Walking along the back streets from the camp they were shocked to see families with bedding and their few possessions out on the pavements, living in absolute abject poverty. Men with missing limbs, looking very sullen, were standing or lying around. Some played cards, some begged, whilst the women – either very thin or bloated and in their shabby black dresses with untidy, unkempt hair – looked on hopelessly. Those same ragged children with their pot bellies they had seen in the barren homesteads of the country were now on the pavements of Naples soulfully, pleadingly watching them pass by, through their large, round, dark brown eyes.

They could hardly walk a few paces without being accosted by prostitutes and women openly offering their young daughters for bars of chocolate. There were the older children begging, pestering them for money, cigarettes or chocolate. They were very relieved to get away from the squalor and on to the main streets of the town.

The centre of the city was a bustle of military activity and seemed clean and orderly, giving no indication of the squalor lurking in the back streets beyond. They found their way to the Royal Palace which the Allies had taken over and converted into a giant canteen/leisure complex for the Allied troops. Among the notices was one announcing an opera in the Opera House that night. Later in the canteen, they enjoyed the first decent meal they had had since they arrived in Italy, and then it was off to the San Carlo Opera House – which was situated next door to the Royal Palace Welfare Club – to see *Il Trovatore*. It was a splendid performance, and was just what they needed to relax them.

The following morning they were bound for Sorrento in a commandeered coach. Reaching the coast, the sea lay below them. The Italian driver did not alter his speed at all as they started to descend, but continued to drive down towards the coast at what seemed to be a breakneck speed. The road twisted and turned and, at each turning, a new vista opened up before them. The views were breathtaking as the cliffs plunged ever downwards towards the sea, their tree-lined chasms blending with the splendid outcrops of rock and foliage.

The sea nestling below the cliffs was a picture: deep Mediterranean blue sparkling as the sun danced lightly over the crests of the otherwise almost unnoticed ripples. Each time they went round a corner a new and magnificent scene greeted them, vying with the previous one to impress them with its beauty. Several times the driver took the coach perilously near the edge of the road as it corkscrewed its way down, causing raucous shouts and laughter as they swung in their seats, clutching each other in anticipation of the next corner. Many times the bonnet seemed to go over the edge of the cliffs, momentarily suspended there as the driver struggled with the steering wheel to take the coach around the sharp corners.

They passed through tiny villages of white-painted cottages and houses, each full of flowering shrubs and window boxes. There were lush olive and orange groves, and gardens with flowers growing everywhere, giving the impression they were all inextricably intermingled with each other by nature to bring joy to the eyes of the weary traveller.

It was a scenic paradise and most uplifting to their tired spirits. It was hard to imagine the bloody battle that had taken place at Salerno just around the headland and the poverty they had just witnessed in Naples.

They arrived in Sorrento, which was situated on a cliff overlooking a

Aircrew at Sorrento. *(IWM CNA 2279)*

small beach. Its quaint narrow streets, shops and *vino* bars gave it an air of antiquity, and they felt as if they had moved back in time to a different age. The coach driver took them to a hotel, taken over by the RAF, in which they were billeted. Joy of joys – there were only two to a room with *real* beds. Len and Lee shared a room. A quick wash and brush up and very soon they were joined by the others and were sitting on the patio looking across the Bay of Naples sipping cherry brandies and drinking *vino*.

Lunch was served in the hotel restaurant by young Italian waiters and waitresses: soup followed by fish, salad and chips, washed down with a glass of *vino*. This was followed by an orange trifle. The battle front seemed very far away.

'Let's all go into town,' Len suggested after lunch. It was warm enough for shorts and open-necked shirts. The town lay about half a mile away down the hill and they found it very picturesque as they enjoyed a stroll along its ancient streets, eventually finding their way to the small beach, which was situated at the bottom of a long flight of winding steps. The sea was warm and inviting and they all longed for a swim. Not having any bathing shorts their first job had been to find a shop which sold them. This wasn't as difficult as they imagined and they were soon relaxing in the calm warm waters of the beautiful Bay of Naples.

On the beach, Jock decided to go for a stroll to relieve himself. Whilst he was away the remainder of the crew got together and decided to buy him a leather-cased replacement shaving kit, which they had seen him looking at in one of the shops on the way down. When it was time to return to the hotel, Len and Lee walked slowly behind the others until

Three members of the first crew on 'holiday' in Sorrento. From left, Jock, Lee and Len.

they came to the shop. Lee popped in, whilst Len kept an eye open for Jock, and bought the shaving kit. Later in the bar, Lee tapped on the table and, calling Jock over, said, 'Here's a little present to the finest rear gunner in the RAF.' Jock was overjoyed.

It didn't take very long for a pattern of relaxation to appear. Between swimming, walking and messing about in a small sailing boat someone had managed to acquire, they were able to forget the cares and squalor of war and enjoy their holiday. They were determined to enjoy it. None of them were heavy drinkers, but they did enjoy ferreting among the bars, sampling the local wines which seemed to appear mysteriously if the price was right. Riggy was the one who was able to make the wines appear. Speaking very little Italian he managed to cajole the plump Italian women behind the bars to bring out their finest bottles by appealing to their mothering instincts, always waiting until the hawk-eyed owner was out of sight or earshot.

It was amazing how none of these Italian men liked Mussolini or the Germans. They had – all to a man – changed loyalties, particularly when trying to sell you something! Therefore, it was always a call of, 'Come on, Riggy, get cracking on this fat Italian momma,' for the best deal at the right price.

A dance organised in the hotel proved to be a very humorous affair. All the women present, reputedly of good reputation and brought in by the entertainments officer, seemed to be either an ex-countess or the wife of a count who had been captured by the Allies. Very few were able to dance, and Lee wondered what else they were brought in for. 'Which countess did you dance with?' was the favourite joke the following day.

There was a day trip to Pompeii organised for them by the entertainments officer. Lee was enthralled by the way in which this ancient city had been preserved and was captivated by its historical connections. The crew had a great deal of fun with the grubby little Italian guide who sidled up to them and, in broken English, offered for a few extra lire to take them to see things concerning the goings on in the past in the city which were normally kept out of view of the ordinary tourist. He took great pleasure in showing them the lewd drawings, which were kept in locked frames out of sight of pre-war tourists. During the guided tour to the brothel, they were shown the fertility symbol of the flying penis carved in stone on the outside of the building. Inside, above each doorway, was a picture of the different position in which the client could have sex in that particular room. This caused a lot of frivolity and laughs among them. However, in spite of the so-called secrecy, outside the walls of the old city they were able to buy a small 'lucky charm', a flying penis reproduced in metal and a souvenir booklet which contained photographs of the 'forbidden' drawings which were freely available.

A trip to the edge of Vesuvius's gaping volcanic mouth with its acrid smell of sulphur ended a tiring but most enjoyable day. Not since Lossiemouth had there been a day filled with so much fun and laughter.

A day out on Capri with a visit to its famous Blue Grotto was another

Lee (in the middle of the back row) with friends in the car they hired in Capri.

81

occasion for complete relaxation and fun. Favoured by the Roman emperors, Capri was another demi-paradise of narrow streets with white buildings garlanded with flowers and looked breathtaking in the glorious sunshine. Some of the lads in the hotel had managed to acquire an old open-backed car capable of carrying eight at a squash. It was in this that they were able to regally tour the mountainous island. A 'must' was a visit to see Gracie Fields' villa and to see the homes of the Italians who were formerly wealthy under Mussolini.

The days were passing too quickly. They had tasted the good life and were now due back to reality. The final evening arrived; they were due to leave for Foggia the next day. The smoke-filled bar of the hotel was crowded. New crews had arrived and were mingling with those about to leave. Talk amongst the crews centred around other crews who had just been on leave and who, on return to ops, had bought it on their first trip out. Rumours also abounded in the rest camp that the losses were much higher then they, the powers that be, would care to admit. Cheerful lot, thought Lee.

The following morning they boarded the coaches for the journey back to Naples, and the crews were in good spirits. Most of the conversation centred around what a jolly good break it had been. The RAF had done them proud, as if to appreciate what the lads were doing out there and the conditions under which they lived. They had had good food, comfortable accommodation in an excellent hotel and it had not cost them a penny. The RAF had really excelled themselves, and all agreed that they could not have been better cared for. There was no discipline and virtually complete freedom of movement and activity. What was more they had had a lot of fun. Lee felt great; the swimming, walking, fresh air and exercise had done him the world of good. He had slept well and, except for last night, they had hardly talked about operations at all. As a matter of fact, it had been taboo in the Mess. If anyone had dared to start talking about them, shouts of 'shut the hangar door', were hurled at them from all directions, more often than not coloured with more expressive expletives.

The journey back up the coast road was even more nerve-racking than the journey down. Most of the time they were leaning backwards in their seats. Whenever they came to a tight corner, inevitably the driver stalled as he tried to swing the heavy coach around the bend. When he did get started again or went slowly up the steep gradients this was greeted with shouts of 'Push! Push!' with much laughter and merriment.

When, at last, they reached the top, a final look back at the beautiful scene that they had just left brought a sense of nostalgia – or was it regret, desire or melancholy? Whatever it was, Lee wished wholeheartedly that Connie had been with him to have shared the pleasure of such a romantic spot.

CHAPTER SEVEN

BACK TO WORK

THEY arrived back at base refreshed and, to Lee's great pleasure, there was a stack of letters from Connie. There was also the news that Lee had been promoted to Flight Sergeant. However, Lee was quick to notice that the crew were unsettled. Although they had needed the rest, the break had disrupted their way of life and their war, and they had no desire to go back to it. They had enjoyed a taste of normality and they wanted to keep it, presenting quite a problem to Lee who became very anxious about his own ability to keep them together as an efficient crew. Their mood had changed. Now they didn't want to continue. Lee hoped that as soon as they got back into the swing of things again they would overcome their reluctance and settle down to the job in hand. It was understandable. The odds were piling up against them. Every operation they did reduced their chances of survival. Unspoken before, now they talked openly about this possible eventuality. It was unsettling.

The first trip, on 22 May, the day after their return, was to support the troops on a battle stooge attacking with nine 500-pound bombs at 6,000 feet. The target was German forces holding the main roads at Ferentino, a small town opposite the Anzio beachhead in Italy. Ten Wimpys were ordered to operate against the main road through Ferentino, with the object of creating a block to prevent supplies being brought by the enemy to the front line in the Idri valley area.

One aircraft burst a tyre on attempting to take off and did not operate. The remaining nine attacked roads in the target area and saw bursts on, or near, the roads and in the adjacent buildings. Bombing was carried out from 6,000 to 9,000 feet, with no opposition. Len dropped two sticks, aiming for a road loop south of the village, and bursts were seen near the aiming point. Photographs, taken with the bombing, later indicated that the main attack was in the Frosinone area some seven to eight miles east of the prescribed area. This was put down to the weather, which was unfortunately not favourable to target identification, there being 4/10ths to 6/10ths strato-cumulus cloud over the target area.

This attack was quickly followed by another the next day on Valmontone, another small town further up on the same road, but just north of the Anzio beachhead. They had a second pilot with them, a young sergeant who had just arrived on the squadron. Shortly after leaving base, the cloud thickened and once again Lee had to resort to flying on his instruments. Looking out of his window he was surprised to see a halo of lights building up around the prop tips of the engines – he was fascinated by the rainbow effect as they whizzed around the propellers. Sparks reported from the astrodome a similar phenomenon building up on the aerial.

'It's getting larger, Lee,' he reported a few moments later.

'OK, Sparks; these halos on the prop tips are nearly a foot across. It's static electricity, known as St Elmo's Fire.'

The aircraft was bumping about in the clouds. Turning to the second pilot, Lee asked him to go back to make sure that everything behind them in the fuselage was secure, a job that Len normally did under such circumstances. As soon as he had gone through the connecting door and Lee had heard it shut behind him, there seemed to be a terrific explosion, and the lights in the cockpit went out. Lee felt the cockpit, with him in it, dropping out of the sky. He was sure that the rear of the aircraft had been blown off.

He felt stunned, and it was a little time before he realised he was still sitting in the cockpit, his feet on the rudder bars. He had a strange feeling of being encapsulated in the cockpit and dropping through space. He just sat there, his mind a blank, for what seemed like eternity.

What's happened? This is it. There are no lights. I'm falling in space. Where are the others?

Slowly he recognised the instrument panel in front of him. 'Where's the control column, what use will it be now?' he said out loud. Half dazed, he reached forward and felt it bobbing around in front of him.

He was brought to his senses by Sparks saying, 'You all right, Skipper?'

Thank God they were still there! Recovering quickly, Lee felt for the cockpit dimmer-light switch, and slowly turned it on. The force of the explosion, or whatever it was, had knocked it from the normal dim position to off. He looked at the altimeter. They had dropped well over 1,000 feet. The compass was swinging violently and the artificial horizon was out of control. Looking out of the window he could just make out the true horizon. He struggled to return to normal straight and level flight. He knew he could not stay at that height very long because of the hills below.

'What the hell was that?' he asked. 'Have we been hit?'

'Don't think so,' said Len, who had been at the back of the aircraft preparing to drop the 'Safe-Conduct' leaflets which called for the German troops to surrender.

'I think we've been struck by lightning,' said Riggy.

Lee looked out at the props. The static had all gone.

'I had damn great flashes of lightning coming from my guns,' said Jock, 'and there was a terrific bang as they left. It nearly knocked me out.'

'All of the instruments have been knocked out,' said Lee. 'The compass is going mad.'

'So's mine,' said Riggy from the navigator's bench.

'We had better get rid of these bombs, Len,' said Lee, 'but we don't want to drop them over land. Our troops might be down there. How far are we from the sea, Riggy?'

'Not far,' came the reply.

'Well, I'm going to try to make it,' said Lee. 'Go down, Len and see if you can spot when we cross the coast.'

Lee strained his eyes on to the darkened horizon, which kept disappearing as the clouds rolled by. He gently headed the aircraft in the general direction of the coast. The second pilot came back to his seat.

'Crossing the coast now,' said Len.

'OK, stand by to release the bombs,' replied Lee. A few moments later the bombs were jettisoned harmlessly into the sea.

Turning the aircraft back to base in poor visibility without the aid of a compass, the artificial horizon, the turn and bank indicator and other instruments called for all the skill and expertise that Lee could muster.

With both of the compasses out of order, the only thing that Riggy could do was to give him some stars to steer by. However, trying to see these through the breaks in the clouds, keeping them in view in a fixed position in the frame of the cockpit window and at the same time fly straight and level, taxed his concentration to the limit.

Lee asked the second pilot, Mac, to go to the astrodome where he would have a much easier opportunity to keep an eye on the stars rather than his own restricted view from the cockpit.

'What do you want me to do, Skipper?'

'Try and keep the tail fin in line with a group of stars at the rear of the aircraft and let me know when we wander off course. Len and I will keep our eyes on those in front when we can see them.'

'Wilco, Skip.'

And so they limped homewards, dodging around the cloud tops whenever they could rather than fly through them without instruments, frightened and dreading the possibility of running into another electrical storm.

Mac, his eyes glued to the tail fin, gave instructions over the intercom in the same manner as Len did on a bombing run. 'Steady as she goes . . . Left, left,' and so on. The journey was traumatic. Flying only on his airspeed indicator and altimeter, Lee would frequently fly into the swirling mist at the tops of the clouds when he could not dodge around them. With the night-darkened horizon broken by the clouds and hardly visible, the compass, artificial horizon and other instruments spinning out of order, whenever he went into the cloud tops he felt completely disorientated, giving him the horrible sensation of spinning down into the hilltops below. In the beginning, every time he saw one looming ahead and having to fly into it, he would have the same traumatic experience, to be relieved only after waiting for the moment when he flew out of the other side to see that he was still flying straight and level. He would remember those wonderful feelings of relief for ever. It was like going through a period of having nightmares and waking up to find it was a bad dream, but then lapsing into another.

It seemed pointless to try to climb above the clouds as they seemed to go on and on ever upwards, and he didn't want to try climbing up through them without instruments. He decided it was better to carry on bashing through them if they looked too big to go around, and hope they were not too thick. Nevertheless, as they flew on, he was grateful for one thing. As it was out of one cloud and into another as they flew homewards, he had no time to feel frightened any more, only pleased when he got through one. It seemed like years before they came to the Foggia plain, and Lee was never happier to see the searchlights.

They broke cloud over the plain, and ahead of them, clearly visible, was the criss-crossed pattern of the searchlights pointing their welcoming fingers to the sky. Foggia was never more beautiful. He could see at last. Thank God he didn't need those bloody useless instruments now.

'Searchlights ahead, lads,' he called over the intercom. 'Should be plain sailing from now on.'

A resounding cheer went up throughout the aircraft. Lee couldn't help feeling a sense of pride. They had done it again! Mother luck was certainly good to them!

The verdict in the ops room at debriefing was that they had either been hit by lightning – in which case they were very lucky to have survived – or, more likely, they had flown from a negatively charged cloud into a positively charged one or vice versa, and the current had discharged through the plane, actually making a flash of lightning itself.

Ten Wimpys had been detailed to attack the roads through Valmontone. The operation was almost completely abortive because of the 10/10ths cloud, electrical storms and icing, which had been encountered, on average, between 4,000 to 16,000 feet *en route* and over the target area. These weather conditions were absolutely different from the Met. forecast. The aircraft carrying the flares to illuminate the target searched for over an hour and dropped altitude in an effort to find the target. However, realising that illumination in such cloud was futile, the Wimpy brought the remaining flares back to base. All but one of the other crews, like Lee, had jettisoned their bombs in the sea. That same night, another Wimpy was detailed to drop leaflets on Spezia, Rapallo, Massa and Genoa. The pilot found good weather conditions *en route* up the east coast and also in the target areas after crossing Italy. He dropped his leaflets from 11,300 feet at the prescribed times to fall on the respective towns. On returning, his port engine cut out, and later the starboard engine also failed. He and his crew baled out over San Paolo, but his navigator and wireless operator were killed. The remainder of the crew were unhurt.

Two nights later they were out supporting the troops again. Eight Wimpys were detailed, and attacked roads at Viterbo, a large town north of Rome, in an attempt to disrupt the German communication and supply route. Bombing was concentrated in the north area of the town where Len dropped one stick of nine 500-pound bombs on a road junction. Direct hits were observed on the roads leading from the built-up area. Bombing was from 7,500 to 9,000 feet and the operation was carried out in good weather and visibility, in spite of some haze.

Opposition consisted of slight heavy and light flak. An intense light and heavy barrage from the Rome area was observed. A single-engined aircraft was seen over the target dropping fighter flares. All the squadron's aircraft returned safely.

It was a brilliant moonlit night when they were told about their first trip into Austria. Ten Wimpys were detailed to attack Feuersbrunn airfield in the Vienna area. From this airfield several crack German air force units were regularly attacking the American daylight bombers on missions in Austria, Hungary and Romania, causing many losses. It sounded simple enough. Because the airfield would be difficult to identify, flares would be dropped over the airfield and they were to bomb on those. The flight up the Adriatic, over the Dolomites and foothills of the Alps was without incident, although flak was observed at places on the way up. It was a lovely night, as clear as daylight, as they flew into Austria. The raid was a huge success, taking the enemy completely by surprise. Many bombs, dropped from 7,500 to 10,000 feet, were claimed to have hit the target. Len's was amongst them, bursts being seen from the one stick he had aimed at the middle of the target where flames and explosions were occurring. Photographs taken with the bombing proved the claims made by the crews. Up to thirteen fires were seen on the airfield.

No opposition was encountered from the target, but intense and accurate flak was met at Graz, one aircraft being hit and slightly damaged. Weather and visibility were good with no cloud or haze over the target. The day after the raid, the American daylight bombers encountered no fighter opposition from the airfield.

The following morning there was great excitement in the camp. Another camp had been built at the other side of the olive grove to accommodate visiting aircrew from England. This was to be a Lancaster bombing force who were to attack targets in southern Germany and, instead of flying all the way back to England that night, they were to stay and carry out another raid on the way back. Lee decided to go and have a look at the camp with some other pilots of the squadron. They were amazed at what they saw. Instead of the small bivouac tents in which they lived, there were large marquee type tents, the type that the American Air Force used. The whole camp looked exactly like the American Air Force camp.

Each tent was equipped with electric light, camp beds and washing facilities. The floors were covered with duckboards and there were duckboard walkways outside. What a difference from the conditions they were forced to live in. If anything was designed to cause dissatisfaction, and lower morale among the aircrews, this certainly was. Obviously the bomber force in Italy was looked upon as the poor relation by the higher command in the UK. The eggs and bacon breakfasts after each op were legendary among the UK crews. They had comfortable beds, were home-based and could see their loved ones whenever they were off duty. If they could build a camp like this for them on a passing visit, why couldn't they do it for the crews already out there, miles away from home? The crews were really cheesed off over what appeared to them as being the forgotten men, 'out of sight, out of mind'.

A day's rest and they were off to minelay the Danube again in the area of Dubravica where there had been another 'sowing' a few nights earlier. Ten aircraft were detailed, but two returned early with engine trouble. The weather was excellent, a lovely night with the river sparkling in the moonlight. But this time the German troops were waiting for them with a balloon barrage on the barges and flak guns along the river bank. Fortunately, for once, as they approached the target area, the moonlight was their ally, as it enabled them to spot the balloons with their dreaded cables hanging from them. All they had to do was to sow their cucumbers a little farther up the river. When they got back to base crews were very critical of the planners. Fancy sending them to sow cucumbers in that same part of the river. Surely they could have chosen another part? One of the Wimpys ditched in the Danube.

It was 1 June and they were on duty again, this time the oil refinery at Szolnok in Hungary being the target. They had only been flying for about an hour when a small oil pipe in the cockpit just in front of Lee burst and spurted oil all over his face. It covered the windscreen and his eyes and he was blinded, but fortunately they were on automatic pilot which gave Lee the opportunity to pull out his handkerchief and wipe his eyes. They smarted terribly and he wondered if his eyes would be permanently damaged.

The oxygen mask saved him getting a mouthful of the stuff and swallowing it. His flying suit was saturated right through to his battledress, with oil seeping into his flying boots, and the cockpit was in a complete mess with oil everywhere. Len, who was sitting beside him, missed most of it and he rushed to help Lee clean up his face whilst putting one hand with a rag in it over the leak. Sparks was called up to help, and the three of them, in the confined space of the cockpit, worked furiously to prevent further damage. Eventually Len was able to stop the flow, but not until the oil in the hydraulic system was seriously impaired. Lee had no option but to abandon the mission, and reluctantly he decided to return to base and asked Riggy to set a course for home.

On the way back he decided, after a discussion with Len, that they should test the hydraulic system to see if they could lower the landing wheels. The system did not work. They would have to be lowered manually when they returned to base. Meanwhile they would have to keep their bombs on board and land with them. Neither he nor Len relished the idea of trying to open and close the bomb doors now. If they remained half open and did not close again it would make landing at night extremely dangerous, particularly with a full bomb load on board!

How he wished he could remember more about the hydraulic system, but Len seemed to know what he was doing. The reserve oil tank was just above the wireless ops compartment and it was possible to see that there would be enough oil to lower the wheels manually. However, Lee did warn the crew that they may have to pee in the tank, if need be, to increase the level. This broke the tension and the crew were in fits of laughter, working out ways in which they could do it by passing up their tin mugs, standing on Sparks' head.

Arriving over base, his eyes sore with the oil in them, Lee asked Len to start pumping the wheels down with the pump handle situated alongside the pilot's seat. Len began pumping away as they approached the airfield, whilst Lee informed control of what was happening. It was no easy task.

'It's like trying to pump up a car tyre with a bicycle pump,' puffed Len. Sparks came up and took a turn. After what seemed to be an eternity, the wheels locked down. Lee breathed a sigh of relief as the little green light came on, and Len slumped over the seat. The crew sat there with bated breath as the aircraft touched down, wondering if the wheels were going to collapse, and if they would all be blown to eternity, but Lee managed to land without mishap.

Because of the superstition they now had, Lee continued to fly in his oil-caked clothing after trying his hardest to wash out the oil in the upturned tin hat which he used for washing. In the sticky, oily pocket of his battledress trousers he continued to carry his lucky St Christopher charm – given to him by Connie the night before he had left England – together with odd coins and the flying penis charm.

The news next day was good – the Allies were advancing on to Rome. The target for tonight was the Ostia Bridge over the River Tiber near Rome to try to cut off the retreating German forces. Eight Wimpys were ordered to attack the bridge and nearby marshalling yards. Len dropped his bombs in one stick of nine 500-pound bombs which were seen to straddle the bridge near the west side. The attack was very successful, the squadron bombing from between 6,000 and 9,000 feet in good weather and visibility. Bombing was well concentrated in the target area and a cloud of smoke and dust covered the target after the attack. No opposition was encountered. That was the night of 4 June. The following day the Allies moved into Rome.

Expecting to hear the news on the British radio station on the morning of 6 June, Lee was a little peeved to hear that they had been outdone by the Allied invasion of Europe. But the news from the UK was good. A tremendous cheer had echoed through the camp as the news came over the radios.

Viterbo was the target the following night. They were to attack the road and rail junction with a full bomb load in an effort to stem the German retreat. Eight Wimpys were detailed to create road blocks and crater the roads through the town. This was as successful as the previous night's attack on the bridge. All the aircraft found their target, which was well plastered with bombs dropped from 4,500 to 9,000 feet. Len dropped his bombs in two sticks aimed at the town centre and south road junction, and bursts were seen at the aiming points. Two 4,000-pound bombs were seen to burst in the town. Outbound and on the return journey many fires were seen east of the Bracciano, presumably from burning motor transport vehicles on the roads. Weather and visibility were good below a layer of 10/10ths cloud with a base of approximately 8,000 feet.

The next detail was to Orvieto in support of the troops again, with a 4,000-pound cookie on board, attacking the road and rail junction from 6,000 feet. Again it was a force of eight Wimpys from the squadron that were ordered to attack a road junction approximately half a mile east of Orvieto town. All the aircraft succeeded in finding this particularly small target area, and bombing was carried out in good weather and visibility. The target was well illuminated by the aircraft detailed to carry the flares. The two 4,000-pound bombs, one of which was carried by Lee, were seen to burst very close to the target junction and each of these two crews provided a photograph taken with bombing showing the target point. Lee was delighted with the result, as this was precision bombing at its best.

One single-engined aircraft was seen over the area flying between 7,000 and 8,000 feet. One crew operating on the target saw what appeared to be an aircraft burst into flames and descend to the ground burning. One Wimpy was missing from this operation. No flak was encountered.

It was probably because Lee was becoming a very experienced pilot and his crew were moving up to be the senior crew on the squadron, that his old fears of trying to reconcile his conscience with his duty hardly bothered him at all these days. He certainly did not lie awake at night worrying about it. Furthermore, he was delighted that he had put those doubts behind him and that he felt far more confident in himself. He still had difficulty in getting off to sleep, but he put this down to being over-tired. But the crew were unable to relax. Months of sleeping on hard boards at irregular hours and, when they were not on flying duty, being cramped up in a tent without so much as a decent chair to sit in, never gave them the opportunity to unwind. His tiredness manifested itself both by his uncharacteristic negative thoughts when he was alone lying there at night in the tent, and by the ever dominant awareness of his pulse racing and pounding through his tired and aching body.

The significance of their next attack was the fact that Pathfinders were going to be used for the first time from Italy. The news was broken to them at briefing. They had been very successful in the UK, but the proposal was not universally welcomed by the crews in the squadrons in Italy who were used to operating independently, mainly because the navigation aids used in the UK were not available in this theatre of war.

The target was the oil storage tanks at Trieste and the crews were ordered to drop their bombs on the red marker flares only. Even if they knew they were not where they felt they should be, the reason given was that the powers that be may have another target in mind in the area other than the one which they had told the crews about at briefing.

Exactly on time, after an uneventful trip, they arrived in the target area. Ahead the red marker flares appeared.

'Lee, I can see that the flares aren't over the oil storage tanks,' said Len. 'I think the target is a bit further over to the east.'

'You have got to bomb on the marker flares,' Riggy called out.

There was no opposition anywhere, no flak or searchlights, only the red marker flares, the smoke from which helped to obscure the ground below. And so it was that Lee's crew, convinced that the flares were not over the oil storage tanks, dropped their bomb, a 4,000-pound cookie, in the centre of three red marker flares on open fields and mud flats, thereby obeying orders.

Unfortunately, in Lee's view, other crews also did the same. Whatever was underneath never showed up on the photograph. All that could be seen looked exactly like mud flats or fields, with the red flares clearly indicated over them.

The 'official' report of that raid said that eleven aircraft were ordered to attack Trieste oil refinery. Only ten crews operated because the rear turret of one aircraft was unserviceable. The remaining aircraft were ordered to bomb on the red marker flares to be dropped by the Pathfinder Squadron over the target. All the aircraft except one duly bombed on the mean of the three marker flares seen at blitz time, the remaining aircraft bombed just before blitz time, at the same time as the marker flares were dropped. Nearly all the crews felt certain at the time of the attack that the red markers had been dropped at the wrong place and subsequent photographs showed that such was the case, the attack having been carried out approximately two miles north-east of the target. Bombing was from 6,700 to 8,000 feet. Weather and visibility were good. Opposition consisted of slight heavy and light flak from the target area, with slight heavy flak from Pola on the return journey.

The skipper and two of the crew of the Wimpy that had ditched in the Danube arrived back in camp. It had taken just two weeks because of the help the partisans had given them, and they had got out of Yugoslavia with no trouble at all. This was quite a morale booster, the message coming back that the partisans were very supportive of the Allies' actions.

Bulgaria was their next trip, to a little known place called Kalova. They were to attack the fighter aerodrome there, and eight Wimpys were detailed for the attack. One swung off on take-off and did not operate. Of the remaining seven, three returned early on account of bad weather (electrical storms) encountered over Yugoslavia. The sky was heavily laden with dense cloud above and, after crossing the coast, it filled in below them. So, once again over the Adriatic, they were unable to take drifts to check their position, and static electricity, together with the very few radio stations broadcasting, meant that Sparks was also unable to get a decent bearing for Riggy to check his course. They were flying blind all the way, relying on winds given to them at briefing. When ETA target arrived, after searching for five minutes, they were unable to find it nor any trace of an attack going on. Subsequent reports showed that a few aircraft from the group did manage to find the target where the weather over it was said to be excellent. Under good illumination they had attacked the southern dispersals with a direct hit being scored on one of the main hangars. At least six aircraft on the ground were reported in flames and the first of the attack were visible from forty to sixty miles away. Where Lee and his crew had got to was anybody's guess, for once again they were completely lost. Turning for home they decided to release the bomb load over the sea as soon as they estimated they had left Yugoslavia.

The estimated time of arrival for the Italian coastline arrived, and Lee was flying at 5,000 feet in thick cloud. He couldn't see an inch in front of him. The mist of the clouds swirled around the wings and engines, lighting them up in an ethereal sort of way. He nosed his way into where the crew thought the coast should be, a second pilot alongside him. Len was lying in the bomb aimer's position trying to recognise some place below, or even see the coastline. Sparks was in the astrodome trying to do the same. With apprehension they flew in, estimating to go in as far as they dared, not being certain of the height of the terrain they were flying over.

Flying in what they estimated was inland for a few minutes, in desperation they turned, and flew back out to sea again. After doubling the length of time they flew outwards – to ensure they started over the sea again – they turned and went back in, searching for a piece of coastline that would give them a clue to pinpoint their position, or for a sight of the three coned searchlights over base.

According to the indicators, fuel was getting low, which worried Lee as he could not remember whether they had started out with full tanks or not. He asked the second pilot to switch to the reserve tanks. It's Crotone all over again, thought Lee. But this time there was no friendly Beaufighter buzzing them. Riggy felt confident about their position. He asked Sparks to see if he could get a radio fix to confirm it, and Sparks went back to his radio cabin to try. No luck. He gave up; another pair of eyes were needed in the astrodome.

This bloody Balkan and Italian weather! Who said, 'Come to sunny Italy' Lee felt like crying with frustration as he felt his nerve going. This is it, he thought, it must be this time. Oh shit! He desperately scanned every inch of the cockpit window searching for that elusive coastline. They dare not go any lower; if they were over land they might crash into the hills just north of base. If the wind speed and direction hadn't changed too much they should be near just about now. Nervously at first, Lee flew in again several more times, but he couldn't see a bloody thing! His nerves started to get the better of him. He could feel himself starting to panic. He was beginning to get very, very frightened. He felt very vulnerable.

He gripped the control column as the swirling mist disorientated him. He looked at the artificial horizon. Christ, the left wing is dropping. In panic he overcorrected and the right wing dropped. He levelled out and looked out of the cockpit window again in forlorn hope. His eyes were popping out of his head. He could feel them red-rimmed and tired. Fear gripped him. He could sense danger. His throat was dry, and it became parched and sore with fright. His tongue seemed to fill his whole mouth. He tried to speak, but words did not come. A strange tingle ran up and down his spine. Someone was walking on his grave. He could feel the goose pimples, cold and damp, on the back of his neck. His hands felt wet and clammy, and his whole body seemed to stiffen up. He tried to say something, anything, but the words did not come. He felt only the dry, hot searing soreness of his throat and the panic in his eyes. It seemed as if he would choke if his tongue became any larger. He was petrified. Realising he was frightened out of his wits, he stopped trying to talk, not wanting to betray himself to the rest of the crew by showing them how much he was scared. He gave a furtive glance to the second pilot sitting beside him. Did he know how scared he was? He peered out of the cockpit window again, desperately trying to avoid meeting his gaze. Dear God, what can I do?

Shall I tell them to get ready to abandon the aircraft, or wait until the engines cut and then try and ditch? But where are we? Over land or over sea? Oh God, I wish I knew. If there is a God – please help me. Please help *us*.

In desperation he closed his eyes and silently tried to pray. But in his despair he realised he couldn't get started. How he wished he knew how to pray in the cramped cockpit of a Wimpy. Would just thinking and talking to God in his mind help? The noise of the engines seemed to shatter the peace he was seeking, the peace he felt he should have in which to pray. In his confused mind he tried again.

Dear God. Please help us, don't fail us now. Please get us out of this awful bloody mess and I will never doubt you again . . . I'm sorry I didn't mean to swear. Oh yes . . . through Jesus Christ our Lord, Amen.

Good God, that didn't sound right. It sounded awful. Oh Christ, what a bloody cock-up. They had about ten minutes' flying time left in the fuel tanks. He was at his wits' end. What can I do? What *shall* I do?

In panic he tried to pray again, this time saying the Lord's Prayer to himself, at the same time trying to convince himself that it wasn't, that it *couldn't* be, the end.

The engines suddenly seemed to go quiet, and he felt a moment of peace and calm. Was this the end? Had the engines cut out? He listened. Yes, they were still purring away.

What was that? He felt sure he had seen something. Subconsciously he looked out of the port side of the cockpit window at the engine. The prop was whizzing around normally. He turned his head to the starboard side, not at the engine. He would have had to look past the second pilot to do that. Instead he peered straight out, looking up into the starboard side of the cockpit window, trying to avoid visual contact with his second pilot. He thought he saw, through the misty cloud, the face of Connie. He looked hard again as the swirling mist rolled by. Yes, it was her. She was smiling at him reassuringly, nodding her head to the port side of the aircraft.

He looked in the direction that Connie had seemed to be indicating and, for a brief second through the murky clouds and mist, he thought he saw the searchlights. It's impossible, I'm seeing things. He looked again. Connie seemed to be saying, 'Go on . . . Go on.' Without a word to anyone he altered course to where he thought the searchlights were, realising, as he did so, that not only had he not spoken during the last quarter of an hour, but neither had anyone else. But he had once again made a decision and he felt the fear slowly drain away, turning to apprehension. Hope came back to him, his eyes felt stronger and, although his throat was sore, he spoke up.

'I think I've seen the searchlights, lads,' he said quietly. Turning to the second pilot, he added nervously, 'Keep your eyes skinned ahead, everyone.'

Sure enough, in a break in the clouds, were the searchlights. There were no other aircraft about. Calling up control, Lee had the green light and went straight in and landed. By the time he reached dispersal the fuel tanks were empty and the weather had closed in over the airfield again.

His legs were shaking as he stepped out of the aircraft, but fortunately the gharry arrived quickly to take them to debriefing and he was able to scramble aboard without anyone noticing. They sat in silence on the way to debriefing, apart from one comment from Len: 'Did you know we only had about a pint of fuel left, Skipper?' and a single word response from Lee: 'Yes.'

Lying on his bed that night Lee felt, and for the first time heard, not just his pulse, but his heart throbbing and thumping loudly inside his body. He couldn't stop it. His ears were ringing with a swishing sound that sounded like water racing like a flood and he imagined he could taste blood in the back of his mouth. As he lay there his heart continued to pound against the inside of his chest as if it were trying to escape – its loud beat seemingly crying out for release.

The noise in his ears and the beat of his heart were so loud and so incessant he felt sure the rest of the crew in the tent could hear it. He could even feel it in his legs. He couldn't get off to sleep the noise was so deafening. He could hardly think, he was so preoccupied with what was going on inside him. After what seemed like eternity, the noise and the pounding became more subdued. He was ashamed at being so scared. Tonight had been a miracle, but nobody would ever believe him. God really was around and knew what was going on. There must be a purpose. He lay there and prayed, thanking God for what he was convinced had been an answer to his prayers, half promising, because he didn't want to become a religious nut, but hoping that some day he could be of service to Him. When he did finally get to sleep it was a shallow, fitful sleep, as he tossed and turned like one demented.

'Christ, I was scared last night,' said Len the following morning.

'Weren't we all?' chorused the rest of the crew in unison.

'Bloody good job you were awake, Skip,' said Sparks. 'I thought you had fallen asleep when we didn't hear from you for ages.'

'Why didn't you call me, then?' bluffed Lee.

'I was too bloody frightened.'

It was then that Lee realised that the whole crew had felt as he had – absolutely petrified – but that they still had had confidence in him to get them home. He decided that he would tell them of his experience, and he did then and there.

CHAPTER EIGHT

MUNICH

THERE was still no news of the Lanc. force that was supposed to occupy the new camp. However, at briefing a few days later, the rest of the crews were advised that they were to fly over the Alps to Munich. They were to carry out Churchill's promise to attack the soft underbelly of Europe.

The raid was to be a grand affair. Ten Halifaxes from 614 Squadron were to act as Pathfinders. The main bombing force for the attack was to consist of thirteen Liberators from 240 Wing, thirty-two Wimpys from 231 Wing, of which seventeen were from 37 Squadron (Lee's Squadron), thirteen Wimpys from 236 Wing and twenty-two from 330 Wing. The Pathfinders were to mark the target and landfall positions, and the whole attack was to be stage-managed by a controller flying high above the target area giving instructions over the area by radio. They were to assemble at the edge of the lake twenty-eight miles from the target at 16,000 feet and run in together, losing height to the bombing height of 14,000 feet.

The edge of the lake, the landfall position nominated 'A', was to be marked with sky markers, and they were advised that it should take eight minutes to reach the target marked with yellow target indicators, at an airspeed of about 210 miles an hour. Extra fuel tanks were installed on the aircraft and the bomb load reduced to six 500-pound bombs. Needless to say, as the crews left briefing, they were grumbling about the raid and what the hell the powers that be were trying to do. Did they realise the conditions under which they operated in Italy? Nevertheless, there was a job to do, and the old saying, 'Theirs not to reason why, theirs but to do and die', was very much in vogue.

It was with some trepidation that they set off. They were airborne at 8.50 p.m. and were expected to be over the target at half past midnight. The weather forecast was fine, with a slight ground haze and about 5/10ths cumulus cloud over the target. Icing level for the whole trip was low. This was the most heavily defended target they had ever been called upon to attack. It was also the most organised raid inasmuch as, instead of bombing independently as they had been used to doing in the past, they now had to attack under instruction from a controller.

Lee's main concern was the weather over the Alps. They didn't have much room for manoeuvre, flying over peaks 12 to 14,000 feet high if the weather closed in. He need not have worried, because when they got to the Alps the weather was fine, although cloudy, and the visibility was very good. They could see for miles around. How spectacular the panorama of the mountains of the Alps looked at night. The peaks of some of them even seemed to be on the same level as they were, whilst others disappeared, their peaks lost in the clouds around them. It was June and Lee was a little disappointed that not many of them seemed to be snowcapped. However, his attention was soon drawn away from the scenic beauty. Climbing was getting difficult for the aircraft, and they were not climbing to the planned height of 16,000 feet at the rate of climb they should have been. The rarified air and the heavy load they were carrying was having its effect, making it extremely difficult for the engines to maintain airspeed, so he opened the throttles a little more. The aircraft was wallowing. Lee looked at the wings. They were flapping up and down like a dying swan. He levelled out whilst he thought out what he should do. He became very anxious as they were at 14,500 feet, barely high enough for safety. They were staggering along just above stalling speed and there were still several miles to go before they crossed over the peaks. God, he hoped he did not have to turn back.

He hated the thought of failure, as he had wanted so much to fly over the Alps and had gained some consolation in looking forward to that part of the op. The thought of what was beyond never entered his mind at this stage of the journey. There was only one thing for it: he must continue to climb just in case they ran into any of those clouds which may be hiding a mountain peak. He started climbing again, concentrating on his airspeed indicator and the 'feel' of the aircraft. The moment there was the slightest sign of a stall, the nose was dropped to regain airspeed, and off the sequence started again.

It was in that manner that they lumbered over the Alps and managed to reach the other side.

As they passed over the foothills, Len was able to pinpoint their position on the ground and confirmed it with Lee; they were on course, but early. Below them, in clear but slightly hazy visibility, lay the contrast of a vast plain, and they were able to drop down to their operational height. The engines purred as they flew smoothly along in straight and level flight. Immediately they had reached the plains below and confirmed their position and time, Riggy worked out a number of dog-legs in order to waste time. A dog-leg meant flying a zig-zag course across the main route.

At nine minutes past midnight they set course for the landfall position 'A'. Visibility was fair with a very slight ground haze. They arrived on time in the outer target area where they should have heard the controller. They listened out for his instructions, but there wasn't a sound. They continued to fly on to the run-in point where they were supposed to assemble, hoping to see the sky marker flares from the Pathfinders. There was no sign of anything. The target area was in cloud, a little over the predicted density, but not impossible to see between the breaks. Lee had never seen so many searchlights – it was reported later as up to 120, concentrated over a wide area which coned several aircraft. Flak was intense and accurate at times. Heavy Ack-Ack, as predicted, concentrated at the apex of searchlights developing into a barrage. Light Ack-Ack was also very intense.

He was confused. No controller, no markers at point 'A', yet they were spot on time and on course. What should he do? They had not been given instructions as to what to do if they didn't see the markers, only that they must act on them. He decided to have another go, even though it meant being late at the run-in point. He turned to go around again.

'Are you sure we have the right place to commence the run in, Riggy?' he asked.

'Positive, Lee.'

'What a cock-up! We'll be going around again to find the sky marker flares and see if we can hear from this controller,' said Lee. 'If we can't see the marker flares, we'll go in anyway to see if we can find the target flares. OK?'

'OK, Lee,' said Len, who was snuggled over the tin hat that protected his privates, as he lay down in the bomb aimer's position.

Within a couple of minutes he had quickly turned over the landfall position again. There was still no sound from the controller or any sign of the flares.

'Right, we're going in,' said Lee.

They commenced the run in to the target.

'Any signs, Len?'

'No, Skip.'

'Can you see anything, Sparks?' He was in the astrodome.

'No, Skip.'

'We must only bomb on the yellow target indicators, Lee,' reminded Len.

'ETA target!' shouted Riggy.

They were in the middle of the target, with searchlights all around them lighting up the cockpit. It was exhilarating, the flashing lights, the crackle of the anti-aircraft fire as the shells burst near them with their orange flames and puffs of smoke, with the clouds scudding by below as if to intensify the action. Below them and reflected on them were the lights from fires and flares, with the occasional silhouette of a bomber aircraft on them. It was thrilling, it was intoxicating, and Lee was fascinated. He had no thoughts whatsoever of the danger they were in; all he wanted to do was to find those bloody target indicators and was quite happy to continue the search for them.

The flak was heavy, but as far as they were concerned not accurate and below them. But there were, alas, no yellow target flares identifying the target. What flares they saw were illuminators, or were hard to recognise as they could have been the fires glowing on the clouds below. They had been over the target area for five minutes. Lee felt the crew were getting anxious.

'OK, let's piss off,' said Lee.

He turned out of the target area, frustrated and confused. What the hell was he going to do with the bombs? What a cock-up after struggling to get over the Alps like that.

'What shall we do with these bombs, Len?' They had just altered course and were flying out of the Munich target area.

'Wimpy caught up in a searchlight behind, Skipper,' called out Jock. A sudden chill ran though Lee's spine. That's Bobby, he thought.

'They've got him, Lee. It looks as if they've shot him down.'

Christ, I hope I'm wrong, thought Lee. There was deathly silence inside the aircraft. Outside, above the noise of the engines, could be heard the dull thuds of the flak. It was uncanny.

'Let's see if we can find something, Skipper,' Len broke the silence.

'OK, I'll circle around.'

'Sparks, will you drop some flares?'

They were still in the area, on a heading back towards base, when Len called, 'Looks like an airport down below, Skipper.'

'OK, I'll turn over it.'

Banking gently, at the same time keeping an eye out for other aircraft, he also saw what appeared to be an aerodrome.

'Drop another flare over it, Sparks.'

Sure enough, in the light of the flares, there was an aerodrome down below.

'OK, let's do a run on it, Len. Make sure you get its position for debriefing, Riggy.'

'OK, Lee. There is an aerodrome at Wessling. That must be it,' he replied.

They circled it again, losing height as they did so. Riggy checked their position.

'Yes, it is the aerodrome at Wessling,' he confirmed. It was all very quiet down below. Obviously the ground defences don't want to give themselves away, thought Lee. They are expecting the attack to be on the city. At 10,000 feet they dropped two more flares before starting their bombing run.

'Steady, Steady, I have the hangars in sight,' said Len.

'OK, Len, let's dive on it.' Lee could now also see clearly the buildings around the edge of the airfield. Putting the nose of the Wimpy down, he raced towards them.

99

'Bomb doors open,' called Len. It was a unique experience as they dive-bombed on to the target to see the ground rushing up towards them, and in the light of their flares, the buildings outlined on the tarmac below. At 8,000 feet they levelled out and released their bombs and headed for home.

As they climbed away, Jock, calling from the rear gunner's position, shouted, 'Well done, Skip. The bursts have straddled the hangars and what looks to be HQ, and a fire has started.'

The clouds obscured any further observations as they headed for home. Without the bomb load and with less fuel, the flight back over the Alps was uneventful.

Back at debriefing it was discovered that two Wimpys had not made it crossing over the Alps and had turned back through inability to gain operational height. One aircraft was missing. Bombing was made difficult as the Pathfinders used both sky and ground markers at the target and *en route*. Night fighters had also dropped flares. Thirteen bombed on markers, but on account of the cloud cover, results were not observed, although one aircraft reported starting a fire south-west of the railway station.

Crews that did make it and returned safely had the same story to tell as Lee: no controller and difficulty in identifying the target marker flares. The Group reports were:

> 614 Pathfinder Squadron. Of the ten Halifaxs ordered, one returned early and one failed to take off. Target was obscured by cloud. Three aircraft dropped sky markers. Three aircraft dropped yellow flares and one aircraft released green target markers using the yellow markers for aiming points. Scattered bomb bursts were observed and one fire was seen at 0028 hours. Unidentified fighters were seen over the target area. On the way home fighter flares were very frequent from the target to the River Po and scattered on a parallel course to the Italian coast.
>
> 240 Wing. Of the thirteen Liberators, three returned early and one aircraft was missing. All aircraft identified the target by the number of searchlights. All aircraft bombed in this area but none were able to identify results, as only reflection of bomb bursts were visible in the clouds. No one reported being able to see the town. One aircraft saw flares and a green target indicator over target area at 0027/0028 hours and bombed on these.
>
> 231 Wing [which included 37 Squadron]. Of the thirty-two Wimpys, one failed to take off and seven returned early. One landed away. Owing to the unpredicted winds most aircraft arrived early at point 'A' and had to lose time in the area. Because of this and much cloud, only a few aircraft saw the route markers. One aircraft bombed Wessling Aerodrome [Lee] and one bombed a road NNE. of target. One aircraft carrying a 4,000-pound bomb was unable to find target indicators or pinpoint target area, and jettisoned

its bomb somewhere north of target area. One aircraft was missing.

236 Wing. Of the thirteen Wimpys, one returned early and eleven reached the target area which was obscured by cloud. None identified the target area visually. A few saw green markers at Point 'A' and bombed on dead reckoning. Two aircraft bombed on flak and searchlights. Results of bombing unobserved. One aircraft missed point 'A' arrived north-east of the city and bombed a road with unobserved results. One aircraft was missing.

330 Wing. Of the twenty-two Wimpys, two returned early. One landed away. Nine bombed on various target markers. Four bombed east of the target markers and three on ETA. Two jettisoned their bombs safe away from the target. Another aimed at a bridge south of Porto Civitanova and one attacked an aerodrome at Ancona. One aircraft was missing.

Of the ninety aircraft detailed from the group, seventy-three arrived in the target area. Sixty-three, including eight illuminators, dropped 106 tons of bombs on the target area and nearly fifteen tons were dropped on other targets. Four aircraft failed to return and were reported missing.

Lee and his crew went to bed at five o'clock in the morning, their exhaustion made worse by the partial sense of failure. They hadn't really been able to do the job they set out to do, and what they had bombed was not the primary target. It was all very demoralising. Lee in particular had a deep sense of foreboding.

Once again it seemed to take ages for him to get off to sleep, even though he felt utterly exhausted. He lay there with his heart pounding away inside its trapped body, and he couldn't escape from this deep sense of foreboding. It was nine o'clock the same morning, after only three hours' sleep, when a corporal in the groundcrew of the wireless section, knowing that Lee and Sparks had friends in another squadron, burst open the flap of the tent. Waking them up, he hurriedly broke the news that Bobby's crew had bought it.

'Oh, piss off!' cried Len.

Bobby and his crew were missing. In his crew was one of Sparks' best friends, the wireless operator. He, too, had been married to a WAAF at Moreton-in-Marsh before they had left. They were all wide awake now and, except for Sparks, lay there talking about the good times they had had together. The whole crew were devastated. Poor Bobby, who would be next?

'Jesus,' remarked Len, 'that guy couldn't wait to get here quickly enough to bring us the bad news.'

Sparks hardly said a word. Even the letters he received later that morning from Connie could not console Lee. He felt wretched and miserable. The whole thing had been a bloody shambles.

CHAPTER NINE

RECONCILIATION OF PURPOSE

THE next afternoon they went for a swim at Bari. The crew were trying hard to put the sad news of Bobby's crew behind them and to get on with the job in hand, so they welcomed the idea that Riggy put to them in the ops room. He had heard that a gharry was going for stores to Bari, a seaside town, and while there, one of his officer pals and his crew were going with it for a swim. Together they felt sure that a day at the beach would be a good thing for them as well, to help take their minds off the loss which had affected them all so greatly.

Ascertaining that they were not on ops that night, Lee asked Riggy if he could organise it for them to go as well. Riggy and his pal did not want to go swimming, so they were to go shopping in the town while the rest of the crews went on the beach for a swim. It was left to Riggy to get permission from the Flight Commander. It had been raining slightly when they left, with the two officers sitting in the cab with the driver and the crews sitting huddled together on empty boxes in the back. Lee was sitting next to the tailboard with the pilot of the other crew, also a flight sergeant, sitting opposite him. The weather forecast was for the sun to come out later but, as it was likely to be cold in the back of the truck, they wore greatcoats.

Soon they were on the move, subdued at first by the cold draught from the air circulating around their faces and ankles as the truck sped quickly on its way. Except for those sitting immediately behind the driver's cab, the others had taken off their hats to prevent them blowing off. They had also turned their greatcoat collars up to protect their necks from the chilling blast. But later, as they sped through the countryside, their spirits rose as, from the sheer boredom of sitting there cold and huddled together, they soon started to tell jokes and sing the usual RAF bawdy songs.

Part of their fun was to wolf-whistle at any Italian girl, whether she was pretty or not, as they drove past them in the village streets. One or two of the more high-spirited lads pretended to want to jump off the truck to get to them. However, when they had nearly reached Bari, the sun came out. It became quite warm, enabling them to remove their greatcoats and to sit with them over their knees, enjoying the warm, sunny morning breeze that had taken the place of the chilly wind.

The two pilots used their influence as captains and told the lads to behave themselves and to stop mucking about as they went through Bari. They were driving into the town, and had slowed down when they came to a crossroads. The truck had almost come to a complete stop when a small Italian boy, who couldn't have been more than about eight years old, jumped up onto the back of the truck. Holding on to the tailboard with one hand, as quick as a flash he snatched Lee's greatcoat off his knees with the other and was off the truck and away with it before Lee and the others had time to realise what had happened. Lee was thunderstruck and mad at himself for being caught out so easily.

Meanwhile, the truck had moved off again and the boy had vanished into the streets as quickly as he had appeared. There was not a cat in hell's chance of catching him. It was goodbye to his greatcoat.

The driver soon found his way to the part of the beach where bathing was allowed, and the crews jumped off and arranged times to be picked up. The truck, together with the officers, drove off to town to carry out the shopping and pick up the stores.

The sea was warm and inviting. A swim in the sea and a game of leapfrog on the beach helped to relieve the past and present tensions of the day. Two crew members took it in turns to look after the clothes. No one relished the thought, after what had happened to Lee on the way in, of going back to base in their bathing trunks.

A friend of Sparks who had come with them had obtained a camera and some film, and they took photographs. Later, Lee sent copies to Connie. On the way home in the evening sun, and having to share Len's greatcoat, Lee mused over the fact that he would never see Bobby again, and in the loss of his greatcoat, he had also lost the eiderdown for his bed! With a start he pulled himself together . . . was he going nuts, equating such happenings? It was some time before he could console himself that the mind can play funny tricks when confronted with a tragedy, or with something it doesn't want to know about.

It was as if the squadron was licking its wounds after Munich, because there were no operations over the next two days. However, a much more interesting operation was awaiting them a few days later.

They were to take part in a combined landing on the island of Elba. The historic connections of Napoleon with the island stirred Lee's imagination and he was quite looking forward to it. Code-named Operation *Brassard*, French troops from Corsica were to be carried and escorted by the Royal Navy to capture and hold the island.

The only thing that marred it from his point of view was that the attack was to be made on Portoferraio at four o'clock in the morning. This meant a take-off time of 1.20 a.m. and, to enable them to get through briefing and all the other jobs necessary prior to take-off, they had to report for duty a couple of hours earlier at 11 p.m. the night before.

The chances of getting a couple of hours' sleep prior to that were pretty remote, because, by this time, with the irregular hours they had been keeping, their bodies' time cycle was all out of sync. What that in fact meant was that they would be up all night and by the time they got back at about 6.30 in the morning it would be 9 o'clock before they could get to bed.

It was to be a low-level attack, and once again Lee's crew had a 4,000-pound cookie on board. The landfall was to be the Piombino peninsula opposite Elba. They were to fly at normal height across the country to the west coast, then head northwards following the western coastline, slowly losing height to 6,000 feet on the way up over the sea to Piombino. From there they were to head west again, lose height to fly low across the sea, keeping under the enemies' radar, identify the target, climb and drop their cookie at 5,000 feet, ahead of the landing barges. This was a very different prospect from the normal attack routine. What made it even more special was that Lee's crew and only one other Wimpy, also carrying a 4,000-pound bomb piloted by a young pilot officer, were detailed to carry out the attack.

On reaching landfall and flying over the sea on the way to Elba, Lee was thrilled to see the French landing barges with the French flags flying, making their way across. One or two of them were a little trigger-happy and let go a stream of tracer as they passed overhead, but they were gone too quickly for it to do any damage. It was a most exciting experience; low flying always was.

Flying into the small harbour, they had to climb quickly to avoid the hills that rose up behind the town. They did a quick reconnaissance of the harbour, turned over the town, and headed out to sea again to make their run-in. The town looked deserted at that time of the morning. Surprise was obviously going to be the order of the day. They made a perfect bombing run and dropped their bomb which was aimed at the southern mole in the target area.

On leaving, Jock reported seeing the bursts of both bombs slightly inland and to the south-west of the aiming point. It was difficult to identify which bomb was which, both aircraft attacking almost simultaneously. The opposition was slight, with inaccurate light flak from the target. Shortly afterwards the troops landed. It had been dead easy. The troops themselves encountered stiff opposition, but it fortunately collapsed after two days. When the invasion and occupation was completed, more than 2,300 Germans were taken prisoner and about 500 awaited burial.

Earlier that night, nine other aircraft from the squadron were ordered to attack the marshalling yards at Timisoara. One aircraft did not take off owing to engine trouble. Another crew were missing, having radioed they were baling out over the Danube, one engine being unserviceable. The remainder successfully attacked the target which was illuminated by 614 Squadron.

The squadron continued to support the ground forces and, a few days later, they were attacking the marshalling yards at Ventimiglia in Italy, quite close to the French border. At briefing they were told that as they were so close to the Vichy French border they had to be absolutely positive that they had the right target. Twelve Wimpys from the squadron were detailed for this attack, but one did not take off owing to trouble with the undercarriage. Although the undercarriage was later adjusted, an accident on the runway to an aircraft from No. 70 Squadron caused cancellation of subsequent take-offs. Eleven aircraft located the target, where the weather was clear with good visibility. No. 614 Squadron, in their role of Pathfinders, illuminated the target which was good, although it started too high. Bombing was well concentrated, and Len dropped his bombs in one stick aiming at the centre of the yards. Bursts were seen in the target area. On leaving the target area one large red round fire was observed just north of the marshalling yards which could have been a gasometer on fire. Other fires were also seen in the marshalling yards, in the dead-end sidings, which had been attacked by 240 and 330 Wings just before 37 Squadron's attack. Opposition came from a few bursts of heavy flak and the light flak was negligible. Needless to say, the attack was very successful and being so close to the Vichy French it was hoped that they had got the message.

Sparks did not come with them, having reported sick with a bad back. Another wireless operator was detailed to take his place. This had an unnerving effect on the crew as it broke their superstitious routine of entering the aircraft.

Then it was back to Budapest. Sparks did not come with them, reporting sick with a bad back again. The same wireless operator from the previous raid was detailed to fly with them once more. They also carried a second pilot, but because he was a different pilot from the one who had been with them on the previous op, it upset the rest of the crew enormously. They were convinced that these two newcomers would be a jinx on them. Superstitiously hating change, they were afraid of breaking a winning sequence. At this time, the whole routine of pre-flight activity was strictly adhered to and anything that was likely to break it became an omen. They were not all happy with Sparks either, for they felt he was letting them down.

Fourteen aircraft were ordered, detailed and operated from the squadron to attack the oil refinery. This was to be the largest raid in which Lee had taken part, with 104 aircraft from the group participating. Only twelve aircraft from Lee's squadron were known to have carried out the attack, because two were missing and did not return. The illumination was poor, some five to six miles north of the target. Len dropped his bombs in one stick and they were seen to burst on a factory on the east bank of the Danube river some five miles north of the target. This was in the area where most of the bombing was taking place owing to the fact that it was where the illuminating flares were dropped. Two other crews reported a large explosion on the north tip of Caepel Island and another small explosion was reported to be near the Manfred Weiss Works. Opposition consisted of moderate, mainly inaccurate, heavy flak and light flak in the target area and some at Lake Balaton. Enemy night fighters were also seen.

The following night, Lee's crew were detailed to attack the oil storage tanks at Giurgiu, but swung on take-off. This was to be an unlucky night for the squadron because, besides Lee's mishap, of the thirteen aircraft detailed to carry out the attack, only seven, for some reason or other, got to the target area. When they did, the illumination was poor, scattered and inaccurate and the bombing was therefore largely ineffective. No crew definitely identified the target, though several claimed bursts in the target area. It had also been an unlucky day. At about 1515 hours a squadron aircraft, Wellington X, LP182, blew up on the aerodrome in two tremendous explosions. A piece of burning debris was blown nearly a hundred yards, and by great mischance fell on another Wellington aircraft, MF351, which was also destroyed by fire. Furthermore, of the 105 aircraft from the group that took part in the raid, five failed to return.

It appeared that the original cause of the explosion was the igniting, by an undiscovered medium, of a faulty incendiary bomb which was being loaded for operations into LP182. Fortunately there was a short time interval between the first outbreak of fire and the first explosion, which gave all personnel the opportunity to get clear, so that no injury was suffered. Good work was done, not only by the fire services, but by a flight lieutenant and a flight sergeant from 231 Wing, and a sergeant from the squadron, who promptly went out while there was still danger from exploding bombs and taxied away three other aircraft in the area to safety. A Court of Inquiry was later convened by the Officer Commanding HQ 231 Wing to inquire into the circumstances of the incident.

The next trip was again to Feuersbrunn, with Sparks still reporting sick. Nine Wimpys were ordered, and all operated, there being no early returns and no losses. They took off at 8.30 p.m., and returned at 2.45 a.m. Illumination by 614 Squadron was again very scattered, and only five aircraft appeared to have definitely identified the target, one of which was Lee's. They identified the target at first by estimating its position in relation to two small villages. A large fire was seen in the target area and also two small fires. Later, the large fire was confirmed as occurring in the workshop hangar in the north-east corner of the aerodrome.

The four other aircraft bombed what was believed to be the target under the illumination, but the photographs were to show that this was not the case. There was a fair amount of opposition *en route* from four or five different towns and, with accurate flak, one aircraft was holed quite badly. Others saw enemy fighters in the area. There was very little opposition in the target area.

The loss of Bobby and his crew had now left Lee and his crew as the only survivors of all of the friends that had come out to Italy together. This knowledge, together with their superstitions, made them very aware of the present situation, which they now found themselves thinking about daily. They liked to call it, 'The survival roulette game', for they were knocking off the ops one by one with the goal of becoming 'Tour-expired'. With each sortie, the wheel of fortune was shortening the odds against them surviving.

In spite of this there was one consolation in the present situation as far as Lee was concerned: although still troubled through the lack of sleep at night, he was no longer kept awake by trying to reconcile his conscience with the job that he had undertaken to do. The rest camp at Sorrento had given him the break he had so badly needed. He was aware that he had gone through that terrible fear barrier he had experienced before going to Sorrento, and he was no longer afraid of what was happening to him as a person. He had now been able to reconcile his conscience with his duty, but just when this had occurred he could not pinpoint. It could have been because of the support they had been giving to the troops recently – tactical raids were always better than strategical. Or maybe he felt that after Valmontone and Kalova, the Grim Reaper was on his side.

It also helped no doubt that as the months turned from winter to spring and then on to summer, the weather in the area greatly improved and flying conditions were not nearly as hazardous as they had been. Whatever it was, he had matured quite considerably and now, with another fifteen or sixteen ops under his belt, he knew and felt that he had become a very experienced pilot. He had become fully blooded to the rigours of war, and in his mind he felt better for it. He was supremely confident in his ability and it was only the shortening of the odds that concerned him now, the game of roulette, their survival against the number of ops left to do. Only another four to go! A four to one chance. Would their luck hold out?

Nowadays, it was body fatigue that prevented him from sleeping easily, simply over-tiredness. Although he could switch his mind off from worrying over events, his body refused to respond in the same way. Even so, after only a few hours' sleep he was able to awake refreshed and did not feel so irked and irritable as he had done in the past. That night's sleep had once again been very hard to come by. All the same, Lee marvelled at the change that had manifested itself in his attitude. The

107

nights of worrying over his reactions had gone, thank God. He didn't want to go through that phase again.

What had supplanted his conscience and suppressed his rambling thoughts as he lay on his bed, was the noise of the blood pounding around inside him and the pounding of his heart that seemed to get worse and worse. He lay there at night fascinated by it, wondering what it was. What other thoughts he had were always more positive.

The change in the weather, besides making the ops more bearable, had brought about a change in the conditions in which they lived. There was more sunshine and warmth which, in itself, cheered them up. The mud had been transformed to dust, so that when the strong winds blew around the airfield, the sandstorm effect had caused one or two operations to be scrubbed, giving them a welcome night off now and again, and easing the pressure on them. The warmer weather brought its own problems, some of which, like the ops being scrubbed, could be turned to advantage. For example, in the tent encampment the dust got everywhere, which meant that, because everyone always felt dirty, almost daily trips were made to town to take a shower in the communal shower blocks, giving them another reason to get off the camp. The British shared these blocks with the Americans or was it that the Americans allowed the British to use theirs? It was always a friendly and good-humoured occasion, with plenty of wisecracks from the Americans. They had a much more relaxed attitude to service discipline than the British, who could not help admiring their cheek.

There was, of course, a downside to this weather: the heat brought out the flies and mosquitoes. Flies were everywhere – in the canteen, in the lavatories and around them when they were trying to have a brew up in the tent – and could the little buggers bite! They had a nip on them which would have been a credit to bugs three times their size. But, by and large, life was much more tolerable.

Lee was beginning to become a little worried about Sparks' future. He would have to make up these missing ops with another crew if he wasn't careful, but if he came back he may be tour-expired with them, as they had only four more ops to do. Lee put it to Sparks to try and get off the sick list. They were standing by the water bowser when Sparks told him he did not want to continue; he had been badly shaken when his pal in Bobby's crew had been lost in the raid on Munich. Lee was shocked.

It was 1 July, a beautiful moonlit night, when they went minelaying the Danube again. Ten aircraft were detailed to lay two Mark IV mines each in the area between Fajs and Baja at midnight at a height of between 200 to 300 feet. Only nineteen were laid as one was returned, hung up, to base. Lee's crew successfully laid both of theirs in the target area. Four aircraft shot up a number of barges seen on the river. The opposition they encountered did not bother them very much, coming from about half a dozen light Ack-Ack guns which, although fairly accurate, were not accurate enough. One enemy fighter, a Ju 88, was reported in the target area. All the squadron's aircraft returned safely.

Once more it was to be on a brilliant moonlit night when they were told about their last trip into Austria – Feuersbrunn again. In spite of the success of the previous attacks, the American Air Force were still experiencing tremendous opposition from the crack German fighter squadron based at this fighter base. Eleven Wimpys were detailed, but one returned early with intercom and guns unserviceable. It was a lovely night, as clear as daylight, as they flew into Austria over the Dolomites at 10,000 feet, engines perfectly synchronised and purring away. Visibility on the earth below stretched for miles. The only other sound to disturb the stillness of the night was the hiss and popping sound from the oxygen masks as they gulped in the precious air. Suddenly, over on the starboard side, an aircraft dropped out of the sky in flames, quickly followed by another, then another. Lee counted seven in all. There was no flak or searchlights, not a sound, only the visual Roman candle effect as the aircraft floated downwards.

Ahead lay the target, marked by illumination flares dropped on time but scattered over the aerodrome. Arriving over the area, the target markers looked to be well placed over the airfield, but in view of the aircraft being shot down around them, Lee decided that it would be unwise to fly a straight and level bombing run at that height, not wishing to be a sitting duck for enemy fighters. From his bomb aimer's position, Len picked up the target marker and asked Lee if he was ready to start his bombing run.

'What do you think would be a safe height to go in at, Len?' Lee asked.

'I don't think it should be less than 5,000 feet, Skipper,' came the reply.

'OK, that's it then,' said Lee. He put the nose of the aircraft down, and the thrill was exhilarating as he sped down to 5,000 feet.

Buildings could be seen through the haze created by the flares and target indicators. Lee levelled out at just over 5,000 feet, and Len held the target in his bombsights.

'OK Lee, I've got it. Bomb doors open. Steady, steady, left, left, right, right. Hold it there – got it! Bombs gone.'

They broke off the attack, but unfortunately, at that height, the target was soon left behind and as they climbed away, they were unable to observe the results in the haze below. Later they discovered that other members of the squadron had also bombed between 5,000 and 6,500 feet and like themselves, were generally unable to observe the results. Nevertheless, the subsequent photo reconnaissance proved that the raid had achieved its objective: the aerodrome was unserviceable.

After bombing and taking the photograph, Len came back to the second pilot's seat. He gave the thumbs up sign to Lee and settled into his seat. Lee had already started to climb back to 10,000 feet to head for home over the foothills that lay ahead. Over in the distance he could see another aircraft going down.

'This is like a daylight raid to those bloody fighter pilots,' he said. 'It's as clear as day out there. Keep your eyes open, everyone,' he warned.

He was just about to level off when he glanced down past Len to the clear bomb aimer's window position in the nose. There, neatly framed in the glass panel, was the outline of a German fighter, a Ju 88! The black crosses on its wings gave him the fright of his life.

'German fighter below!' he screamed down the intercom and immediately flung the aircraft into evasive action.

'Do you see it, Jock?' he called out to the rear gunner.

'No, just got a glimpse of it as you broke away, Skip,' came the reply.

'Well, keep your bloody eyes open and your fingers on the trigger,' shouted Lee. 'What the hell were you doing letting him get underneath us like that?' He was furious. It must have crept up from behind, but he couldn't dwell on it, his job now was to get back safely. He had been badly shaken and he knew that at that height he was a sitting target.

'Bastard's back, Lee,' came an excited shout down the intercom. He couldn't recognise the voice.

'Give him a burst, Jock. Let the bastard know we've seen him,' he shouted.

He put the aircraft into a dive once again and down and down he went to treetop level, determined that the fighters would not get below him again. He skimmed over the tops of the trees and buildings and headed in the general direction of home. His pulse was racing, he was angry; fancy being caught like that. Christ, they had been lucky! He tapped Len on the shoulder.

'What the hell were you doing? You had a better view through your panel than I did,' he said.

There was no reply.

'Is the bastard still chasing us, Jock?' he called.

'Can't see him, Skipper,' replied Jock.

No, you couldn't see a bloody brick wall if it was in front of you, thought Lee.

He turned his concentration to the job in hand, and soon his anger abated as the thrill of the low-flying chase gradually took over. They were skimming over the hilltops now. Rooftops of farmhouses and village buildings flashed underneath them as they sped on their way. They raced gracefully up and down, following the contours of the land over ploughed fields, meadows and woods.

The tops of trees waved as they flew rapidly over them. They fled on crossing roads, railways and streams glittering in the moonlight, past homesteads and villages, as if they were trying to outpace or outstrip the very land itself. Lee had to keep his eyes firmly fixed on the objects looming up in front of him as they in turn raced towards him. He dared not look either to his left or his right for fear that he might hit something. It was exhilarating. They had no idea where they were. At that height it was impossible for them to pinpoint their position, the ground was going past them so quickly. Riggy gave Lee a course to steer, and he reckoned that if they kept on that course they would probably end up somewhere near Venice.

After a while Lee relaxed. They must be out of that fighter's range by now. He started to climb to give the crew a chance of pinpointing their position. Flak ahead on the port side made them think that they must be nearing Venice, but low cloud, or the mist of a moonlit night, obscured the outline of the coast below and prevented them from getting a definite fix.

It was then that they saw another Wimpy also heading for home in the same direction. This convinced Riggy that it must have been Venice they had just passed, and a new course for home was set.

'That was a damn good course you gave me, Riggy, when we were scurrying back, considering the number of times I had to deviate to get round the odd hill or so appearing in front of us. Bloody good effort.'

The raid had been very successful. The following day when the 15th USAAF made the double passage past Vienna to bomb the synthetic oil plants in Silesia, fighter opposition, although heavy, was undoubtedly lessened by the knocking out of this very important fighter base. Nineteen out of thirty-eight enemy single-engined aircraft were destroyed or damaged on the ground. But the cost had been high.

The cost to the Squadron was bad in itself: two aircraft out of the ten that operated were lost. But to the Group, the cost was very high indeed: eleven Wimpys, two Liberators and one Halifax; losses which were attributed to the necessity of penetrating the strong fighter organisation of Vienna in brilliant moonlight. Lee only had two more operations to do. Would they survive?

Whilst waiting in debriefing, Len came over to Lee.

'Sorry, Skip,'

Lee shrugged his shoulders. 'That's OK, Len, it happens.' They were pals again.

A South African lieutenant was the senior crew. He was a dedicated, extremely caring pilot and easy to get along with. He had finished his tour, which cheered Lee up immensely, having overcome the dreaded, 'he bought it on his last op' story. Lee was now the captain with the highest number of operations to his credit, and therefore became the senior crew. Besides his bomb load he would have the responsibility of marking the target with flares for the squadron.

Brod in Yugoslavia was their thirty-ninth op. It was a comparatively easy target, where twelve Wimpys were detailed to attack the Brod Bosanki Oil Refinery storage tanks. This was to be a follow-up of a very successful attack of about a month before, which had destroyed the oil refinery proper. Riggy had no difficulty in getting them to it and Len no difficulty in illuminating it on the first run, and successfully bombing it on the second. The bombs dropped in one stick across four or five tanks. The target was reported to be a mass of flames by aircraft leaving it, reporting fires visible up to 110 miles away. In this attack it is believed that the storage tanks to the south were just about finished off. Opposition was slight and there were no losses.

But their last op was to be the Milan Lambrate marshalling yards again. Remembering their previous experience on that particular target, the crew were convinced after briefing that this was it. Their luck could not hold out any longer. After all, they reasoned, the last crew to finish had got back safely from their last op. It couldn't happen twice on the trot. Theirs must be 'the last op story'. It had to be.

Why, oh, why, could they not have given them an easy target to end up with? However, Lee still discouraged them from writing 'the final letter', which was considered among bomber crews to be the ultimate jinx. But what was more significant was the fact that the crew due to take over the senior crew mantle had only completed thirteen operations. If the losses had been sequential the next should be doing thirty-nine and so on down the scale. Milan for their last one. It wasn't fair!

Twelve Wimpys were detailed, but only ten operated; one did not take off due to a mag. drop and another returned early with intercom and guns unserviceable. The journey across Italy and up the coast was uneventful and, in spite of their previous misgivings, the crew were in good heart. The wireless operator who had taken Sparks' place had fitted in well with them and had been a permanent member since Sparks had reported sick. He was referred to on the ground as 'Sparks number two', but in the air just as Sparks again.

On reaching the target, the illumination and markings were good and well concentrated, and an accurate attack resulted. Len dropped his bombs in one stick on the red target indicators and one large fire was started. Many incendiary fires covered the yards, especially the central and eastern yards, and fires were visible for forty miles. Flak consisted of up to four heavies and some light guns, but they caused little inconvenience.

After taking the obligatory photograph those final thirteen seconds' flying straight and level felt like thirteen hours. After Len had called 'Bombs away,' it seemed like an eternity. As soon as it was over, Lee broke off the attack and turned for home. Putting the nose of the aircraft down they sped back to base as fast as he could make it. Once they were back over Allied territory the excited chatter started. Was this their last op? Were they really through it?

All they had to do now was get back home safely. Fortunately, the weather conditions were favourable, and when the three searchlights came into view as they headed back home they let out a terrific cheer. Lee was the first back into the circuit. They had taken off at 8.40 p.m. and it was now 2.10 a.m., six and a half hours, but he wasn't tired. Receiving instructions to land, he gently touched down his Wimpy Wellington X 'H for Harry' LP502 (his, for it had been his aircraft for the last seven operations) on to the metal runway and together they taxied triumphantly back to dispersal.

It was 10 July. They had carried out forty ops in the space of just over four months. They were tour-expired. The crew were delighted they had done it. They had made it. Their delight and joy knew no bounds. At debriefing that night it felt as if someone had waved a magic wand over them and lifted all their cares and worries. What was more, they were pleased to learn that there had been no squadron losses that night that would mar their celebrations. Although it still had to be confirmed, it was a moment to treasure. They were virtually walking on air.

When they finally got to their beds, Lee had his usual troubled sleep. Now his heart and body was again throbbing with exhaustion, it seemed like hours before he succumbed to that precious gift of sleep. What if his calculations were wrong and it wasn't confirmed? What was going to happen now? Would he be able to stay on the squadron for his rest period? He must get his other tour done so that he could get back to Connie.

When they awoke later in the morning, he and the rest of his crew went to the ops room. Riggy was already there. Yes, it was confirmed, they were tour-expired. The Squadron Commander came in and congratulated them and thanked them for their efforts as did the rest of the flight leaders who were on duty.

Lee went down to dispersal and thanked the ground crews for the help and support they had given to them, and he felt six feet tall. It was finally over. Other congratulations, mixed with envy, came from the very junior crews who now made up the bulk of the squadron. The losses had been high.

Poor Sparks was left behind and, although present, took no part in the joyful celebrations that evening. Before that Lee had sent a telegram to Connie and his mother, saying, 'Anxiety unnecessary. Operation over. Condition satisfactory. Fondest Love.' That was the secret code message they had agreed upon to let them know that it was all over at least for a little while. The crew went to Sorrento again on their tour-expired leave, having first visited the Opera House in Naples to see Rigoletto.

The mood was completely different from their last visit, and they were able to relax and rest. When they returned to Torterello, their postings

The coded cable (complete with spelling mistakes) sent to say that Lee's first tour had been completed.

had come in. Riggy, Len and Jock were going to the Middle East but because Lee had volunteered for another tour in order to get back home to Connie, he was staying in Italy. Sparks was to stay on to finish his tour. Lee was posted to No. 4 Parachute Training School (PTS) based in the south of Italy.

They spent a few more days hanging around the camp, one day of which was spent going into the town of Foggia to get a shower and go to the pictures. The cinema was in an old Italian theatre. The projector continually broke down amidst catcalls and shouts from the frustrated servicemen who made up the audience. The films themselves were fairly up-to-date and provided very good escapist entertainment.

The day to leave the squadron soon arrived, but before they left there were the obligatory drinks in the evening in the Mess. Len and Lee popped over to the American camp to swap some Scotch whisky for beer. This was about the only thing the British had which the Americans did not, and the Americans were always willing to do a deal. The British and the American airmen got on extremely well together, despite the tales of the Yanks back home attracting all the girls, buying them nylons, taking them out and so on, and their better pay and living conditions out here. Here there was a bond of comradeship and friendship between them, brought about because they were both engaged doing the same job against the same enemy targets. The American airmen couldn't understand how the British managed with those very small Wellington bombers at night, which they knew as the 'Rag Bombers', so inadequately armed compared with their heavily armed Flying Fortresses. Conversely the British had a deep admiration for the Americans' fearless encounters with the enemy fighters in their daytime battles over enemy skies.

Armed with their cans of beer Lee and Len returned to camp. After a few celebratory drinks in the Sergeants' Mess, they left and went over to the Officers' Quarters where Riggy was having his farewell party in his tent.

Riggy was sitting inside amongst a few of his fellow officers in the gloom. He called out to them, 'Come in, you chaps,' emphasising the words in an English accent, his face breaking out into a warm welcoming grin. 'Sit down if you can find somewhere to sit. What'll you have?'

Lee could just make out some of the faces of the ground crews in the tent also. God, he thought, why didn't I think of that? They squeezed into the tent, but it was standing room only and they could get no further than just inside the tent opening.

One of the flight commanders, a regular (the name given to pre-war members of the RAF), was there sitting next to the opening with his hat on. He was an older man, one who had also married (for the second time) in Moreton and one for whom Lee did not have a great deal of time. Lee soon realised that the ground crew were also acting as waiters. Maybe that was how Riggy had managed to invite them, thought Lee, since other ranks are not normally allowed to socialise with officers in their quarters. That made him feel better over what he thought had been an omission of recognition on his part of the valuable service that ground crews provided.

Being Riggy, it was 'A Party' that was going on. Somehow he had managed to acquire a various mix of sandwiches, snacks, Italian sparkling wine and plenty of beer and whisky. There was the usual plentiful supply of toast and butter – the aircrews' staple evening snack. The party soon got into full swing, with the usual stories of wine, women and song. When these stories were coupled with stories of action, determination and valour, it made Lee wonder why the war was taking so long!

A few more drinks and it wasn't long before the subject got around to the Flight Commander's bald head. Someone had taken off his hat complaining that he shouldn't be wearing it at a party. At the same time this revealed his smooth bald pate, much to the embarrassment of the Flight Commander, and the amusement of his fellow officers. Advice started to come in from all quarters of how to make his hair grow again, including, amidst howls of ribald laughter, stopping playing with himself!

Lee said he had a cure for it and, picking up the remnants of about half a pound of butter, he plastered it on the Flight Commander's bald head!

Before he could recover, Lee said a quick cheerio to Riggy, waved his fond farewells and quickly departed.

The following morning Lee had to rise early in order to catch the truck that was to take him to the railway station for his journey to his new posting to southern Italy. His belongings were all packed, but Len, Sparks and Jock got up to help him with his kit, and it was a very moving moment when they said their goodbyes. They had been through a lot together, and had remained, at all times, the very best of friends. All had matured from young fresh inexperienced airmen to reliable experienced crew members, developing the comradeship that can only come from facing death together as a team, each relying so much on the other to do his job correctly. It had been a long slog from the time they had joined up together at Lossiemouth, and now, at this moment of parting, they wondered if their paths would ever cross again. Sparks was almost in tears – they had finished, and he had to carry on without them. But this was not the time for recriminations. Loyal Jock had left Riggy's party early to go back to his pal, knowing that he would feel left out. They wished each other luck, exchanged the usual promises to keep in touch, and went with Lee to HQ.

At that time of the morning the camp was deserted. It looked very forlorn and insignificant as they walked between the tents. Much to his amazement, Lee felt a touch of sadness in leaving it. Passing the water bowser he saw there was still mud under the giant taps, but limited now to the place where the cans overflowed, whereas around the rest of the bowser the ground was caked hard. Lee reflected on the conversation he had had with Sparks, when he said he wanted to finish. What a hell of a shame he had felt like that. He could be celebrating with the rest of them now. He looked over at Sparks, but not a word passed between them. Lee wondered whether they were thinking the same thing.

Passing the Mess, Lee noticed for the first time how rusty it had become and wondered if it would be painted or would the aircrew be lucky enough to get an old barn similar to the one recently converted to become the airmen's canteen? Last month, at the suggestion of the Airmen's Mess Committee, a barn in a farmhouse close to the domestic site had been taken over for conversion to a canteen. In a matter of a few days, by the Herculean efforts of a few airmen, decorations, lighting and a large bar were installed. Using the same ideas adopted in the Sergeants' Mess, furniture was made out of bomb tail fin and flare boxes.

The whole effect was excellent and, on the night of 26 June, it was 'officially' opened by the CO. The night had been a great success. That was possible with the airmen, thought Lee. They were permanent staff, probably on a three-year tour, and time was on their side. Not so for the aircrew. He had only been on the squadron six months and, unlike many, he had survived.

Eventually they arrived at the HQ where the truck was waiting. Lee climbed aboard and sat next to the driver, waving goodbye as the truck moved off. It was 6.30 a.m. No one else was about, and he felt sad. Once more in his life he was on his own, but now he was more mature. His life would never be the same. He had grown up, and felt very much older and a hell of a lot wiser.

As they drove away, he realised that it had been less than six months since all this had started. He was still only twenty-three. He was to find out later that, during the eighteen weeks he had been on operational duty with the squadron, the group as a whole had operated on eighty-four nights. Lee had been on forty of those, nearly half. The group losses for the period had been 122 aircraft 'missing in action' and a further twenty-six had crashed returning to base. Little wonder that he had felt the strain emotionally and his heart and pulse had thumped so loudly. Except for the two-week break in Sorrento, it had been almost eighteen weeks non-stop, with no time to mourn the loss of friends and colleagues.

And he had volunteered for another lot! He must have been mad – or, in his case, in love.

CHAPTER TEN

A WELL EARNED REST?

I T was a sunny afternoon when Lee arrived at the Parachute Training School in southern Italy after a slow, uneventful train journey in which he had dozed for most of the time. An RAF Military Police Sergeant had pointed him in the direction of a truck that was at the station from 4 PTS, presumably to meet him and to pick up supplies. The first thing that struck him, as he drove into the town of Gioia Del Colle which housed the HQ of the unit, was the lack of bomb damage compared with Foggia. The town had either been very lucky because it held no strategic position, or the townsfolk had done a good job in tidying the place up. Passing through one of the streets he noticed quite a number of soldiers and airmen queuing up outside a house in the warm sunshine and the heat of the day. Some were leaning against the wall, smoking.

'What's going on there?' he asked his driver as they went past.

'That's the local brothel,' his driver told him.

He arrived at the headquarters and was taken to the CO, a wing commander who was himself a pilot. The CO made him very welcome, saying how pleased he was to have been given a pilot of Lee's experience. He then called in the Flight Commander and introduced him to Lee, and the Flight Commander also confirmed what the CO had said about having an experienced pilot on the team. With that attitude, it was natural that Lee liked them both immediately and they continued to ask him questions about where he had been trained and the RAF stations he had served on. The Flight Commander had been on the unit for some time and was most disappointed that he himself had not been on operations. Leaving the CO's office the Flight Commander was very interested to hear about Lee's tour and was rather shocked to hear that they were still under canvas and about the conditions under which the aircrew lived.

'Not at all like the image I had of them. I thought all aircrew had egg and bacon breakfasts,' he commented.

He suggested that Lee should get through the preliminaries of joining the unit before being taken to the Sergeants' Mess, as all things that had to be done could be carried out in the house they had commandeered for the HQ. That agreed, he passed Lee on to the admin. section for him to be taken on to the strength of the unit.

Once again the usual routines of checking into a new RAF station were

118

undertaken. The medical, FFI (Free From Infection) examination, (Lee had lost count of the number of times he had dropped his trousers and coughed!), next of kin, pay details and so on. After all the necessary routines were carried out, he was taken by Jeep to the Sergeants' Mess which also served as their billet. The Mess was a very large Italian four-storey house that had also been commandeered by the RAF. The ground floor consisted of a lounge which had a bar built into it, a smaller lounge used as a writing room, a dining room and a kitchen. All were very well furnished. Upstairs, on the third floor, were the bedrooms which the sergeant instructors shared two to a room, whilst on the second floor warrant officers and pilots had their own rooms.

Lee was delighted with the room that had been set aside for him, particularly as it had a small balcony. He was even more delighted when he saw that his kit had been taken up to his room by the driver and placed neatly at the end of his bed. There were very few men about when Lee arrived, but the Station Warrant Officer (SWO), an Australian who introduced himself by his nickname of Cobber, made him very welcome, and another friendship was born. After the usual preliminaries, the SWO suggested that, after his long journey, there was time for a wash and brush-up before the evening meal. The bathroom was at the end of the corridor on the same floor as his room.

For the first time since he had been promoted to Sergeant, Lee was getting the full treatment that his rank warranted. Previously, during his operational training, he had only been one of the many sergeant pilots on the course. Furthermore, during his operational flying, he had been too busy, and was just another one of the many NCOs in the tent camp to merit such individual treatment. He was beginning to enjoy this new-found respect for his rank. This became even more paramount when, again for the first time since leaving England, Lee was able to enjoy the privacy of a bath in peace and absolute quiet. Even in Sorrento, other men had been around the place. He soaked up the warm water and just lay there, listening to the silence around him. It was so peaceful and he was so content, he could have laid there for ever.

After unpacking, he sat down on his bed which was, joy of joys, a real one, and he wrote to Connie and his family at home. He felt safe and secure as if he was a prisoner who had just been released from prison and was on parole. Footsteps on the stairs and the sound of voices in the passageway were the signals for him to make a move. Obviously the others were coming in off duty and he was curious to meet them. He finished dressing and went down into the Mess where the SWO was waiting for him. Cobber was standing among a group of suntanned, extremely healthy-looking NCOs.

It was obvious that Cobber had been telling them about the new arrival whilst they were having a drink prior to their meal, and he introduced Lee to them. This had never happened to him before. Usually, when he had arrived on a station, it had been left to him to find his way around and meet people. It usually turned out to be the chap who had the next bed space to him or who happened to sit next to him in the Mess or in the canteen. But these chaps were professional NCOs and followed the traditions and rules of the Mess down to the letter. He was immediately offered a drink and bombarded with questions about his tour.

'How were things up at the Front Line?'

'Were there many losses?'

'How many ops have you done?'

'What was it like over a target?'

'Were you frightened?'

'We would shit ourselves if we had to do it.'

Lee tried to answer the questions the best way he could, as he did not want to talk about it. On the other hand, he did not want to appear unsociable. He had been on enough new stations to know that to keep things to yourself was a sure way to get people's backs up and to become known as a toffee-nosed bastard. God knows what the SWO had told them about him, but it wasn't long before he began to realise that they were treating him like a hero, which was the last thing he felt or wanted. Having just found this new way of life, he did not want to ruin it by having to live up to a reputation which was unfounded anyway. He certainly did not want to become a bullshitter. His mind alerted, he immediately tried to dispel this image right away by explaining that the targets were not the things that worried him and his crew. It was the weather which gave the crews their worst problems, with the lack of navigational aids, W/T silence and complete blackout everywhere. Trying to find your way over unfamiliar hostile enemy country in pitch-black darkness and poor visibility was no picnic. That, to him, and to other aircrew, had been far more dangerous than the ops. It was the same for everyone operating in that theatre of war. Furthermore, the conditions in the British camps from which they were to carry out this work, were less than basic!

This brought on more questions about the camps. Just like the officers had been earlier, these men were also staggered to hear of the living conditions in the camp he had just left. He was destroying the image of 'Brylcream Boys' and the glamour that surrounded aircrew in the UK. He also tried to explain that, in the early days, and as the tour progressed, how he had been so frightened and unsure of his motives night after night when they had returned from a raid, but that only made things worse; particularly when he went on to say that, after about twenty-five ops, he had finally sorted himself out and had just got on with the job. That ops had become routine work.

However, it became obvious to him after a while that, no matter what he said, it was going to make no difference to their attitude towards him, so in the end he gave up, and started to ask them questions.

'How many pilots are there on the unit?'

There were two other pilots; both were officers and lived in the Officers' Mess, neither of whom had been on operations, but had been with the unit for some time and were extremely well liked. Both had been in the desert with them. One was the Flight Commander whom Lee had already met. The unit had recently returned from the Middle East, having moved from Palestine to Egypt, and then on to Italy.

The instructors came from varied backgrounds, and the majority seemed to be school teachers from the Manchester area, where the unit had been based at Ringway. Nearly all were ex-physical training instructors and had been together for a long time. At that point, the dinner gong went and they all went for their meal. Sitting four or six to a table, they were waited on by Italian waiters wearing white gloves. As members of the Mess they had got themselves very well organised; Mess duties had been allocated to individual members and it became apparent to Lee that they were all going to be extremely kind to him. He was on a rest, and a rest they were determined to give him – the excuse being that they had been together for so long that it would upset their routine if they were to start allocating him Mess duties. Lee protested, and he was reluctantly given the job of assistant catering.

After an excellent meal they retired to the bar. Jimmy, a sergeant from Manchester, soon stood out as a leader and, on his initiative, as if they needed an excuse, it was decided to give Lee a party to welcome him. The songs were sung with great enjoyment and each member was called upon to do his party piece. There was one particular sergeant instructor, Bill, who had a wonderful singing voice, having been on the stage before the war. His rendition of 'Bless this House' brought tears into the eyes of many, while Harry's version of 'Eskimo Nell' brought howls of laughter.

The English beer and *vino* flowed quite liberally. Then, much to Lee's surprise, they decided to show him what parachuting was all about, by doing 'a quick stick off the bar'. Propping a chair against the bar they clambered on to it and, shouting 'Geronimo', they ran along the bar, jumping off at the end and upon landing, broke their fall in the special way that paratroopers did.

Lee was quite certain that one of them would break a leg or something, but they knew their job well, having carried out this particular exercise in the Mess on many, many occasions. Nevertheless, no amount of persuasion would entice him to take part.

It was a most enjoyable evening, truly a welcome that brought Lee into the group on his very first day. He had never met a bunch of fellows like them.

*   *   *

121

The next morning Lee was taken to the airfield to meet the ground staff and other members of the unit. It was a very small unit, where everyone knew everyone else but, what was more important, it appeared to be a very happy and cheerful group.

Nearly a month had passed by since Lee had been airborne, so his first trip was a familiarisation trip at night as second pilot with the Flight Commander. The airfield was some miles out of town so, after an excellent dinner in the Mess, the Flight Commander drew up in his own Jeep to take Lee to the airfield. The instructors who were on duty had left earlier to make their own way to the building in town they used as a ground training base, there to meet up with the trainees who were to take part in this particular exercise. A great deal of training took place in this building before the trainees ever got to see an aircraft. The emphasis was on learning to land properly when they hit the ground to avoid broken limbs, and to be ready to spring into action as a fighting force.

Arriving at the airfield, Lee was delighted to see the familiar dark outline and tall tailplanes of a couple of Wimpys standing on the apron. One was being warmed up by the ground crew staff getting it ready for take-off. The airfield was primarily an American Air Force base, in one corner of which the RAF had a facility. The RAF quarters consisted of one large spacious hut in which everyone gathered very informally, and a smaller building which housed the stores and maintenance section. The larger building served as the nerve centre for the flying operations of the unit and as the canteen-cum-waiting room for ground crew, instructors, trainees and pilots, irrespective of rank.

Everyone mucked in together and, that night, in spite of the lateness of the hour, it had a very friendly and cheerful atmosphere. Collecting their 'chutes from the stores, Lee and the Flight Commander made their way to the waiting aircraft. Together they made the pre-flight checks, the Flight Commander signed the Form 700, and they were ready for take-off.

It was a marvellous feeling to climb into the cockpit of a Wimpy again; the smell of the fabric 'dope' (the paint used on the fabric to make it weather-tight), mixed with that of the oil and petrol, all combining with the dimmed lights of the cockpit made an atmosphere of nostalgia which, as it came over him, made him realise just how much he loved these old Wimpys. It was very comforting, as if he had met up with an old friend once again, but in more cordial and pleasant surroundings. As the engines came on to power and the prop tips whizzed around outside just missing the fuselage by inches, he felt completely at home and relaxed. What is more and, much to his surprise, he had a strange longing to take off on a long op. He would never have thought that only a month after his tour had ended he would have missed the excitement so much. But then, he was no longer a 'sprog' pilot and felt, ashamedly, a little superior

to the Flight Commander in spite of his rank, as he had not had his operational experience.

They were to drop trainee paratroopers at night at the dropping zone
which was a few miles away. On the face of it, it was a fairly mundane
exercise. The actual flying came as an eye opener and quite a shock – it
was nearly as bad as flying on operations. His attitude towards his Flight
Commander soon changed. Flying a heavy Wimpy low at 300 feet, at
90 mph with quarter flap, just above stalling speed, was hazardous
enough, but at night, with a load of trainee paratroopers on board moving
about in the back then dropping out and upsetting the trim, coupled with
flying tightly around the dropping zone in the dark, and at the same time
trying to concentrate on just where to give the signals to release them,
was a very precarious operation to say the least. No wonder they had
wanted an experienced Wimpy pilot for the job!

The Flight Commander and the other pilot must be damn good pilots
to have kept this up for so long, Lee thought, because it must also be
bloody boring. If the aircraft stalled and spun in at that height, you would
not stand a cat in hell's chance of recovering. That would be the end . . .
curtains. He would need to keep all of his wits about him. Lee realised
that his 'rest period' was not going to be quite what he had thought.

The Wellington bombers used for this purpose had a hole cut out of
the floor of the fuselage through which the trainee paratroopers jumped.
The very low flying speed was extremely crucial to those jumping out of
the aircraft because any faster would mean they may become caught up
in the fast slipstream being created underneath the aircraft. This would
be fatal if the airflow carried them upwards and they became wrapped
around the tailplane, or if they were spun round and round, winding up
their 'chutes which, of course, would fail to open! In addition to the effect
of the airflow as they jumped, consideration was also given to the effect of
the windspeed and direction upon them as they were floating downwards.

In order to minimise the adverse effect of the wind after they had left
the aircraft, and to ensure they landed within the dropping zone, dropping could only take place when the winds were light. Therefore, because
light winds in that part of the world occurred mainly in the very early
morning or evening, flying normally took place at that time of the day.
And so it was that Lee found himself getting up at four o'clock in the
morning to be at the airfield at five o'clock in order to pick up the trainees
to take them to the dropping zone – a complete reversal of his old way
of life when he was lucky if he got to bed by four o'clock in the morning.

The procedure for each trip was fairly routine. The pilot would
approach the dropping zone, check the wind sock to see which way the
wind was blowing and then fly into the wind at 300 feet, keeping his
airspeed constant at 90 mph. Troops were dispatched from the aircraft

through instructions given by lights above their heads in the fuselage. These were controlled by the pilot, green for stand-by and red for dispatch. There were set procedures to go through involving 'dummy runs' before giving the signal to jump. First the pilot would carry out a dummy run to estimate where he should press the green light button. Then, a little later as they flew on, the pilot would have to estimate where to press the red light button to indicate to the dispatchers when to let the troops go out one at a time.

The object was to land all of the troops as near as possible to a marker, in the shape of a target, set out on the ground below. However, before any troops were allowed to leave the aircraft and in order to estimate where to signal more accurately, the pilot would carry out another 'dummy run'. The purpose of this second run was for the dispatcher, who, when he saw the green light come on, got ready to release a parachute with a weight attached, equivalent to the weight of an average man. He would dispatch this from the aircraft when he saw the red light.

Whilst all this was going on the pilot made a mental note of ground positions, a tree, a spot in the hedge or some other mark on the ground where he had pressed the buttons. He would then have to keep his eye on the weighted parachute as it floated downwards, note how far from the ground marker it landed and adjust his previous calculations and visual ground positions accordingly. He would then go around again for a third and final 'dummy run', this time for one of the instructors to jump. The object was for the instructor to drop so close that he would land bang in the middle of the target on the ground, which was marked with a bull's eye. Later, Lee found out that bets would be taken on how close the team got to the middle of the bull's eye. Needless to say to hit the bull's eye, with that amount of accuracy, was not achieved very often. The instructors were, of course, experts and were able to control their descents by pulling on the cords of the parachute, slipping air out of one side of the parachute or the other. They would, on most occasions, land standing up, either in or by the circle, having released their 'chute a few feet above ground level. Woe betide the pilot who miscalculated, and dropped them too far out so that they could not reach the circle and they had to walk back to it carrying their 'chutes with them.

Finally, the troops would go out in 'sticks' of six to eight troops. The number of times he circled the dropping zone after that depended upon the number of troops he had on board. There was an instructor on the ground, giving instructions through a megaphone to the trainees as they were coming down. It was very difficult to estimate what time they would return to the Mess, but they were usually back in time for a wash and brush-up before lunch. Lee had the rest of the day off, as did the instructors who had been on duty that morning. It was only a few days after his arrival, that 'the after lunch bridge school' came into being.

Lee reflected, after his first game, what a lot had happened to him since he had first started to play bridge before going to Canada, and how his knowledge of card games had helped him to make friends in the many air force camps that he had been to since joining the RAF. It had certainly proved to be an ice-breaker in the past, and here it was again proving to be a valuable asset. He remembered how he had first met Smudger Smith and Chalky White. It was at Heaton Park in Manchester whilst they were waiting to be posted to either Canada or the USA to do their training. They had only just arrived and he was watching the two of them playing Solo for money; they had been winning, but by 'stacking' the cards against the other two players. He and Tommy Thompson, a cadet he had palled up with, had seen what was going on and, when the two losers had pulled out, had offered to join in with Smudger and Chalky.

They had played them at their own game, which Smudger and Chalky had been quick to realise, and from then on the four of them had teamed up as a foursome at bridge. This foursome had lasted for the months they were hanging about at Heaton Park. It had continued on the journey on the boat over to Canada and at Moncton in Canada; it had continued until, in fact, until they had all been posted to different training camps. (He often wondered what had become of them and if they had ever got their wings.) During this time Lee had become a very proficient player.

Now Lee teamed up with Jimmy who was also a very good player. By playing regularly together, it wasn't very long before they became champions of the Mess. Not only did bridge dominate his off-duty hours, but it also helped him to ease the pain of being away from Connie who was constantly in his thoughts. He and Jimmy became good pals in the Mess, mainly through bridge. If they were not playing they were talking about it and the various systems associated with the game. If their duties did not coincide for a game after lunch, after dinner in the evening they usually had a game or two before joining the others in the bar. They would then retire to the bar with their opponents who would hold a post-mortem on what they should or should not have done, whilst Jimmy and Lee looked on. Much to their annoyance, Jimmy was always on hand to give them unwelcome advice!

A sing-song in the bar usually followed. Jimmy had altered the words of the song 'Just Molly and Me' to 'Just Connie and Me' and, in the regular 'party' sessions, this was sung with great enthusiasm by Lee's new-found friends.

It was one night after the usual excellent dinner in the Mess that an event occurred that had a profound effect on Lee and made him decide to go in to the bar each evening after their meal. He had that evening decided to take a walk after eating to help his meal digest. Looking out from his balcony before the meal he had thought that it was such a lovely evening it would be ideal for a stroll to familiarise himself with the neighbourhood and local surroundings. By the time the meal was over and he was ready, the sun had almost gone in, but it was still quite warm. He left the Mess. The evening air was still. The trees that lined the pavement threw long shadows on the road ahead, their leafy branches overhanging the pavement forming a canopy of light and shadow which made the path ahead appear very spooky. There was not another person in sight, and the only sound came from his own footsteps.

As he walked along, he became acutely aware of his own loneliness on this desolate road. He felt a chill creeping through him, and he felt sure that someone was watching him, but dismissed it as imagination. But, as he walked along, the feeling persisted and he thought about the stories he had heard and the films he had seen of the Resistance in France, of the way the Resistance thought nothing of killing German soldiers as they walked alone through dark narrow streets.

What if there were some Italian Resistance workers here, despite the fact that he hadn't gone more than a few hundred yards from the Mess? A feeling of apprehension came over him, followed by a slight moment of panic, and, turning sharply around, he walked quickly – almost ran – back to the Mess. That was the first and only time he ventured out on his own! Fortunately, he had not told anyone that he was going for a walk, so he had no explanations to give about his speedy return.

Back inside the Mess he realised that everything was still not all right with him, for although he was sleeping a little better, it did not take much to make him jumpy. He changed into something more comfortable and joined his friends in the bar.

Meanwhile, in spite of the apparent state that his nerves were in, Lee had quickly become very skilful over the dropping zone, which gave him a good reputation and made him very popular with the instructors. He thoroughly enjoyed the esteem in which he was held, and in particular his friendship with Jimmy.

Shortly after the feeling of nervousness he had experienced when out walking, he was delighted to receive a large, coloured photograph of Connie. She had gone into Glasgow whilst on leave and had it taken especially for him. He was overjoyed. It was lovely, and in it she looked absolutely beautiful. He placed it on the locker unit beside his bed and it was much admired by everyone who saw it.

The photograph and the circumstances in which he now found himself helped him considerably and, as the next few weeks went by, he soon found that he was sleeping much better and was becoming much more relaxed. Nevertheless, he did not want to chance going out by himself again. Lee had some misgivings, therefore, when he heard that two new NCO pilots had arrived on the unit; he was sure their arrival would take away a little of the patronage that he enjoyed through being the only pilot in the Mess. They were both Hudson pilots from Coastal Command, but had not been on any sorties. He need not have feared; neither could play bridge and they both kept themselves to themselves. Nevertheless, soon the rivalry of which aircraft was better for the job became the topic for the Mess. Troops were dropped out of the open door of the Hudson and they could therefore jump clear of the slipstream. However, the Wimpy was more stable at low speed and could therefore fly that little bit slower and be more accurate over the dropping zone.

There was a lot of friendly rivalry about the performances of the two types of aircraft: the clumsy size of the Wimpy against the nippiness of the Hudson and the amount of runway a Wimpy needed to take off and land. Lee was very proud of the capabilities of the Wimpy and his prowess with it which had served him so well. To prove his point he asserted that it was easy to do a three-point landing in one and stop within 250 yards on the runway. His claim was quickly taken up and it was agreed that he should attempt it on his next flight. One of the Hudson pilots was to be with him.

The next flight was to be an air test, so off they went. Lee had no worries about the three-pointer itself; a Wimpy three-pointed beautifully but he had always had the whole of a concrete runway to land on during training. During operational flying, it had been customary for them to land tail-up quite fast, in order to cover as much ground as possible before letting the tail come down as the aeroplane lost its momentum. This enabled them to get off the runway quickly so that the next aircraft could land. He had never before had reason to attempt a limited landing run on a metal runway, particularly without the weight of a rear gunner in the tail to help bring the tail down. However, he did have his experience of Crotone behind him. In due course they took off, completed the air test and came in to land.

Reducing his airspeed and with full flap, he flew low over the perimeter. Just as he reached the beginning of the metal runway, he gently eased the stick back, as he had done many times before, particularly in his single-engined aircraft days. The Wimpy behaved magnificently. Lee had judged it absolutely perfectly: there was no sign of a wing dropping or a stall. Quietly it nestled down to a perfect three-pointer and, when asked to stop, as Lee immediately put on the brakes, it rolled gently to a majestic halt well within the 250 yards limit. Lee and the Wimpy enthusiasts were delighted. Later, he said in the Mess that the lady knew she was on trial and had given those Hudson upstarts a lesson on how to behave perfectly, action speaking louder than words.

One of the dreads of the instructors was the 'candlestick'. This was when a parachute failed to open and the poor man dropped straight to his death below.

Lee only ever witnessed one of these tragedies. This was on an occasion when, having finished his flight, he went back to the dropping zone in the gharry to wait for the rest to finish so that they all went back to the billet together. It was an experience that Lee hoped he would never have to witness again. As the trainee left the aircraft a shout went up that his 'chute wasn't opening, and everyone just watched helplessly as he vanished behind a hedge, plunging into the ground below a couple of fields away. The stand-by ambulance rushed to the scene but needless to say the parachutist was dead. Lee was told later that he was a young Yugoslav boy partisan, about sixteen years old. What a waste!

But one of the worst mornings occurred when coming down to breakfast he was told amidst a deadly silence that one of the Hudsons had spun in on its first run, catching fire and killing everyone on board including one of the new pilots and the two instructors. One was Bill, the sergeant who had sung so beautifully: 'Bless This House' in the Mess the night he had arrived. No one was sure what had happened, whether an engine failed or the aircraft had stalled, but those waiting at the dropping zone said that no one in the fated aircraft had stood a chance. It had just plummeted down, bursting into flames the moment it hit the ground. An inquiry was to be held, but the Mess were very subdued until well after the funerals had taken place.

One morning at the airfield Lee was surprised to see what appeared to be a group of extremely young soldiers about to board his aircraft.

Calling Jimmy to one side, he asked, 'Who are they?'

'They're Yugoslav partisans,' said Jimmy.

'But they are only kids,' replied Lee.

'Yes,' said Jimmy. 'Fourteen- and fifteen-year-olds, and rumour has it that if they refuse to jump, Tito will have them shot when they get back. So it is up to us to give them a push if they do refuse.'

Occasionally, they had visitors to the Mess: two in particular were on special attachment to the Yugoslav partisans, one with Tito and the other with Mihailovic. The stories they had to tell were quite hair-raising, particularly with reference to the feuding between these two groups of partisans. Often they would find themselves fighting against each other when caught up in a skirmish between the two groups.

After he had been with the unit a few months, a great opportunity came for Lee, Cobber (the SWO), and Jim, one of the other pilots, to visit Rome on a long weekend. Lee jumped at the opportunity, and off they went on a grand sightseeing trip, following the proverbial saying that 'All roads lead to Rome', with Lee determined to visit all of the main tourist attractions if he could.

The city looked as if the war had never touched it. Its triumphal arches and historic buildings were unscathed. Only the passage of time had left its imprint on this magnificent and most beautiful city. Lee had never

seen anything like it. Everywhere there were the most beautifully decorated churches, palaces and dignified residences. These, together with the
art treasures found inside – the paintings, mosaics, icons, sculptures and
statues – together with the ancient walls and buildings, fascinated him.
He couldn't see enough of them or find out enough about their history.

Standing in the Colosseum he experienced the same feeling of history
as at Pompeii a few months earlier. In the arena of this great building the
stories of the gladiators and the Christians he learnt at school suddenly
became alive. The Italian guide told them that the seats of stone housed
87,000 spectators in fifty terraced rows. Here, the Emperors had held
their gladiatorial battles with gladiators fighting each other using various
weapons such as swords, nets, and tridents. Some had fought on horseback, while others had fought wild beasts. It was here they had held their
public meetings, circuses, chariot races and had thrown Christians to the
lions.

He stood in the middle of the vast arena with his friends and gazed up
at the spot where the Emperors had sat and imagined the cries of, 'Hail,
Caesar' echoing around the amphitheatre, and the thumbs-down sign
being given for some poor soul to be put to death. Now in Germany, in
their amphitheatres, the call was 'Heil Hitler', for his persecution of the
Jews. He felt that civilisation had not progressed that much after all.

Their guide pointed out – with a sly, meaningful smirk on his face –
the seats where the virgins sat. Lee could not help thinking, while remembering his experience at Pompeii, that this seemed to be all these guides
thought about. He was amazed to learn from the Italian guide that, by a
series of water conduits and watertight doors, the whole area could be
flooded to turn the arena into a giant lake on which mock galley fights
had been staged to further amuse the Romans.

Bridges seemed to be everywhere in Rome, and looking down on the
Tiber, the words of Shakespeare came back to him, particularly Cassius's
denunciation of Caesar. Cassius recalled how he had saved Caesar from
drowning in the Tiber . . . 'and now this man has become a God and
Cassius a wretched creature who must bend his body if Caesar carelessly
but nod on him.' How true those words were to some people.

They visited the Victor Immanuel monument and paid their respects
to the Tomb of the Unknown Warrior. They visited the famous fountain
and threw coins into it. Lee wished that the war would soon be over and
that he could quickly return home to his beloved Connie.

However, the highlight of the trip was a visit to the Vatican City where
they were blessed by the Pope. They had been staggered by the opulence
of the tomb of St Peter and the vaults which held the treasures, including
the golden robes in which the statue of St Peter was dressed on special
feast days. It was after they had visited the Sistine Chapel, admiring the
fresco of the Last Judgement by Michelangelo, together with the frescos

by Botticelli and Ghirlandaio, that a priest came up to them and, in very good English, told them if they wanted to see the Pope they should go right away.

Walking through the vast corridors, past the Vatican guards in their splendid uniforms, they came to the entrance of a large room where the guards on duty asked them to wait. They were among the first to arrive. It wasn't long before servicemen of all nationalities, together with civilians, priests and nuns of all denominations queued up behind them and they were eventually ushered into this great room. Being in the front they found themselves sitting in the front row of chairs that had been set out. These were set out before a dais on which there was an altar with golden lamps and other objects upon it. Standing around, and in continual prayer, were several priests or bishops. They had only been waiting a few moments, by which time everyone had entered the room, when they were asked to stand as the Pope was carried in on a sedan chair by four people in white robes. The room was hushed; one could hear a pin drop as he stepped out of the chair on to the dais. He was dressed in white flowing robes and carried a simple gold cross in his hand. Saying a short prayer he bade everyone to sit down. He then addressed the audience, speaking in several different languages, welcoming them to the Vatican and saying a prayer.

Sitting in the front row, Lee could not help querying in his mind the pomp and ceremony which was so evident on such an occasion, and wondering if this was the true meaning of the Christian religion. The Pope being carried in on a chair did not at all reconcile in his mind Jesus going into Jerusalem on a donkey. He had also been dumbfounded to see that, with all the poverty and misery just outside of the city, there was so much richness inside. He was completely unable to reconcile the differences and had been shocked when he saw the foot of the statue of St Peter which had been worn away over the years by people kissing it.

He realised then that, in his heart, he was a protester and, for the first time in his life, he could understand the reasons for the difference of opinion that fragmented and dominated the Christian religion. His thoughts were interrupted as the Pope came along the front row, blessing each individual as he passed and giving a general blessing to all of those standing behind. The Pope stopped in front of him and, as if he read his thoughts, blessed him. Lee felt a tremendous thrill run through his body. *He* had been blessed by the Pope! However, all good things come to an end; the break was all too short, and he soon found himself back on duty.

It was on a day visit to Taranto when, sitting in the RAF canteen, Lee met one of the ground crew from his old squadron. The news was not very good. Someone had told him that Sparks had been court-martialled and sent to the 'compound' for ninety days. Apparently, he had resisted all attempts to get him off the sick list and, when they eventually succeeded, he had been put on an op with the Flight Leaders to try to restore his confidence, but he had tampered with the radio and they had to return to base. He was condemned LMF. Lee never did get confirmation of this, and wondered whether or not it was another of those rumours that swept through the camp.

The squadron had also been awarded a number of DFCs and DFMs for the work it had done. The pilot who had only done thirteen ops when Lee had left had been shot up following a raid on Ploesti. He had flown to Turkey on one engine after the other engine had been put out of action by the Turkish ground defences. The crew had baled out, but within ten days had been returned to the squadron. The skipper had also been awarded the DFM.

The success of the minelaying of the Danube was becoming a legend. This vast river had become a very important lifeline for the German forces connecting the oilfields of Romania and the grain fields of Hungary with the German war machine. One barge could carry a load equivalent to that carried by a hundred large railway wagons, and hundreds did so. Because of the Allied air attacks on the road and rail links, the river had been used by the Germans extensively, but now it had been put out of action for months – a most serious blow to the enemy. Reports had come back that barges had been stuck in ports which had become overcrowded and storage facilities strained. The barges were forced to disperse along the banks of the river. Canals were blocked and the barges were easy targets for Beaufighters which, in support of the minelaying bombers, regularly attacked them with cannon fire. By the end of August the traffic on the Danube had been reduced by some 70 per cent. Bargees were afraid to go out on the river, and crews deserted because attempts to minesweep the river were not very successful. Chaos was widespread on the German front in northern Italy because of the lack of supplies held up on this previously untroubled route. Not only this, but the Germans had been forced to protect it, which used up vital anti-aircraft equipment including guns and the trained men to use them. They had also set up a base from which to use mine-detecting planes, and had to employ minesweeping ships; all of this additional activity at a time when they were hard pushed on other fronts and could ill afford to spare the men and equipment.

In addition, considerable help had been given to the Russian forces in their drive towards meeting up with their Allies. So far 205 Group, of which 37 Squadron was a unit, had sown over a thousand mines on about eighteen missions. Lee was thrilled to hear of the success in which he had played a part, having participated in three of the eighteen missions, particularly because on the last time he had been there, the night of the 1/2 July, he had been told that this was the biggest mission of the

131

campaign. Sixteen Liberators and fifty-three Wellingtons had dropped a total of 192 mines.

Christmas came and the catering staff did everything they could to make it a Christmas worthy of the occasion. Each table was decorated and menus in the shape of parachutes adorned the place settings. The Mess was decorated, evoking the feeling of a Christmas at home. It was a magnificent effort, and the cooks had gone out of their way to make it as enjoyable as possible. They even had a Christmas pudding. Finally, the evening was rounded off with a sing-song, with carols being sung in the bar.

New Year came and Lee's mind went back to last New Year which he had spent with Connie and her parents in Glasgow. It was then that he had asked them if they would give their consent for Connie and him to get married. It was in January, almost six months to the day, that his posting came in for him to return to Operational Duty; he was devastated. But, after all, he *had* volunteered for it and it did mean that when he finished this tour he would at long last be on his way home – home to Connie. The thought of that spurred him on; it couldn't come quickly enough.

The farewell party given to him in the Mess was a magnificent affair and it was very late that night when he retired 'half-cut' and tearfully to bed with the accolade of 'For he's a jolly good fellow!' ringing in his ears.

The Flight Commander offered to fly him to Foggia. During the journey back as a passenger he had time to reflect on the numerous comings and goings he had had. There had never been a send-off like the one last night and he tried hard to bring to mind if there had ever been an arrival on a station which had given him so much pleasure. It had to be his arrival years ago in Torquay.

As very newly accepted aircrew cadets they had left the Aircrew Receiving Centre in Brighton early one evening during January and had travelled down overnight to Torquay. The carriages had been over-crowded and men had been standing or sitting in the corridors on their kitbags. Luggage racks and corridors had been filled with kitbags and haversacks and there had been hardly any room to swing a kitten. They had been cramped, and had had sore bottoms through sitting so long on the hard uncomfortable seats. The atmosphere had been stale with smoke and beer. Their hands and faces had been dirty with the smut and grime from the train which, when the windows were opened to let in badly-needed fresh air and to ventilate the overheated carriages, had merely added to their discomfort because of the sulphur smoke which came belching in. To add further to the discomfort of the journey, the lavatory-cum-washroom on the train had had no water in it for the wash basin, and had smelt strongly of stale urine. They had arrived tired out and hungry the following morning after numerous delays owing to enemy air raids *en route* along the south coast.

The journey had been terribly slow, having been shunted into various sidings and left for what had seemed an eternity. Air raid sirens had gone on and come off. The dim blue lights in the carriages, which were normally reduced to one bulb only, had been turned off completely, so they had had to sit there in the dark, sleeping fitfully whenever they could drop off. There had been no refreshments, and when they had arrived at Torquay railway station the buffet had been closed at that time of the morning.

They had been bundled into lorries and taken to the ballroom of the Torbay Hotel and left there. The ballroom was very dimly lit and there had been palls of cigarette smoke everywhere. You could have cut the atmosphere with a knife. Bodies had been lying, sitting or standing about all over the place amongst their kitbags and other paraphernalia. The hubbub had been nerve-shattering. Any moment he had expected someone to stand up and shout, 'Shut up, the lot of you'. Everyone had been fed up, sick, sorry and tired.

To relieve the tension, an airman had gone to the grand piano that was in the ballroom and started playing Chopin, and other classical music, which had been most uplifting. The noise had abated as their tired spirits listened intently. But the moment he had started to play 'The Rustle of Spring', someone had drawn back the heavy velvet curtains and the morning sunshine had come flooding in. Over the green lawns had lain the calm and peaceful sea, the morning sunshine heralding a new day. It had been such a magical moment, so full of hope that one had been able to feel the atmosphere change as spirits had been renewed.

Thinking about that at this time, Lee's own thoughts were again uplifted, something that he very badly needed as they touched down on the drab grey metal runway, seeing the squalor of the tented camp as the grimness of the battered buildings around the airfield came into view. Whatever else happened he was determined to make the best of it, because after this he would achieve what he most wanted: to be on his way home to his wife of just a few days.

CHAPTER ELEVEN

GETTING READY
TO START AGAIN

A FTER Lee had reported in at Foggia Main he was posted to
40 Squadron, where he was warmly welcomed by the squadron
commander. The war had changed dramatically in the Balkans
and in Italy since he had left 37 Squadron the previous July. Romania
had surrendered, and had changed sides, declaring war on Germany in
August. In September, Bulgaria had asked for an armistice and, a few
days later, they also had changed sides and declared war on Germany.
In October, Belgrade had been freed of German forces and the Russians
and Marshal Tito's Yugoslav Partisan Army had joined hands. Also in
October, Hungary had asked for an armistice, but it wasn't until later,
even though Budapest was circled by the Russians in December, that it
finally fell. In fact, it fell on the day that Lee carried out his first air test
with his new squadron on 13 February 1945.

Those long hazardous trips over the Balkans were no longer part of the
squadron's activity. The war in Europe had progressed beyond his
wildest dreams. The Allies had landed in southern France, Paris had been
liberated and they were fighting on German soil. In Italy the Allies had
moved up into the north, but had been bogged down once again during
the winter months through snow and mud, this time in the Apennines
at the entrance to the Po valley. However, the Gothic line had been
broken by the Canadians after some bitter fighting, and now, as soon as
the weather broke, the American Fifth Army was poised to take Bologna
and move northwards to the Alps and westward to Milan and Turin,
whilst the British Eighth Army was preparing to head for Venice.

Meanwhile, after the fall of Belgrade, Marshal Tito's Yugoslav Army
was moving up through Yugoslavia, heading towards Trieste, the ultimate aim being for the Allied forces in Italy to join up in Austria with the
advancing Allied D-Day landing forces for the final thrust into Germany
and Berlin itself.

It was this new battle line, mainly on the fertile plains of northern Italy
rather than the treacherous trips across the Balkan mountains with their
atrocious weather conditions, that gave Lee the heart to look forward to
completing his second tour. Maybe, he thought, who knows – the war
may even be over before I complete it. The way things were moving –

events seemed to be happening so fast – it certainly looked as if it would be sooner rather than later that he would be on his way back home.

But first he had to get through this second tour, only thirty ops this time. His rest period had restored all of his earlier confidence and he was raring to go. The self-doubt which he had overcome during the final stages of his first tour were a thing of the past, and now he felt better equipped to tackle the job ahead. He was no longer the inexperienced rookie in the field of operations he had been a year ago, but he now felt himself to be a mature, experienced and confident operational pilot, which he indeed was. That was why he was back on a second tour. The squadron commander, who was very sympathetic to his desire to get home as quickly as possible, set about getting him organised with a crew. He felt that it would be better if Lee had a crew of his own, rather than have him hanging about as a make-up pilot whenever one was needed. A job like that could have meant him hanging around the squadron for months.

There were other crew members in various stages of their tour, and Lee was given the choice of making up a crew from them. This did not appeal to Lee at all, as this would have meant that, as a member became tour-expired, the rest of the crew would have to wait for someone else to take his place. On the other hand, there was one crew who were without a pilot, which the squadron commander was understandably very concerned about. They had had a pretty rough time with their previous skipper, who had a very nervous disposition, and apparently it had been impossible for anyone to fly with him as a crew. His attitude to his crew, and other members of the squadron, had been so appalling that he had been taken off flying duties. The crew were in a state of disarray and lacked confidence. The squadron commander asked Lee if he would like to take them on and see if he could make a crew out of them. The advantage to Lee was that he would have a permanent crew rather than a made-up one which would be subject to change throughout his tour. Naturally he could have a few days with them on the camp before he committed himself.

Lee was delighted with the confidence and the esteem that the CO seemed to have in him, and the CO went up in Lee's estimation as an absolutely smashing guy with a very human touch. Some COs would have told him what to do and that would have have been that. However, thinking about it later, he remembered they had been allowed to pick their own crews at Lossiemouth. So it was that he crewed up with Mac the navigator, Frank the bomb aimer, Geoff the wireless operator and Joe the rear gunner. All were RAF sergeants and what a smashing bunch of chaps they were. They, in turn, were delighted to have been given a skipper with Lee's experience.

One of the first things that Lee noticed about the crew was how well they all got on together. He seemed to develop a friendship with them

Lee began his second tour in February 1945, with 40 Squadron. His new crew, pictured above, were left to right: Geoff, Frank, Lee, Mac and Joe.

immediately, something which he did not build up as quickly with his first crew. Although his first crew had been a first class bunch of fellows, he had been very young (in reality, only a year younger, but now he felt a much older man), very raw and inexperienced at being an aircraft captain. Also, when they had met, it was at a time when he was more concerned with learning about flying a Wimpy than developing friendships. Furthermore, when he had first met them they had all had their own individual friends with whom they had trained. Their friendship as a crew had only developed and matured towards the end of the tour, probably after they had learned to have respect for each other's capabilities. Now it was different; these chaps had been hanging around the squadron for months, virtually friendless, so it was natural for them to stick together like limpets. They had seen other crews come and go and had taken no part in the squadron's activities. They had felt like outcasts, a ship without a rudder. There was a bond between them that they immediately offered to Lee on an open plate and which he was delighted to accept.

Mac, as his name suggested, was a Scot. He was an habitual smoker, a cigarette always drooping from his mouth. He had lost his battledress and

went about in his best blue, which was stained with beer and had cigarette holes and ash on it. He liked his drink, and Lee wondered how that
would affect him on duty. In complete contrast was Frank, an ex-
policeman who was tall and very smartly turned out. Quiet of manner,
his appearance radiated efficiency. Geoff, the wireless op, was very
young, just turned twenty, with an air about him of the raw freshness of
youth seeking to establish itself. He had an extremely pleasant and
friendly personality, and Lee felt a naturally protective, almost fatherly
attitude towards him. Finally, there was Joe, the rear gunner. Lee liked
him on sight. He was a lovable rogue, reputedly brought up with gypsies
at some stage of his life, but one of those reliable men who could turn his
hand to anything.

Lee had been allocated a tent on his own, but it was decided that Frank
should move in with him to give the others more room. This time,
however, his tent had a camp bed and a canvas washing bowl. Changed
days, thought Lee. The crew had their lucky mascot, Percy. This was a
pigeon with a broken wing that Joe had found and was looking after.
The pigeon waddled around the floor of the tent that the others shared
and was allowed to stray outside. If ever he wandered too far away and
became lost, someone in the camp would always bring him back. He had
his own box with a food and water dish alongside it. He was fed with
morsels from the leftovers on the plates and whatever Joe could scrounge
from the field kitchen.

10 February came – Lee's first wedding anniversary. He sat down and
wrote long letters to Connie. He wrote one of each kind that they were
permitted to send, to make sure one got through dated the tenth, sea mail,
airmail and airgraph. He longed to tell her about his new-found
colleagues, but censorship would not allow it. He did manage by impli-
cation to get the message across that he was now on his second tour, and
when that was over he would be on his way home to her.

Joe came up to him. 'We can't let this night go by without a celebration,' he said, so off to the Mess went the crew. The bar was in a large
Nissen hut – a much more civilised Mess than that of his previous
squadron. It had decent chairs and tables and had a much friendlier
atmosphere. Of course, it would have now that the war was nearly over,
thought Lee. It had probably been just the same as his old squadron's six
months ago when he was on his first tour and, when the front line was
just a few miles away. He would try to pop over to 37 Squadron to see
what things were like there nowadays. However, no sooner had he got
the idea when he dismissed it again. After all, what would be the use?
Nobody over there would know him now. The Mess was as crowded as
it had been the previous night because ops were scrubbed again.

The radio was blurting out one of Moaning Minnie's tear jerkers, 'We'll
Meet Again', which was quickly followed by the seductive voice of a

German *fräulein* announcer – German Lil, as the troops had nicknamed her – who told the men in the British forces in Italy that they were the forgotten army. This had a ring of truth about it, because the fighting in Italy was bogged down and what action there was had received very little mention in the British papers or on the radio. All the publicity was now being centred on the advances and setbacks being experienced by the Allied forces following the D-Day landings in France. The announcer was purring away in a sympathetic voice, telling the troops in Italy that their so-called Allies, the Americans, were taking their girlfriends away from them in England, and that more and more troops in Italy were receiving 'Dear John' letters. (Dear John was the name given to those letters sent by the wives or girlfriends of the forces serving overseas, telling them they had found someone else and that the marriage or romance was over.)

She went on to say in the most beguiling tone, that they would never do what the song said and meet their loved ones again. And, was it right that they should be fighting in Italy whilst this was going on back home? In the Mess such pronouncements were met by howls of laughter, derision and coarse jokes, but in the loneliness of their tents these songs caused much unnecessary heartache to those missing their loved ones and families at home – and the German propaganda machine played on it.

Very soon, the other men in the Mess became caught up in the celebration of Lee's anniversary. The radio was switched off and, as the *vino* and beer flowed, the songs became more and more raucous. Anything for a sing-song, thought Lee. That had not changed. 'Bless 'Em All', 'Old-fashioned Wimpy', and the RAF Italian version of 'Lili Marlene', all mixed up with some of the desert versions.

Lee looked around the Mess; there were not many of the types who had served in the desert around now, certainly very few, if any, aircrew; just the ground crews, still clinging to the glorious legend and the exploits of the Eighth Army in the Desert Campaign. They had got 'their knees brown' and were rightly very proud of it. What was more, they were not going to let anyone forget it.

It had been a good night when they finally left the bar. With arms around each other's shoulders they made their way back to Joe's tent, where Joe, who had slipped off a little earlier, had gone to prepare a meal for them – eggs, baked potatoes and toast. After they had eaten, Joe filled their mugs with *vino* and proposed the toast, 'To Connie and Lee'. They all stood up and, banging their mugs together, stood around Lee who remained seated on Mac's bed and drank the toast. Lee was deeply moved. He had only known them a short time, they had never met Connie and they were all bachelors. How could they know how he felt? But such was the nature of his new-found friends.

The following morning, after they had breakfasted, they went to the ops room to see what was going on. A stand-by rota had been drawn up for ops that night, but they were not on it. They decided they should have a get-together to discuss what was expected of each one and to ensure that each crew member knew what was expected of them on ops. This idea went down extremely well, and so they spent the day on the aircraft at dispersal, practising parachute drill, dinghy drill (which they practised until Lee was satisfied that they couldn't do it any faster), and the positions to take up in, over and out of the target area. He wanted to make sure that they hadn't forgotten, in their enforced lay-off, their very elementary responsibilities and what he, as captain, expected of them. They discussed all the aspects of their individual responsibilities, before, during and after the flight, as well as the position they each had to take up when approaching, and over, the target; they also made sure that they were fully acquainted once more with the various levers and switches, and where to find them at a second's notice. Because of their training it wasn't very different from what Lee had expected, and it did him good to refresh his memory.

Together they tested their knowledge of each other's jobs and what they were to do in the case of emergency. The only complaint came from Mac, who, after the morning session, would have preferred to have gone through the rest of the refresher in the bar! What Lee was determined never to do was to start again the pre-flight rigmarole which had become so much of a superstition on his first tour. They spent an extremely hard-working, serious but cheerful day together and all came away feeling the better for it. Lee had the feeling that this was the sort of thing they had been longing to do since they had arrived on the squadron.

In the evening they rounded the day off by getting together in Joe's tent again and had another slap-up meal of bacon, eggs and fried potatoes with the inevitable toast – fare which Joe had managed to buy from the Italian workers who came into the camp.

They sat by the drip stove around a home-made table upon which was an oil lamp, acquired, somehow, by Joe. It was extremely cosy, pleasant and warm. Lee, Frank and Mac were sitting on Mac's bed whilst Joe and Geoff sat opposite. Percy was under the table strutting around looking for titbits. A couple of bottles of *vino* drunk out of their cracked enamel mugs complemented the meal. After they had been sitting on Mac's bed for some time it was noticed there were very many lumps under the blankets and, after chatting and joking for a while longer, Frank's curiosity got the better of him. He couldn't resist the temptation to investigate, so he decided to see what the lumps were. To the amazement and hilarity of everyone, the first thing to come out of the bed was Mac's revolver, followed by an old canvas shoe, followed by an assortment of bits and pieces which included his haversack, torch, an old tin mug and dried up crusts of toast!

Amidst howls of laughter, Mac said, 'I wondered why it was so uncomfortable, but usually I'm too pissed to notice anything when I crawl into bed.'

In the morning of 13 February the crew went on air test together. This gave them the opportunity to put into practice the things they had gone through on the ground. That night they practised take-offs and landings: night circuits and bumps, as it was called. Although they never left the orbit of the aerodrome they were able to go through some of those same tasks under night-time conditions. Lee was extremely pleased with the whole performance and was very confident about the way they would react on ops. However, he wasn't at all happy about the age and condition of some of the aircraft that he had seen. Although the ground crews kept them in the best condition possible, these old war horses had done their duty and were looking a little the worse for wear. He was told that they were being phased out and 40 Squadron, like other bomber squadrons in Italy, were converting to the four-engined Liberators which could carry a much larger bomb load.

CHAPTER TWELVE

SECOND TOUR

THE first trip that they were scheduled to do together turned out to be a non-starter, confirming Lee's fears on the state of the Wimpys he had seen. They were to fly to Tuzla, code-named 'The Toffee Area', in Yugoslavia. The flight would take them about halfway to Belgrade in daylight to drop supplies in support of the Yugoslav Army. This was to have been Lee's first daylight operation ever, and he had been quite looking forward to it, particularly as in the ops room they had been told by other crews how weak the defences were nowadays in that part of the Balkans. This was not the first supply drop the squadron had carried out in daylight, and it was the lack of, or limited, opposition which made a daylight operation feasible. They could expect very little opposition from enemy fighters, if any at all, and the ground defences *en route* to the dropping zone were negligible. Furthermore, it was to be the first operational trip in which a Liberator (Lib.) aircraft (with which the squadron was being re-equipped) was to fly with the Wimpys. Nine Wimpys and the one Liberator, captained by the CO, were detailed to be airborne. The target was a triangle marker placed in a field by the partisans.

At dispersal they had taxied to the end of the runway in line with the other aircraft, received the green light from the Aldis lamp in the control box and set off. Lee was thrilled to feel the power of the engines as he opened them up to full throttle, first the port and then the starboard to avoid the torque and to keep the aeroplane straight and level as they thundered along the runway. Lifting off, they crossed over the boundary of the airfield, wheels now up as they started to climb away. It was a lovely day and quite something to see other aircraft in front of them. They had been airborne for about thirty minutes when the starboard engine started spluttering and cutting out. He flew on but the problem persisted, and after about another half hour's flying time decided that it was too risky to carry on.

Much to his disappointment, he had no alternative but to return to base bringing the containers back with him. Lee cursed his luck that, with such an easy trip, he would not now be able to knock that off the number of trips he had to do. Trust him to miss out on an undefended target, a target where the people waiting below were eagerly looking forward to their coming. He was back to square one after all the preparation . . . Shit! The remaining nine aircraft found the triangle marking the dropping area and successfully completed their mission, reporting that the drop was well concentrated, although some Liberators were dropping from excessive heights. This apparently was a problem with that kind of operation. The opposition was, as reported, negligible, except for aircraft that strayed off course where flak was reported from some batteries on the way to the target.

The following day they were on duty again. This time it was a bombing raid in daylight, and again in Yugoslavia. Eleven Wimpys were briefed to attack the armament depot at Pola, with a secondary target of the oil storage tanks at Fiume, should they be unable to locate the first and main

Lee's raid photo taken at Fiume in February 1945.

one. In addition to the usual nine 500-pound bombs, they carried a further three 250-pounders. It was the heaviest bomb load that Lee had carried and, of course, this target would have to be fairly heavily defended. Once again it was a beautiful February day, with the sunshine filling the cockpit as they crossed over the coast to the sea. However, this soon turned to cloud as they flew over the Adriatic, so much so that, when they reached Pola, the target was covered with 8 to 10/10ths cloud, completely obscuring it. Nine of the aircraft then moved off to attack the secondary target of Fiume, which was clear with a visibility of some fifteen to twenty miles. The other two attacked a nearby town. Lee reached the target area of Fiume flying at 15,000 feet at 2.59 p.m. Frank identified it by the mole south of the target. They dropped their bombs in one stick aiming for the warehouses on the southern edge of the target, but because of the dust and smoke they were unable to observe the results.

The attack generally was reported to be well concentrated, with several bombs being claimed as direct hits on the target. Subsequent reconnaissance showed that, although the refinery suffered some damage, the main weight of the attack fell on the marshalling yards immediately adjoining the refinery where much damage was done. Dust from bombing, and smoke from burning oil rising to 4,000 feet obscured the target for some of the other aircraft. Nevertheless, two storage tanks were seen to receive direct hits and a 4,000-pound bomb fell on the east side of the target. A large ship, possibly a cruiser, was reported to be lying in the naval construction dock and another was seen to be anchored nearby. Three destroyers were also sighted. Opposition was nil at Pola, probably because of the cloud and, knowing the attacking aircraft could not see their target through it, they did not want to draw attention to exactly where they were. But there were about six heavy guns and some light guns at Fiume, both mainly inaccurate. Good God, thought Lee as they headed for home, if the rest of my tour is going to be like this it's going to be a doddle.

The next raid was again a daylight flight, this time on the much larger city of Trieste. This was a little further up the coast and on the other side of the peninsula, a target of Lee's previous tour. This time the target was the naval docks and shipbuilding yards. Pathfinders were to identify the target with red marker flares.

Lee told the crew about his last visit to Trieste to attack the oil storage tanks. He told them that he had been ordered to bomb only on the target indicators, and under no circumstances on any other target. He also told them that the Pathfinder's target indicators were so far off target on that trip that they had 'bombed' the mud flats. He hoped they would be better this time.

The bomb load was nine 500- and three 250-pounders again. Eleven

Wimpys were detailed and all found their way to the target. Lee's crew identified the target visually as did many other crews, although three crews reported red target indicators burning at the west end of the target. Dropping his bombs in one stick, aiming for the buildings on the waterfront at the east end of the target, Frank saw the first three small bombs hit the water, whilst the nine larger bombs burst along the sheds and other buildings on the quayside. Other crews saw some of their bombs going into the sea and all concluded, upon their return, that the actual wind was stronger than the broadcast wind they had been briefed to use.

Several sticks were seen to burst in the oil fuel stores area and near the oiling pier south-east of the target. A fire was reported at the west end of the target and another in the oil storage area. Many crews were confused by smoke from the previous bombing which had drifted in that direction to make positive identification and reliable results of their efforts difficult to assess. Three large ships were seen on their sides in the port area when the crews arrived. A large liner was observed in the commercial port and a warship (destroyer or submarine) was seen leaving the harbour during the attack firing tracer. Opposition came from twelve heavy AA guns (including some which burst with an unusual red flash) and slight, light, mainly inaccurate, flak. However, in spite of all the activity going on in the target area, without the tracer, flares, searchlights and incendiaries, the excitement didn't seem to Lee to be so great as at night. It lacked the colour and the intensity of a night raid, even though one could see more of the smoke puffs from the flak bursts in the daylight than you could see in the dark at night time. In daylight the whole area was one large picture. From 10,000 feet the terrain below could be seen for miles around. This meant the attack lacked the compactness of a night attack, where flares, searchlights and fires concentrated the vision into one relatively small area. There were far more Liberators than Wimpys from the group and Lee was astonished to see how close all the aircraft came to each other as they approached the target. It was a good job that they did not have that to worry about on his first tour. But although it lacked the intense excitement and couldn't compare as the same experience, the bombing run had all the same thrills and concentration of a target being successfully attacked. Lee decided that he liked daylight bombing raids.

It was back on night duty for their next raid, returning to rail communications in Italy. This time the target was on the west marshalling yards at Udine, an important rail link between Italy and Austria. This was the anniversary of the day that he left England to come out to Italy. Lee wondered about when they had made that decision in Algiers to come to Italy. Would he make that same decision now, or would he now opt for India? Would it have been better or worse? He chuckled to himself as he thought of the saying, 'Out of the gloom a voice said, "Smile and be happy, things could get worse", and behold he did smile and was happy, and things did get worse.' So could it have been with India.

The German forces were fighting desperately in northern Italy. Their links for communication were being overrun by the Allied troops in the west of Europe. It was therefore imperative that they should try to keep open what links they had. Nine Wimpys were detailed for Udine and took off. However, one returned early with engine defects, the crew jettisoning their bombs in the sea. All the remaining aircraft carried out a very successful attack on the yards which were marked by target indicators. These were well placed near the rail junction to the east of the yards. One cluster was seen to be burning on the locomotive repair sheds. Frank bombed on these in one stick, from 7,500 feet, aiming for the centre of the markers and was pleased to see his bursts exploding in one straight line right along the yards. It was ascertained that four other sticks had fallen on the target indicators and a very good concentration of bombing resulted. Incendiaries were seen to drop in two sticks, one on the target indicators and one to the west of them. Two fires were started and four minor explosions were reported. Bomb strike photographs and subsequent reconnaissance both confirmed that the raid produced some excellent bombing. All of the through railway lines were found to be cut or blocked by wrecked rolling stock and a fire was still burning at noon the following day in a stores building some distance to the east. A 4,000-pound bomb had fallen just north of the rail junction and had caused considerable destruction in that area.

Opposition came from twelve heavy AA guns which were accurate during the blitz period in the target area. There was also some light AA but this was in the main inaccurate. Udine was quite heavily defended for a town of its size, illustrating its importance to the enemy. They had carried out the attack with nine 500- and three 250-pound bombs, this now seeming to be the standard bomb load. Unusually for Lee, the time of the attack was early in the evening, at 8 p.m., which meant that they arrived back to base at about 11 p.m. Getting to bed early was definitely a plus, thought Lee. He got the excitement he loved without the feeling of exhaustion.

Pola, the shipyards on the tip of the Croatian peninsula in Yugoslavia, was the target on the very next day. Five days had passed since they were last detailed to attack Pola, but Lee had not been able to because of the weather over the target. Lee should have realised that there was going to be a snag to getting back early from a night operation – it made them available for a daylight operation the next day.

Seven Wimpys were detailed to attack the naval armament base from 15,000 feet at 4.30 p.m. with the now usual bomb load. It was a lovely, sunny day, with a very powerful strike force of Liberators and Wimpys. Once again Lee noticed the predominance of Liberators over the target.

Some bombing had obviously taken place before zero hour as a lot of smoke covered the area when they arrived, with flames up to about 1,000 feet. Nevertheless, the target was strikingly visible in the sunshine, showing clearly the harbour installation and docks set against the turquoise and deep blue sea. The flak was quite accurate: up to thirty heavy guns in a very concentrated barrage, confirming Lee's suspicions of why they had kept quiet on the last trip. Lee likened it to Chinese fire-crackers with the sudden flashes of flame cracking out of the puffs of smoke as the shells exploded. One of the other points which Lee found most interesting on these daylight raids was the fact that one could see the bombs going down and could follow them into the target. There were aircraft all around, above and below with bombs flying past him, and as he watched, fascinated by the scene of the activity on the target, he was horrified to see a bomb going right through the wing of a Liberator immediately below, just as they were about to go into the attack them-selves. They were on their bombing run and Lee had to concentrate on what he was doing before he could ascertain what had happened to the Lib. Later, it became clear that this was a 37 Squadron aircraft which returned with a damaged engine and a hole in its wing. Another Lib. was reported as being shot down by flak and others were seen with smoking engines as if hit by flak over the target.

They carried on, dropping their bombs in one stick aiming for the centre of the smoke coming from the east end of the target. Bomb bursts were seen through the smoke with an explosion, followed by a large yellow flame and thick black smoke billowing up through the smoke already there. One crew reported target indicators burning north-west of the target, but the remainder, like Lee, identified the target visually. The 4,000-pound bomb fell slightly north of the west part of the target causing an explosion with smoke rising up to 8,000 feet. The whole area seemed to be covered by a good concentration of bursts, with the smoke and flames being visible 120 miles away on the return journey. Reconnaissance subsequently showed that at least eight buildings had been obliterated as well as many others severely damaged. Wooded areas had been cleared by the blast, disclosing the foundations of other build-ings which had been there. A few scattered sticks had fallen into the sea.

Brescia, in northern Italy, was their next op and they were back once more to night flying. The target was the east marshalling yards, in an attempt once again to destroy the German communication lines in support of the Allied troops. Nine Wimpys were airborne and all reached the target. The target indicators were well placed, one cluster of reds being in the centre of the yards and the greens being some distance to the west. Frank used the green for the aiming point of one stick, which was seen to burst across the yards. Haze limited observation of their results by some other crews. Incendiaries fell on the yards and a large fire was seen to commence there, sending a column of smoke some 500 feet into the air. Bomb strike photographs confirmed a good concentration, and subsequent reconnaissance confirmed new craters in the yards, although one through line remained serviceable. The gas works were completely destroyed. Opposition was from six heavy AA guns and a few light AA guns in the target area. Enemy aircraft were encountered but no strikes reported and all of their aircraft returned safely.

The following night they were to drop supplies to the Yugoslavian partisans at a place called Icarus. Lee liked the idea because it had the touch of a special mission about it and it made a change from the usual routine ops. Furthermore, it made up for the daylight supply drop he had missed earlier. They were to make the drop in a large field with a marker, set out in the shape of a St Andrew's cross illuminated by small fires and placed in the middle of the field. They carried nine special containers which were to be dropped at 300 feet. It turned out to be one of the most frightening experiences of Lee's operations, not because of weather or enemy activity but because of the activities of his fellow pilots. It was so unexpected.

They reached the target area spot on time and could see the cross clearly marked out ahead of them. They flew in at the height of 300 feet as planned but, as they approached the field and headed nearer to the cross on the ground, they found themselves flying into a mass of parachutes, with containers hanging from them, dropping down all around them, their billowing 'chutes glistening white and looking for all the world like celestial bodies arriving from outer space. Lee watched them anxiously as they flew on. Luckily they missed hitting the wings, tailplanes and engines of his and the other aircraft by inches. If they had become caught up in the engines or wrapped around the wings, they could have sent the receiving aircraft crashing to the ground. There was also the added possibility of colliding with other aircraft as they went out of control. When the parachutes landed it looked just as if they were flying over a field of enormous mushrooms. It was so unexpected, unreal, like a bad dream. It was so frightening it seemed like a nightmare.

Lee realised immediately, recalling the stories he had heard, that the aircraft that were above them were releasing their loads too high. And what was worse they were coming in on the wrong headings.

'Look what these other silly bastards are doing to us,' he said to Mac who was sitting next to him.

However, before Mac could think up a suitable answer, Frank called up his instructions from the bomb aimer's position.

'Cross ahead. Steady. Bomb doors open.' Lee concentrated on the job in hand. 'Steady. Keep her there, Lee. Steady. Groceries away!'

They were through the dropping area and Lee quickly turned away out of danger. 'It was like walking through a minefield,' Lee said to Mac a moment or two later. It wasn't until they got back to base that it was reported that some Liberators were again dropping their containers too high, dropping them from as high as 2,500 feet. Why they did this, Lee never did find out, but it was a bloody silly practice to adopt when the aircraft that were flying in at the right height below them were having to contend with this mass of slowly dropping parachutes all around.

In the space of the few seconds they had spent over the field what should have been an easy, simple operation had turned out to be a most horrific and nerve-shattering experience. Other than that episode, the mission was uneventful, although some aircraft encountered some light flak from batteries on the way to the field.

One of the last raids Lee took part in was on Verona, where the rail yards (*top and left*) were badly damaged. (© *1992 MoD reproduced with the permission of the Controller of HMSO*)

A couple of nights later they were detailed to attack the west marshalling yards at Verona, with two 2,000-pound cookies. Lee felt a little sad remembering his Shakespeare, because this city had always had a schoolboy's romantic dream about it for him. Nine Wimpys operated. Three crews, including Lee's, saw sufficient detail to make a visual check and considered that the red target indicators were on the yards. Subsequent photographs showed that they were well placed on, and immediately north of, the eastern part of the yards. Lee's and three other crews saw their sticks fall amongst the target indicators right across the target. Ground haze and much smoke from the bombing restricted visibility of ground detail for the remainder.

The opposition came from ten to fifteen heavy AA guns, which were mainly inaccurate, and slight inaccurate light AA fire in the target area, both having more of a nuisance value than anything else. There were also guns firing as they flew along the railway lines into the area and at various other points, but this was very scattered and did not deter them. Flak was seen *en route*, but as it was well away from Lee's course it did not present a problem. Interesting were the various lights that were reported on the ground *en route* and Morse letters from the Castelmasa area.

Joe didn't come with them on that trip because he had a most shocking cold, but he did say he would have a slap-up meal for them when they got back. So, it was a successful raid, in clear weather, and the crew were soon on their way back to base.

CHAPTER THIRTEEN

TREVISO

JOE was a remarkable character, completely without a sense of discipline. One of his favourite pastimes, when off duty, was to visit the local farms selling blankets and kit of all descriptions. After he had disposed of all of his own, he acquired further supplies from other airmen who were short of cash, buying up what items he could because he knew he had a ready market (the authorities would call it a black market) with the local farmers. He was also well into currency exchange, which was forbidden by the Service authorities. New airmen coming on the squadron from the UK were offered lire slightly above the camp rate, in exchange for English pounds. Airmen returning to the UK were sold English pounds slightly below the camp rate for their surplus lire which they would otherwise have to forfeit. This was a practice very much frowned upon, and for which one could be court-marshalled if discovered.

Joe was also very generous. With the profits he made he would buy, or barter for, food – particularly eggs – from the Italians which he would share with his crew mates. He used to get so many that he was able to sell eggs amongst the other crews. He also knew that he could sell as many eggs as he could obtain. It was probably this that saved him from being reported. No one was going to kill the goose that laid the golden egg! The rest of the crew were the same. Although frowning upon what he was doing and always being ready to criticise him for doing it, they were always eager to participate in the fare that he so frequently provided. Even so, whenever Joe went off on these trips, they were very anxious for his safety, half-expecting to hear that he had been found dead with his throat cut, or that some similar fate had befallen him.

Needless to say, Joe always returned with the goods, for there was one other very necessary thing he knew: that he had to know the people he dealt with extremely well. He had to trust them and they had to trust him in this mini black market he was involved in. In this respect, to avoid them becoming suspicious he always went on his own. He would never invite anyone else to go with him, and would flatly refuse any such requests. It was with eager anticipation that the crew were looking forward to the repast that Joe was hopefully going to provide on their return this time.

He was waiting for them at debriefing. Normally, after debriefing, they would have gone straight to the field kitchen for a meal but he had come to meet them to make sure that they didn't go. As soon as debriefing was over, they all clambered into the lorry that was to take them into the tent encampment.

'What have you got for us tonight, then, Joe?' asked Lee, offering him a cigarette and quickly lighting one up for himself before they moved off. Lee was standing up holding on to one of the cover stanchions in order to stretch his legs after sitting down in the cramped cockpit for so long. It would have been almost impossible for him to light a cigarette standing up once they had moved off, as he would be bumped and rocked about as they travelled along the unmade roads leading to the camp.

'I have done a bit of Gypsy cooking, specially for you,' replied Joe, leaning over to light his cigarette off Lee's.

'Good show,' remarked Frank, who knew from experience that it meant something special was on the stove.

'Why's that?' asked Lee.

'Well,' replied Frank, 'Joe has been known in the past to cook a piece of chicken or pig by encasing it in mud and putting it inside the drip stove to cook. When the mud is removed the feathers of the chicken or the skin of the pig are stuck in the dry mud and come away with it. What is left is a very, very tasty, mouth-watering delicacy.'

They arrived at Joe's tent. Joe had been busy. He had set up a table of kind in the middle of the tent. What is more, he had been to the tent that Lee and Frank shared and had got their plates, knives and forks and had laid the table. Bread was by the side of each plate and there was a big slab of butter in the middle of the table. A couple of bottles of wine were also present. The stove was on, giving off a warm glow from its hotplate, and the tent was warm, light coming from a couple of candles also placed on the table.

When they popped their heads inside the tent flap, the whole scene was warm and inviting. Seating them all around the table he proceeded to remove from the stove the rolled-up balls of baked mud. Joe broke open the mud and there within them lay perfect baked jacket potatoes. He opened another three larger ones and in these was the meat. Washed down with the *vino*, the meal was marvellous and the setting serene.

'That meat was delicious Joe; pity there wasn't more of it!' was the general consensus of opinion. The meal finished, they sat and chatted about the night's adventure, but soon it was time to go.

Scraping all of the leftovers onto one of the plates, they good-naturedly called for Percy the pigeon, their lucky mascot, to come and eat up the scraps.

'Where's Percy, Joe?' asked Frank. 'Has he wandered off again?'

'No. I managed to get hold of a couple of pigeons. Two wouldn't have

151

been enough to go round, so I killed Percy and you've just eaten him,' said Joe calmly.

A ghastly silence fell over the rest of the crew. They didn't know what to say. Joe carried on clearing up.

The next trip was non-operational. The crew were asked to ferry a Wellington, which was being removed from service, to Blida in Algeria. After an early morning take-off, they flew under dark, laden clouds over the Mediterranean. The sea looked cold and uninviting. The spindrift on the waves below, feathery white on the now dark-blue, almost black, background of a turbulent sea, made them feel thankful that they were airmen and not sailors.

They landed at Tunis in sunshine to refuel and spend the night, before flying on to Blida the next day. The following morning it was a dull, drab sort of day. The clouds they had flown under over the Mediterranean had arrived and were with them all the way to Blida. After landing at Blida, they were told to move off the runway whilst a Jeep came out to marshal them to their standing point. As they taxied around the perimeter track, following the Jeep, they were amazed to see the number of aircraft parked there. It reminded Lee of a junk yard. Hundreds of all types of aircraft were lined up either side of the perimeter track for what looked like miles around. It was like driving through a cemetery, with the aircraft standing there like gravestones, wing tip to wing tip, forlorn and unwanted in the dull grey drabness of the day. As they taxied past, Lee could not help feeling sorry for them. Fantasising on how their once proud noses pointed upwards to the sky, as if trying to form a final guard of honour, or to protest against this humiliating degradation. Behind them their tailplanes pointed dejectedly downwards towards the ground as a mark of defeat, knowing that for them the war was over. There were German, Italian and Allied aircraft, Wimpys, Dakotas, Fortresses, fighters of all descriptions – an aircraft-spotter's dream. An awesome sight, stripped of their armament, they were now mere skeletons of once vibrant and powerful machines of war. It was a graveyard of tour-expired aeroplanes. Another memorable experience.

The next day they were flown back to base in a Liberator, one which was replacing the Wimpy that Lee had delivered to the graveyard. He felt quite depressed. It was a sorry sight to have seen those once proud monarchs of the air reduced to that, destined for the scrapyard. They had been gone three days.

Upon their return they were detailed to attack the marshalling yards at Germona, a small town in the foothills of the Karnische Alps, but owing to bad weather they had to return to base. Eight Wimpys were detailed and were airborne for the attack. It was to be an abortive effort. Only two aircraft arrived in the target area and aimed for the target indicators, recording unobserved results, although subsequent plotting showed these aircraft were a reasonable distance north-east of the target. Weather conditions caused the remainder to abandon the operation and jettison all bombs. Three other aircraft, one of which was Lee's, returned early having encountered cloud with severe icing conditions within a short distance from base. One temporarily lost control and a second also experienced the same misfortune, having been forced down to within 50 or 100 feet of the sea before regaining control. Two other aircraft arrived in the general target area, one abandoning the operation when arriving at the run-in point with defective instruments, and being unable to see any illumination or markers in the target area. One of these aircraft reported that there were about twenty heavy AA guns in opposition over the target. However, it was the weather which was the main enemy, and with these weather conditions, the squadron was fortunate in not losing any aircraft on the mission. This had not been the case about a month earlier.

It was just about the time that Lee had arrived on the squadron when their other enemy, the bad weather, had taken its toll. Three Wimpys had crashed into the hillside owing to low cloud, and thirteen aircrew members had lost their lives. The squadron did not want a repetition of that night.

They were due to attack Verona again in the early evening with two 2,000-pound cookies on board. The aircraft in which they were due to fly looked just about on its last legs, and it was obviously due for replacement very soon. They had only just become airborne when the oil pressure gauge on the starboard engine indicated a very high reading. In addition to this, the rev. counter was showing very erratic revs with very high fluctuations. Lee reported this over the radio to the ground control, who then asked him if he felt he should return to base. Lee decided to fly on for a few minutes to see if the engine would settle down, but shortly after decided to tell control that he was going to return to base and that he felt that he should not attempt to make it to the coast to jettison his bombs into the sea.

He was instructed to return to the base, but also to fly over an area just south of base out of the way of other aircraft while jettisoning the fuel he had on board, whilst waiting for all of the other aircraft to finish taking off. He circled the base and, whilst doing so, told the crew that he thought that he was going to try and land with the cookies on board.

'You can bale out if you want to; we are over land, and it's still daylight,' he said over the intercom, 'It's going to be quite a dangerous landing.'

They unplugged their intercoms and gathered around the open door leading from the cockpit.

'What are you going to do, Lee?' Geoff asked.

Lee's mind went back to the night of Szolnok when he had landed with the nine 500-pounders on board.

'Oh, I've landed with a full bomb load on board before, lads; mind you, they were not as sensitive as these cookies, but I think I can make it OK. You don't have to make up your minds right away; we have got to get rid of all this fuel on board first.'

They were flying at 3,000 feet, slowly circling around. The rev. counter was going mad and the oil pressure gauge was still reading high. If the engine packed up, he would have to feather the engine to come in to land. Feathering the propeller on a dead engine reduces the drag caused by windmilling blades, allowing the remaining engine to support the aircraft unaided without having to overcome the heavy resistance caused by an unfeathered propeller. Christ, he had only practised this a couple of times at OTU, and that was ages ago. He hoped if he had to do it he would do it properly. He silently prayed for the engine not to pack up on him now. He had no wish to try landing with these cookies on board with only one engine serviceable. Ground Control advised him it would be OK to land when he was ready. He called up the crew again on the intercom.

'I'm going in, chaps. If you want to leave, now is the time.'

The crew, as one man, decided to stay with him and take their chance. Lee was very grateful for this show of confidence in him. This was more than he could say for the staff on the ground: as he made his approach to come in to land in the evening light he could see them running in all directions. The only man to stay in the control tower was his Flight Commander, who stayed there with him talking him down.

'Look at them running, Mac,' he remarked. He looked at Mac who nodded in agreement. Lee was determined that he would show them that they had no need to run. 'Oh ye of so little faith', he thought to himself, at the same time hoping that they had not jettisoned too much fuel in case he cocked up his approach and had to go round again.

The Flight Commander told him it was all clear for him to come straight in and, as soon as he was safely down, to switch his engines off. With the runway in sight he could see the windsock hanging limply on its pole. Thank God there were no crosswinds. As he came in to land, with the ground rushing towards him, he just caught a glimpse of the ambulance and the fire tender waiting at the end of the runway, and it occurred to him that they might be the last things he saw on this earth. These thoughts were soon dismissed for, as he floated the last few feet downwards, he concentrated on the landing itself. Once again his training came to the fore and he made a perfect landing. The wheels hit the metal runway so gently that there was hardly a bump as they touched down, coming to rest after a perfect three-point landing with the bombs safely on board.

His crew jumped on him, shaking him by the hand, and delighted that they had made the right decision to stay with him. At debriefing, the Flight Commander congratulated him on such a calm approach, but Lee was quick to thank him warmly for standing by him in such a crisis.

The following night seven Wimpys, including Lee's, attacked the north-east marshalling yards at Padua. Incendiaries fell early in the attack and obliterated one cluster of target indicators. Red target indicators were, however, judged to have been well placed in the yards and this is where Frank aimed their bombs, dropping them in one stick of nine 500- and three 250-pounders. This was subsequently confirmed by photographic plotting. All the other aircraft also aimed for the TIs (target indicators) and a number of sticks were seen to explode in the correct area but, like Lee, crews found it difficult to pinpoint their own bombing or distinguish it from the remainder.

Ten small explosions were reported in the target area and a fire, which started up during the attack with much white smoke, could be seen for fifty miles on the return route. Opposition in the target was from about six heavy guns and several light guns and once again, because they didn't hit anyone in the squadron, it was reported as accurate only for height. There was slight light Ack-Ack fire in the Chioggia area *en route* and two searchlights which seemed to be indicating the bomber track. The weather was good and there was no cloud at the target. Visibility was good at first, but became limited by smoke from the bombing when the attack commenced.

The next night, 13 March, one month after he had been on flying duties with the squadron, Lee undertook an attack on Treviso against the north-east marshalling yards. Six Wimpys were detailed, with Lee carrying a 4,000-pound cookie. On reaching the target five crews aimed for the red target indicators, which were judged to have fallen close together on the yards at Zero minus 3 hours. One crew claimed, however, that the TIs did not fall until Zero plus 1, and bombed visually. The target indicators were, in fact, on or close to the south part of the triangular yards. The crews aiming for the TIs also reported that bombing commenced before Zero hour. Lee's 4,000-pounder fell to the west of the TIs, but near them. Two crews claimed bursts at the mean point of TIs, and the crew bombing visually claimed their stick fell right across the yards. Incendiaries fell at the correct time during the attack, but were scattered over a wide area around the target. Lee's bomb was seen to explode in the centre of the yards and bombing was judged to be reasonably well concentrated.

An explosion was reported, and fires, which commenced beneath the incendiaries, could be seen for fifty miles. Subsequent photograph plotting showed that the TIs were on the yards, but that many bombs fell to the south of the target. The defences were moderate, about six heavies and some light guns, both being inaccurate. Frank was able to do an excellent run into the target. Joe reported a terrific explosion as the cookie landed and they headed for home contented.

*   *   *

On 14 March, the Wellington crews were briefed for what was to be their last operation but, owing to weather conditions at base – fog – the operation was cancelled. The squadron then ceased to be operational for a short period during which Liberator training was in progress.

The following morning Lee was sent for by the CO. The Flight Commander was there also. The CO told him that Treviso was the last raid by a Wimpy and that had been the last cookie a Wimpy would drop in the European theatre of war. The squadron was going to convert completely over to Liberators. Then followed the most unexpected piece of news that Lee was to hear.

'In view of the total number of operations you have completed, we are not going to ask you to convert to Liberators unless you really want to. You have completed nearly fifty operations – you have done enough. The war is nearly over and there are many who still have yet to do one operation; they can carry on.'

Lee was flabbergasted. He could feel the tears well up in his eyes in gratitude and respect for this man, who was still speaking.

'You have now completed your two tours and you can go home to your wife which is, I know, what you want to do.'

Lee fought back the tears. 'What about my crew, sir?' he asked.

'They can go home also,' came the reply.

'Thank you, sir,' said Lee.

'Don't thank me, Flight Sergeant,' replied the CO. 'Thank *you*. You have served your country well.'

Lee felt a lump rise in his throat and the tears coming back as a surge of pride came over him. He hadn't flunked it. It was great to be told that you had served your country well. The words of his schoolboy hero Nelson flashed into his mind: 'Thank God, I have done my duty.' What a relief. What a moment. Bursting with pride he tried to concentrate on what the CO was saying. He had continued talking, saying something about the Flight Commander who would be making arrangements about leave and Naples and troopships. But Lee was unable to listen, his mind was in a whirl. He couldn't believe what he had just heard. Was it really all over?

Lee left the CO's caravan walking on air. Outside, he remembered he had forgotten to salute!

It was all over at last. He could go home to his beloved, his darling Connie.

His crew were waiting for him when he got back.

'OK, lads, you can pack up,' called Lee before he had even reached them.

'What are you talking about, Lee?' asked Geoff.

'It's all over for us, lads, we've been tour-expired.' He explained what

156

had happened. They went delirious, pumping his hand up and down so much he thought it was going to drop off.

Telegrams were sent home, letters were written while they were packing up; the next few days went like a dream. Then they were on their way to Sorrento. Lee loved the place, but never so much as now. One of the crafts that the craftsmen of Sorrento were noted for was their carvings and inlaid wood. The crew visited the souvenir shops. Lee bought Connie, his mother and new mother-in-law, cameos in the form of necklaces, rings, bracelets, and brooches.

Joe insisted on buying a wedding present for Lee and Connie. It was a beautiful wooden inlaid bridge box, the lid of which had a scene of Sorrento, on it. The forces' newspaper was available in the hotel. It carried the following report, entitled 'Wimpy has Retired' :

> After more than four years as the night striking force of the Allied air power in the Mediterranean, Wellingtons have been placed on the retired list as far as this theatre is concerned.
>
> Their last raid, on the railway yards at Treviso, northern Italy, was made a few days ago.
>
> It was in December, 1940, that the first Wellington wing was formed in the Middle East. The wing lost no time; before the end of the year the enemy in Benghazi were on the 'Wimpy – mail-run'.
>
> They were in action all through the see-saw desert fighting, right up to Cap Bon. They crossed the Mediterranean to blast the Balkan capitals, mine the Danube, carry supplies to the Yugoslav army and rush British troops to Greece. Two squadrons which were with that first wing in the desert are still with the heavy bomber group in Italy. They are now flying Liberators. But all who have served with the Wimpys in the air or on the ground, are sorry to see those familiar shapes go.
>
> Probably the best-designed bomber yet produced, the Wellington just cannot carry the vast bomb loads needed nowadays. But probably a few will see the war out with Mediterranean Allied Coastal Air Force.

It was with some sadness that Lee read that report. He had grown to love that aeroplane. It had stood him well. He had trained on it, flown strategical and tactical bombing raids, taken part in combined ops, laid mines in the Danube, dropped paratroops and supplies, flown above mountain ranges and skimmed above sea-level. It had been with him in the most critical danger and had brought him home safely. In all it had been part of his life for the last eighteen months. He had flown over 500 hours in it. Good God, he thought, all of that, most of it at night. Fifty ops, forty paratroop drops in the last fourteen months. It seemed like a lifetime, and he was still only twenty-four.

He was lucky to be alive. He wondered how the crews who had left

Moreton with him but had gone on to India from Algiers had got on. He was the only pilot going back from those that had chosen Italy with him. He felt a deep sense of reverence and humility. That brought a sense of guilt and shame when he realised that, since Kalova, he hadn't said a really meaningful prayer – except for that dreadful night when he had been very, very frightened. The dryness of his mouth, the soreness of his eyes, his prayers, his promise, the face of Connie. Was he the type that only prayed when he was frightened or wanted something? It wasn't good enough. God had been good to him; was that part of his destiny? Could he live up to whatever was in store for him? He was thankful, but hoped that this war would not turn him into a religious bigot.

He wondered just what was going to happen when he got back to the UK. He would probably go on leave for a week or two and then be posted to a training unit as a rest period. One thing for sure: he would do his utmost to get a posting near Connie. It had been worth taking the risk of doing a second tour to get back home, the way things had worked out. Yes, he had been very lucky. Extremely lucky.

CHAPTER FOURTEEN

FINI

S ORRENTO in the middle of March was not as colourful as it had been on his previous visits. However, it didn't matter what conditions outside were like; the fact that they were all on their way home created in their minds all the holiday atmosphere they needed. Going home was the sole topic of conversation.

They let the next few days slip idly by, and then came the news that they were to go to the transit camp in Naples to wait for the troopship back home. The news was electrifying. At last. That morning, after hearing the news, they went for a walk and arrived back for a drink before lunch. They were sitting in their shirtsleeves out on the patio of the balcony of the hotel sipping their favourite cherry brandies when a mosquito landed on Lee's left forearm. He gave it an almighty swipe and killed it, but not until after he had felt it bite him.

'That's it, Lee,' laughingly joked the crew. 'You've had it now; no boat home for you, no Connie for you.'

Lee joked with them. It was impossible for him to get malaria; his eyes were yellow with the mepacrine tablets he had taken so faithfully since he had arrived. He was a walking anti-malaria advert.

They moved into the transit camp in Naples the following day. A few days later, Lee woke up in the morning with the start of a terrific cold. He had a very bad sore throat and felt terrible. He had slept badly and felt sure he had a raging temperature. They were due on parade each morning for a head check and to hear the Standing Orders for the day. He asked the crew to cover for him, and they begged him to report sick.

'Not bloody likely,' said Lee. 'Not until I'm on that boat.' He stayed in bed whilst the lads went on parade and was soon fast asleep.

He woke up with the excited chatter of them coming back. The news was good, for it meant that they all had to report again in the afternoon with their pay books for some form of document check to do with embarkation. It was important that he did not miss that otherwise he would not be on the next boat out, which, by the way things were going, could only be imminent. Lee stayed in bed, missing lunch. The sore throat had moved down to his chest and he had terrific chest pains. He got up, but his legs were like jelly and he had a splitting headache. His chest hurt like hell. It hurt him to breathe. His eyes were watering, and he could hardly see out of them. He clambered into his battledress, putting it on over his pyjamas. He made a supreme effort to wash and shave in the ablutions. God, he felt terrible. One moment he was boiling hot and the next he was freezing cold. The lads helped him out on to the parade.

Lee felt himself coming to, waking up out of a blackness. He was conscious of lying on a white bed, which was floating away in a dark void. His head felt like a lump of clay, numb and weightless on the pillow. He tried to open his eyes wider to see where he was, but he couldn't see anything. He could hear voices around him, but he couldn't see anyone. There was only complete blackness. He tried to force himself to see, but he lacked the strength, or whatever it was, to open his eyes wider. The whiteness of the bed started going round and round, and the more he tried, the more it went round. He stopped trying. He lay there, devoid of feeling. Eventually, he could make out a light bulb shining above his head. He tried to focus on it. Funny, it was framed in one of those white lampshades, the type that looked like the headgear of a Chinese coolie.

The blackness and the bed seemed to be moving around the light. It got brighter, almost filling the void. He felt giddy and he wanted to vomit. He could feel himself saying something, but could not hear the words. Suddenly he was sick.

He awoke again; the voices were still there, out of reach. He tried to speak to them, but they carried on talking. The light bulb started to swing violently. The lamp shade had gone. Then the bed started to go round and round again gathering momentum. He wanted to get off, but he couldn't move. He became frightened, and vomited again.

He awoke once more. In the blackness he felt the room swinging and swaying. He just lay there. He didn't want to move, in case it started the bed going round again. Something told him that he couldn't move anyway.

He couldn't feel his body, neither could he see it. It was a strange abstract feeling, then he was sick yet again. This seemed to go on and on. Now he felt sure he was lying above a hot stove. It started burning him. He shouted to be taken away. It was getting hotter and hotter. He shouted, almost screamed, to be taken off, but no one took any notice. The voices were still there talking. How could he make them hear him?

He was bathed in perspiration. He felt as if he was suddenly floating on air. The light bulb now started to race away from him at a terrific speed, and he tried to reach out to stop it in panic. He realised his arms were not moving and he watched the bulb as it became a tiny pinprick of light, and it stayed that way for a short while then vanished away into the distance. The void became darker and darker. In panic of the dark, he tried again to call out.

The void closed upon him. Then there were those voices again, nearer now. One said, 'We will have to take him off liquid quinine. It's making him sick. Try giving it to him in tablet form.'

He tried to speak. Words seemed to be pouring out, but nobody took any notice. Someone lifted his head up and put something into his mouth. He saw the light bulb. He took the glass of water that was offered, and the blackness engulfed him once more as the light bulb faded away.

He awoke again and felt someone lifting his head. Again something was put in his mouth and the water was being given to him to drink. He was unbearably hot. His body and his bed were soaking wet. He was aware of this happening to him several times, each time followed by the uncompromising darkness of the void that swallowed him as he lost all feeling and consciousness of his bodily surroundings.

It was a lovely, sunny morning when he finally woke up. The warmth of the sun was shining through the window on to his face as he lay in bed. He remembered that, just before, the bed had been soaked with sweat – but now the sheets were clean and fresh and his head was lying on a snowy white pillow.

'Nurse,' said a voice alongside him, 'I think he's coming round.'

The sun was blocked out by the shadow of a face. He could make out a most gentle face that was looking down at him – the face of an older, but kindly-looking nurse.

'Oh good,' she said. 'You're awake now. Can you open your eyes? Don't try to sit up; just lie there and relax a while.' She moved away, and the warm sun fell on his face again. 'The doctor will want to see you in a little while, but have a little sleep if you want to.' With that she moved away from his bed.

Lee lay there, wondering what had happened to him. He felt extremely weak, drained and helpless, but he was warm and comfortable. The glare of the sun made him close his eyes and he dozed off again.

He woke up with a start. The sun had gone in and he was feeling cold. He raised himself up on to one elbow and looked around him. On a locker beside his bed was a coloured photograph of Connie. It was the one which he had received at the PTS and which had been acclaimed by the instructors there. It really was a most beautiful photograph of her.

He turned his head. In the next bed was a ginger-headed chap. He must have been the one who called the nurse, thought Lee. He looked over and smiled at him.

'How do you feel?' asked Ginger, 'You've been in a bad way for days, mate,' he said in a Cockney voice. 'Would you like a drink?' Lee nodded.

Ginger got out of bed and slipped on a jacket over his regulation pyjamas. As he came towards him Lee noticed a Warrant Officer's badge on his jacket. He gave Lee a drink of water from the carafe that was on the locker.

A number of white-coated doctors were moving towards them. Quick as a flash, Ginger nipped smartly back into his bed.

'Hello, old chap,' said one of them, who, Lee presumed, was the head doctor. 'How d'you feel?'

'OK, I think,' replied Lee. 'What's been the matter with me?'

'You have had a very severe attack of malaria, old son, and because your resistance was low, you have had a rough time. Fortunately, we know how to deal with it here. Soldiers in the front line, suffering like you from battle fatigue, are very prone to attacks of malaria.'

'Even with all that mepacrine?' asked Lee, not really convinced that getting malaria could have happened to him.

'That helps the fit men,' came the reply, 'but never mind. You'll be better now, then we will have you out of here and on a long convalescence.'

A check-up and he was gone. The nurse remained.

'Where am I?' asked Lee.

'You are in the Military Hospital just outside of Naples,' she replied.

'How did I get here?'

'You were brought in from the transit camp after you had collapsed. You had all your friends with you. They have been in every day since and brought that in,' pointing to Connie's photograph. 'You have a very beautiful wife and some very loyal friends,' she added.

'How long have I been here?'

'You have been in this ward about three days, but you were in the reception wing before that. But no more questions, try to get some rest.'

'Just one more,' pleaded Lee. 'Has the ship gone to the UK? Will I be able to . . . ?'

The nurse interrupted him. 'No more questions, you must rest. I know what you are going to say. We will have to see the doctor about that.'

Lee lay there feeling sorry for himself. He turned his head into the pillow and sobbed his heart out.

Fancy, after all that! After leading a crew into battle nearly fifty times, he had to be stopped by a bloody little mosquito. It had done to him what the enemy could not – stopped him from going home. It would be months now before he would be fit enough to get away and then he would have a job to get on to another boat going back. He cried himself to sleep, feeling mad with himself for behaving like that. Fancy crying like a baby at his age, but that only made things worse. The more frustrated he became, the more vulnerable he felt.

It was lunchtime when he woke up again. He didn't want to talk to anyone, feeling pretty sick with himself for letting his emotions take over.

And then, in came the lads from his crew, full of concern for him, but the moment they realised that he was on the mend, their attitude changed. He was better off there. The bullshit in the camp was terrible.

They were bored stiff hanging about in this God-forsaken hole.

It wasn't until the day after that they told him they were leaving for the UK the very next day, and they wouldn't be coming in to see him any more. Joe and Mac promised that the first thing they would do would be to go up to Scotland and see Connie and tell her that he was all right. Lee tried to be cheerful as they left, but the moment they had gone he broke down again. His illness had made him extremely weak, vulnerable and emotional.

The nurses and doctors in the hospital were marvellous, kind and generous; they couldn't do enough to make him comfortable both in mind and body. He was told that he had come in with a very high temperature, that he had been delirious for days and at first had not responded to treatment, and they thought they were going to lose him. Lee asked them about the change from liquid to tablet quinine and they were absolutely amazed that he had heard them talking about it, because at that point he was in crisis and it had been touch and go whether he would live or die.

Lying in bed, Lee had lots of time to think and reflect on the lucky breaks that he had had and the circumstances that had led up to him being a pilot. He recalled the time when, after leaving Torquay, they had gone to a small aerodrome, Clyffe Pypard in Wiltshire, to be 'graded' by their flying capabilities to see if they were pilot material or not. They had to go solo within twelve hours on Tiger Moths. Lee, with two others, had been given a pilot instructor who had just come off a tour with single-engined fighters. That poor chap was a nervous wreck, very highly strung, who nagged the life out of them over every little mistake they made – God, he hoped he wasn't going to turn out like that.

Fortunately for them, this pilot officer's failings were quickly noticed and he was soon taken off further flying instructor duties. They had been given another instructor and Lee had managed to go solo in ten hours. He wondered what pattern his life would have taken if that instructor had not been changed and he had failed to go solo within the required time. His mind went back to the time immediately after that when he had been posted to Manchester where they had hung about at Heaton Park. This was a reception centre for cadets going on the USA and Commonwealth Aircrew Training Schemes. He had hoped that he would go to the USA for training, but, because America had come into the war, he and the guys whom he had chummed up with had later been posted to Canada.

They had gone up to Greenock to embark on the *Louis Pasteur*, a French liner converted to a troopship. At first they had been escorted by two destroyers, one on each side of the troopship, but after a day or so, because of its speed – which could outstrip German submarines – they had crossed over the remainder of the Atlantic unescorted. They had landed in Halifax in Nova Scotia and had been given a wonderful reception at the docks by the local population when they arrived. He recalled how immense the trains had looked compared with those in England. The women volunteers had come along the platform and gone through the train giving them oranges, white bread, meat, ham and cheese sandwiches and as much milk as they could drink. The food and drink was something they hadn't seen in England for years.

There were the weeks they had spent hanging about in the transit camp at Moncton, New Brunswick in Canada waiting to go to Elementary Flying School. This was brought about because, now that America had entered the war, they had their own aircrew to train and for a while there was a hiccup in the system. He had been lucky there, because being a corporal wireless operator he did not have to take part in the endless picking-up of litter, painting coal bins and all the other non-productive tasks that the other aircrew cadets had to do to fill in the time.

Then on to his Elementary Flying School at Oshawa, in Ontario, to train on Tiger Moths. It was still a civilian flying school when they had first arrived and all of the instructors were civilians, not yet having been caught up in the changes that were taking place. This, of course, meant that there was an almost complete lack of service discipline. Another lucky break. He would never forget the day they were shown into the Mess for their first meal on arrival. There were individual tables and chairs, set out to seat twelve cadets. All the tables were laid with snow-white tablecloths, flowers, jugs of fresh creamy milk, carafes of water and bowls of fresh fruit.

This lasted just over a month until the camp was taken over by the RCAF, when, overnight, the instructors all became sergeant pilots and the Mess became a regulation Mess with long wooden tables and benches to sit on. Gone were the fruit, flowers, milk and tablecloths.

He remembered the day when he almost blew it. This happened during flying training in the field that the instructors used to show the cadets how to practise emergency landings. The instructors would slip the aircraft into the area of the field and when they were just a few feet above the ground open up the engine and fly off. They never actually landed in it and this is what the cadets were taught to do. However, they used to say, 'We could quite easily have landed here if we wanted to, but we won't waste time doing it.' He had finished this part of his training on how to do an emergency landing; his instructor, being quite pleased with his progress, had got out of the plane and told him to go to the field and spend the next forty-five minutes practising them by himself.

'Well done. You don't need me with you any more; go to the field and practise by yourself.' He knew how much these young cadets liked to fly solo.

Lee, in all innocence, thought that meant he had to go and land in the field – the sort of thing that Pilot Officer Prune would have thought. (Pilot Officer Prune was a cartoon character, used by the RAF in the training manuals to illustrate the stupid things that airmen did.)

He flew over the field, switched his engine off, got his glide path just right, glided into wind side and slipped in exactly as he had been taught, the only difference being he had actually made a perfect three-point landing in the field. He was surprised to find that it was full of small scrub-like bushes. Not a very good field, he had thought to himself as he started up the engine again and taxied to the far side of the field with the bushes brushing against the underside of the wings. Nevertheless, feeling quite proud of himself, he turned into wind and prepared to take off again to do another 'practice landing'. Meanwhile, other instructors who had seen him land, came down close to see if he was in trouble. Lee found that he couldn't take off whilst these other aircraft were around. Eventually it was safe to do so but, by this time, his time was up and he had to return to base, quite pleased with himself that he had made at least one successful emergency landing.

When he arrived back, Tommy Thompson, his instructor, was absolutely furious with him because, not only had he disobeyed orders by landing in the field, but now that everyone knew that he was OK, they were having a good laugh at them both for him being so stupid.

Tommy told him the reason the instructors never actually landed was because it was considered to be too difficult to take off from that small field again! In any case, they would never get through the course if they all landed and took off again.

'How could anyone be so bloody stupid?' Ignorance is bliss.

Later, he discovered it was only by the good representations made on his behalf by Tommy Thompson that he hadn't been thrown off the course for that episode, because the scrub had damaged the fabric on the underside of the wings, tearing it off and leaving great holes in it! And to add to the trouble he was in for landing in the field, he had also flown an aircraft that was unserviceable. He had been very, very lucky to have got away with it.

How he had loved those Tiger Moths: doing aerobatics, formation flying and flying around the clouds playing hide and seek with his friends. How innocent and naïve he had been in those days, just a kid who thought he knew it all. How things had changed in two years. Now he felt like an old man. But still lying there, he had time to muse on, like the time that having passed out, Tommy had taken him up on a last flight. After trying to do a reverse loop, the aircraft straining almost to breaking point, Tommy had given the controls to Lee to see if he could do any better. But after he had tried unsuccessfully it was decided that it was time to go home. It was then that the real point of the final trip was revealed. Tommy calmly passed over a handful of condoms to him and told him to blow them up. They then 'dive bombed' the tarmac, dropping out the condoms which they had blown up like balloons!

The town of Oshawa hadn't been his favourite place. The bars were drinking saloons with no atmosphere and, during the summer they were there, the weather was very humid and close, which made it difficult to breathe. Going for a walk along the side of the lake in an attempt to cool off was itself a nightmare as the lakeside was plagued with midges. But he had loved the flying and had thought the world of Tommy. They had

2 SFTS at Camp Borden (*l to r*) Ken Slough, Dick Hale, George Peakman, and Lee with two Canadians on the course, Bill Rhodes and Bill Whittaker.

been really good friends. But, like so many, he had hated the various tests that so many of the young hopeful cadets had failed on the way. The sadness which prevailed when another hopeful packed his bags and was posted in sheer desolation to some unknown destination affected them all. None of the course wanted to fail and were selfishly thankful if they were far enough up the 'exam results list' not to be 'scrubbed'.

Then there was the final excitement of passing out and being posted to the SFTS at Camp Borden, flying Harvards. There were anxious moments as the inevitable tests came and went and the exams became more difficult and complicated with the subjects becoming more specialised. The Harvards had a much more sensitive touch than the Tiger Moths and it was very easy to overcompensate when flying them. This, plus the added power and speed on take-off and landing, meant that more failed not only the written tests but the flying exams as well, particularly as most of the time they were taking off and landing on impacted snow. Where the runway was marked out by the branches of fir trees it was only the distance between these, as you came in to land, that gave you any idea of height or distance. Thus more hopefuls bit the dust. The Canadians and the Americans seemed to take failure more intensely than the British. They took it very badly. Maybe it was because they were nearer home.

One of the things that Lee reflected upon was the kindness of the Canadian population in and around Camp Borden and Oshawa. They used to come to the camps at weekends and take the British boys into their homes for the weekend. Over there things had been so good they had not been aware that there was a war on. For over a year he had missed the full impact of the war and the bombing that had been the lot of the British people.

The runway at Camp Borden in the winter was formed from snow which was rolled hard and had small fir trees planted as markers.

Yes, he had been lucky to have survived thus far. Lee made good friends with Ginger and began slowly to regain his strength. Nearly two weeks had gone by since the crew had gone home, and he was resigned to spend his convalescence in Italy.

It was on 12 April, the day that President Roosevelt died, that he was allowed out for the first time from the hospital ward, and Ginger went with him. They made their way to the Royal Palace Canteen. Allied servicemen were standing around on the steps, reading newspapers, their banner headlines in large black bold print informing the world that the President of the United States had died. Lee and Ginger stood there reading and at the same time listening to a group of Americans who were anxiously discussing the probable outcome.

A shout of 'Lee!' made him look up from the paper he was reading. Running towards him was his old pal Mickey, a friend he had trained with in Canada. He had got his commission and was now a squadron leader. They clasped each other warmly and together the three of them went into the canteen for a drink. They chatted together relating experiences, and Mickey told him he had been flying Bostons, but was now awaiting the result of an inquiry. Apparently he had come back from a raid and had crashed into an American Air Force camp that was on the airfield, killing a number of airmen. While he was waiting he was flying Warwicks – the transport version of the Wimpy – between England and Italy, mainly for the VIPs.

It was as if a miracle had happened for these two to meet after such a long time, when Lee's need to go home was so great and yet the prospects seemed so bleak. Mickey was flying back to the UK in a couple of days with an almost empty plane. If Lee could work it, he most certainly could fly back with him, so could Ginger. He told Lee how he could get in touch with him and the friends separated.

Lee was delighted; back they went to the hospital. The doctor had at once said agreed that it was OK for them to go, providing they did their convalescence in the UK, adding that going home was in itself convalescing. The administration were delighted to be able to off-load them so easily and did everything possible to speed up their documentation. Lee was convinced that the doctors were instrumental in that respect.

It was a beautiful, sunny morning when they left Italy. Sitting comfortably in the passenger seats of the Warwick, Lee and Ginger were on their way to Lyneham in the UK. Passing over France, and later the Cherbourg peninsula, Lee could clearly see the Channel Islands, and in particular Guernsey and Alderney outlined below, set in the silvery sea. He wondered how his relatives, who had stayed behind in Guernsey, were faring, as the Islands were still under German occupation. The occupying German forces, although surrounded and starving and in a state of siege, had not, as yet, surrendered.

Crossing the Channel, he felt a thrill as they flew over the English countryside on their way to touch down at Lyneham. He could not help feeling a deep sense of pride and patriotism at the clean, fresh, green look of the countryside, with its neat patchwork of green and brown fields and clusters of trees below. What a contrast to the barren, sun-scorched land of Italy.

They landed safely at Lyneham, said warm 'goodbyes' and 'thank yous' to Mickey, and set about trying to go on convalescent leave. However, it couldn't be done at Lyneham; it was not an official re-embarkation centre, therefore they couldn't stay there. The re-embarkation centre was at West Kirby, near Liverpool. They would have to go there by rail.

When Lee telephoned Connie at her new RAF station at Errol in Perthshire, she wasn't there. He left a message to say he would be in touch from West Kirby. Railway warrants were then obtained, and they were able to leave immediately for West Kirby. Ginger helped Lee with his kit for, by now, Lee was feeling very weak after such excitement and the long journey. Together they made their way up north.

West Kirby was virtually deserted when they arrived very late in the evening. They were put into deserted billets for the night and told to report early in the morning to check in officially. They had no trouble or delays checking in, going through the medical, and general documentation. They had officially arrived in the UK!

Within a couple of days they had received their railway warrants and were ready to leave – Ginger to London, and Lee on nearly a month's sick leave to Scotland. He was given warrants to go to Errol, and then a return one from Errol to London in order to report to the Air Ministry in London on 10 May. Meanwhile he was to keep in touch with them by telegram, and his pay would be forwarded to him by money order. They were about to leave when a party of airmen arrived in by troopship. Who should be amongst them but some of Lee's crew; Joe, unfortunately, had been left behind. They had just over an hour together and were delighted to see Lee up and about again. The journey had been quite uneventful and very boring. However the good news was that the crossing had been smooth and none of the lads had been sick. They enquired how he had managed to beat them. Lee told them about his meeting with Mickey.

'Christ, Lee, if you fell into a cesspit you'd come out smelling of roses,' said Mac.

Lee, who had worried about how Joe would get on over his kit, needn't have done so as the lads told him he had been given a completely new kit in Naples. Now it was Lee's turn to wave farewell to them. It would take at least a week to get them all through the incoming routine.

'You lucky old bastard,' said Mac as he bade farewell. 'But nobody deserves it more than you. Do keep in touch.'

Lee made a phone call to Connie to tell her he would be arriving in

Glasgow at 9.30 p.m. She was home in Glasgow having obtained special leave at a moment's notice as soon as she had heard that he was back in the UK. He was thrilled to hear her voice again as they chatted excitedly together. Then it was 'cheerio' to Ginger, and once more he was on his own. The train was crowded, but Lee managed to find himself a corner seat which someone had just vacated and, leaving his kitbag in the corridor, sat down and stared out of the windows as the train sped through glorious, wonderful England on its way to Scotland and to Connie.

The train journey seemed to take forever. Lee was tired and kept dozing off. He still felt unwell, but knew that he had to keep going. After all, this was what it had all been for. He hoped and prayed that he wouldn't collapse again like he did in Naples. He must not give in now.

He stepped off the train at Glasgow Central and there, waiting for him on the platform in a lovely check suit, looking more beautiful than ever, was his Connie. They flew into each other's arms. He had survived; he was home!

EPILOGUE

AT West Kirby he had been given a very thorough medical, having carried a letter from the medical officer in Naples setting out his condition. He was immediately sent on sick leave to convalesce. He spent a few days with Connie's family in Glasgow using up the compassionate leave that Connie had been granted on his return to the UK. Connie was still in the WAAF and had been posted to Errol, where they returned together. She had asked to be posted nearer to her home when she had returned from Moreton after they had been married.

They were able to rent a room in a small cottage near the RAF Station and they stayed there until the war in Europe ended. The rest did him good and, slowly but surely, his strength returned, so much so that he used to go daily with Connie to the stores where the equipment officer was very sympathetic, allowing him to sit with her during the day whilst she went about her duties. Towards the end of April, Connie was able to obtain some more leave and they decided to go to Gosport to visit his family.

On the way down in the train they talked over the last time they had been to see them. It had been on a leave from Lossiemouth when, on arriving at Waterloo Station, Lee had asked directions from a lady pushing a tea wagon along the platform. The lady had replied in a broad Cockney accent and Connie had been absolutely thrilled to hear her voice as it had given her the feeling that she had really arrived in London. However, later that morning they had had a shock, walking through London's West End, admiring the shops in that crazy way that two young people in love do, window shopping and spending money they didn't have and dreaming dreams of the future. Connie, upon Lee's request, had removed her WAAF uniform cap in the train and her lovely, brown tresses were cascading down her back. Arm in arm, laughing and joking, they had been in a different world, completely forgetting to put the hat back on.

Suddenly, they had heard, 'Sergeant! What on earth do you think you are doing, behaving like that?' The voice had come from one of two young WAAF officers standing directly in front of them. They had stood frozen together, the ground seeming to open up in front of them.

The reality of wartime had come back with a startling jolt.

171

'You are improperly dressed, Sergeant. Put your hair up and your hat back on immediately!' the voice had continued. 'Give me your name and number, and report to your station when you go back.'

Connie was in deep trouble. Hastily they explained what they were about. It had seemed so cheap having to explain to those two young upstarts why they were so happy. But grovel they did, anything to get Connie off a charge and have that hanging over them for the rest of their leave. And so it was that, with a warning, they had got away with it.

How he loved that girl with her laughing eyes and flawless complexion snuggled up beside him, giggling and laughing at her efforts. Italy had been worth every minute for a moment like this. As they talked about it, the train thundered on, trees, meadows and houses flashing by with Connie sitting next to him, with her lovely hair once again falling over her shoulders. Lee caressed it with his hands and their lips met. The hat that had brought them together and had nearly got them into trouble was squashed on the seat between them!

Just what had happened in Glasgow with Connie's parents, after a few days, happened to them in Gosport. Her parents had asked why had they not had them to the wedding. There were veiled hints of whether or not it had been a 'shotgun wedding' – in that day and age almost unspeakable. Once again there had been reassurances and, after that, their leave together was unblemished – until the telegram arrived.

Lee was to report to the Air Ministry in London. He felt just a little flattered to be summoned to such a prestigious venue and, in due course, reported to the Ministry. It happened to be on VE day plus one. He was to go before a board to discuss his future and it was from this that he was later posted to Honiley to undergo a very thorough medical. He failed every aspect of it. He was found medically unfit for flying duties and was grounded.

Two months later he underwent another medical and, although feeling stronger and more confident in himself when he went there, he failed to pass the stringent medical examination needed before he could resume flying again. This time the news devastated him, and he was told that it would be some time, if ever, before he would be fit for flying again. The malaria from which he had suffered and so nearly died was, apparently, the recurring type!

Lee was shattered. All his confidence left him, and he felt his old weakness overtake him again. He had no reserves left in him to take this blow, and the disappointment welled up in him. Tears of frustration rolled down his cheeks and, the more they fell, the angrier he became with himself. He just stood there. This behaviour was lamentable. On the one hand he felt he had just been branded a physical wreck, and on the other, instead of fighting it, here he was proving that he indeed was a bloody, nervous wreck. What on earth did the Medical Officer think of him,

172

snivelling like that in front of him? He felt so embarrassed and ashamed he longed for the ground to open up and swallow him.

He heard the MO saying something about not worrying – he wasn't the only one who was reacting like that after ops, and this was a problem many would have to face. Lee saluted and, with tears still running down his face, he left. He stood out in the fresh air. The sun was shining, and he slowly composed himself. God, what an idiot. What a stupid, bloody idiot!

Ruefully, he looked down at his pilot's brevet on his tunic. What now? Little did he realise when he did that last raid on Treviso that, not only was that to be his last operation, but it was also to be the end of his flying career. That little mosquito in Sorrento had sealed the end of his days as a pilot.

For about seven years after that, each March, he would go down with a most flaming and roaring temperature, followed immediately by an attack of the shivers. Staying in bed, which used to get soaked with perspiration, for two days, sometimes longer, was the only solution, as it made him very susceptible to an attack of flu, and this, if they were not very careful could last for weeks. After a while, Lee became blasé about it, and called it 'going into his furnace for his little spot of hell.'

After Honiley, Lee had been posted to RAF Atherstone, near Stratford-upon-Avon, and promoted to Warrant Officer. While waiting for the results of his medical, he was given the job of organising the Educational Vocational Service, designed to help airmen and women fit into civilian occupations. Once it became known that he was not going to fly again, he was left in that post. Connie was demobbed and came down to join him. They managed to obtain digs in a boarding house near the river and spent the summer of 1945 lazing about in the punts on the River Avon, feeding the swans and going to the pubs and theatre. He was demobbed the following December.

For years Lee wanted to do something to ease the nagging feeling of conscience that he frequently had, often concerning how many innocent people had been killed by the bombs they had dropped, particularly as doubts about Bomber Command's activities during the war were being raised in some circles. To try to ease his conscience, he always found himself coming back to the fact that maybe his crews didn't kill anyone, but they would never really know for sure. How could they? Neither could he ever really put it to bed under the heading of 'doing his duty'. Like so many of his colleagues, he never talked about their experiences. Maybe in his case, subconsciously, he still felt ashamed. However, maybe now that he has told the story, his conscience has been finally put to bed.

Having left the RAF, his career finished, Lee set out to re-establish himself, now with his young family to support. He chose selling, first domestic appliances and then business systems. This background enabled him to settle in Guernsey in 1963 in business administration. Eventually, he retired as the Director of his family's own microfilm company.

It wasn't until May 1968, when he was invited to join the Lions Club of Guernsey, that the opportunity for him to honour his promise was presented to him. He had never heard of Lions Clubs International, or for that matter realised the tremendous amount of good that they and other Service clubs do for their local, national and international communities. The Guernsey club was formed in 1967 by a group of businessmen getting together under the sponsorship of a club that had been formed in Jersey many years previously.

After a few years, as an active member finding his feet, he served as Welfare Officer and Secretary and was involved in many major club projects. Lee was given the honour of being President of the Club during 1973/74 and, during this time, he also served as a committee member on The Guide Dogs for the Blind Association. It was during his term as Welfare Officer that the late Dr Sam Gregory approached the Club for help in setting up a screening and research unit for heart complaints. Lee helped in the setting up of a Steering Committee and became a Founder Member of The Guernsey Chest and Heart Association.

At the end of his term of office he was appointed Youth Officer in 1975, a position he held for fifteen years. Part of these duties were to take part in Lions National Youth Award project.

In 1976 he was invited to join the Panel of Prison Visitors and later became their Chairman. In 1978 he was asked to become the Chairman of The Guernsey Society for the Mentally Handicapped, and was responsible for them becoming affiliated to the National Society – MENCAP.

In 1980 he set up an investigation to provide meaningful work for mentally handicapped adults, and served as Chairman on the Steering Committee. It was through this work that Grow Limited, a Horticulture Training Centre and Sheltered Workshop for disabled people, was officially opened in 1984. Being the Founder, he was elected Chairman of the Board of Directors. In 1986 he became President of The Guernsey Committee for The International Year of Youth.

Earlier, for his work, he had been awarded the Lions Club of Guernsey's Community Service Award, an award normally given to non-Lions Club Members and, in 1985, was also awarded the International President's Certificate of Appreciation for Humanitarian Services. In 1989 he received one of the highest awards given to a member of Lions Clubs International: The International President's Award.

During this time the Lions Club's many welfare projects and those of the other charities had to be funded, and Lee has either initiated or taken part in the raising of the many hundreds of thousands of pounds needed to finance them.

There are many unexplained phenomena which have happened to many people, particularly in the answering of prayers. Lee says, 'All I know is what happened to me on that dreadful night, my night of absolute panic and fear, and the promise I made. It must be left to the readers to draw their own conclusions.'

POSTSCRIPT

IN my acknowledgements I referred to the fascinating experiences I enjoyed while writing this book. These have now been supplemented and enhanced by the wonderful responses I have received from readers, particularly from 'those who were there'. It has also made me many new friends locally and pen pals far and wide who have enjoyed reading it and who have congratulated me on my work.

Simon Parry of Air Research Publications, my first publisher, telephoned me to say that we had virtually sold out of the first print run and suggested that we should go for another as the demand was still there. He asked me to write this postscript for the second edition. To accomplish this I felt that it would be nice to relate some of the anecdotes that have been related to me after the publication of the first edition. However, before I start on these, I must say that the dedication in the second edition included our new grandson, Sam, born shortly after the first edition was published. Furthermore, before that event, after twenty-five years

Twenty years after the war ended Lee and Riggy met up again, this time in Guernsey.
(© *Guernsey Press Co Ltd*)

Reminiscing: Lee and Joe at the Moreton-in-Marsh Wellington Aviation Gallery, with the geodetic framing of a Wimpy behind them.

membership of the Lions Club of Guernsey, I was pleased to be offered Life Membership of Lions Clubs International and now proudly wear the badge of Life Member.

Another notable event was brought about, thanks to the efforts of a fellow 205 Group member, Reg Rogers. Reg kindly put me in touch with Joe (our second tour rear gunner of 'pigeon' fame). Joe and I met up at the Wellington Aviation Gallery at Moreton-in-Marsh after fifty years. He hadn't changed a bit. He recounted some experiences including not being able to take his air firing test because he was prone to air sickness. He got around it by getting a pal to do it for him. Now he tells me!

One of the first letters I received was from George Peakman, a pal who trained with me at Oshawa and Camp Borden in Canada, again over fifty years ago. We are now in regular contact. George has a better memory than I have and was able to fill in a lot of names on photographs we had. He also told me of the fate of some of our friends who were on courses with us, including a particular chum who used to say to me that he wasn't going to survive the war. He was killed on his first op, to Nuremburg, in March 1944.

177

George also tells me that the Americans did not keep their crews together as we did, but on each sortie would mix them up – a completely different philosophy to that of Bomber Command. Now that it is all over it would be interesting to know if one method was better than the other. On balance, mainly because I experienced it, I would be in favour of the *esprit de corps* developed through the British way. George also reminded me that it was the *Empress of Scotland* in which we returned from Canada.

Another story was told to me by Peter Gadbury, ex-70 Squadron. His crew had arrived in Foggia on a cold, wet night and had stumbled about in that school building looking for bed spaces. From one room came a stream of light from a bulb soldered directly to the mains wires and under it a WOP/AG (wireless operator/air gunner) was cooking a meal on a Primus. He called out, 'There are three bed spaces in here if you are not superstitious. We lost a crew last night.' He also offered them part of his food, which Peter said was '. . . fried bread and jam and highly popular'.

Peter remembers the four/eight-seater open lavatories. His crew kept a pair of binoculars and an umbrella on the tent pole. The binoculars were to check whether there was a vacant seat before setting off, and a brolly to keep the hot sun or the rain off them during their sojourn! Peter was in the horrific attack upon Feuersbrunn airfield on the night of 6/7 July 1944, when we nearly bought it. Out of the sixty-one aircraft taking part, thirteen were lost. He says that most of the seven Wimpys that were shot down came from 70 Squadron. He has a German ex-fighter pilot friend who did not know where Feuersbrunn was. Fortunately I still have my navigator's log of that trip and was able to give him the exact location.

Peter Elliot, ex-40 Squadron, told me about a remarkable coincidence, having been in touch with the son of a former 40 Squadron aircrew member. He discovered that his crew's rear gunner reported, at debriefing, seeing a 'plane shot down over the Danube.' This turned out to be the aircraft the son's father was in.

Lewis Williams was in 37 Squadron during some of the time I was with them. He was pleased to tell me how many memories my story brought back to him; the olive grove, the mud, the water bowser (which he hated) and the rotting desert-bleached tents. He reminded me that the hotel we stayed in at Sorrento was the Minerva Hotel.

Ken Westrope was the rear gunner in the 37 Squadron Liberator that had the bomb go through its wing. Our dates and places do not coincide, so what we thought we saw – a bomb going through the wing – must have missed. We were so sure that the bomb we saw going down must have gone through it. When we were later shown the photograph we immediately jumped to the conclusion that it was the event we imagined we saw. Things happen so quickly over a target.

I have struck up a good companionship with Tom Cranmer, the Honorary Secretary of No. 205 Group Reunion Association. Tom and his family came to visit us while in Guernsey. He passed on the stories of Tony Brown of 70 Squadron, who had returned to Foggia. Tony had reminisced about the hot summer days in the tent encampment, the biting winter winds, the dug-out tents with their home-built drip stoves (with stories of tents catching fire and the loss of eyebrows and hair when blow-backs occurred), the return from ops to find the tents flooded and the beds afloat.

These are priceless anecdotes. Very few talk about the ops themselves, particularly as I have since discovered that the targets we attacked were considered to be rated third after Berlin and the Ruhr. Most memories rekindled seem to centre around the appalling conditions of camp life in those days.

Finally, I must thank all the reviewers of the earlier editions of this book in the various magazines. I have been fortunate in having many very good reviews based on its readability, factual research, historic content and a story of events hitherto untold, but had to be told.

I do hope that you have had as much pleasure reading it as I have writing it and being involved in all the events surrounding its publication.

Maurice George Lihou, Esq., MBE was appointed to be a Member of the British Empire in 1996 for his services to the Young and to the Mentally Handicapped in Guernsey.

MAP

The Mediterranean Theatre of Operations from mid-1943

THE map illustrates the approximate location of targets during the operations carried out by 'Lee'. It also gives a clear indication of the strategy adopted by No. 205 Group to assist the Allied armies in their advances through Italy, the Balkans and southern Europe.

Tactical operations can clearly be seen by the attacks carried out on the sea ports on the west coast of Italy and the close army support on road and rail junctions as the army moved up from Naples to Rome and beyond.

Furthermore, the strategic operations further afield involving the cutting of communication and supply links can also clearly be followed. The pattern shows that to cut off supplies reaching the enemy, action consisted of attacks on the railways across northern Italy, minelaying in the river Danube and attacks upon oil refineries and the large marshalling yards in capitals and major cities. The targets chosen clearly highlight the *modus operandi* of the Group during this phase of its activity.

In addition to these activities, support was also given to the Allied air forces by bombing airfields. As the war progressed and the enemy armies retreated, support was given to partisans by the dropping of much needed supplies.

The illustration also shows some of the other places of interest mentioned.

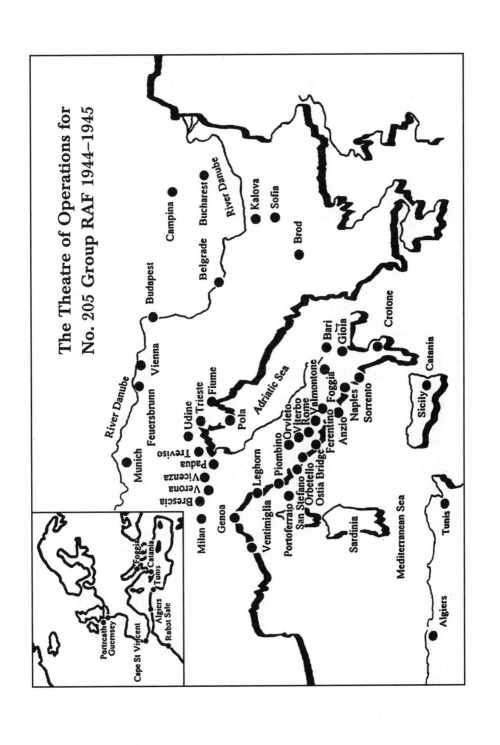

The Theatre of Operations for
No. 205 Group RAF 1944–1945

Appendix I

Organisation and Equipment of No. 205 Group

February 1944–May 1945

231 Wing:
37 Squadron. Equipped with Wellington Xs and operating from Tortorella, re-equipping with Liberator VIs in October 1944.
70 Squadron. Equipped with Wellington Xs at Tortorella, re-equipping with Liberator VIs in January 1945.

236 Wing:
40 Squadron. Equipped with Wellington Xs at Foggia Main, re-equipping with Liberator VIs in March 1945.
104 Squadron. Equipped with Wellington Xs at Foggia Main until February 1945, then re-equipping with Liberator VIs.

240 Wing:
178 Squadron. Equipped with Liberator VIs throughout the period, initially operating from El Adem, moving to Celone in March 1944 and on to Amendola in July.
462 Squadron. Operating Halifax IIs at Celone until renamed 614 Squadron on 3 March 1944.
614 Squadron. Renamed from 462 Squadron and moving to Stonara on 10 May 1944 and finally joining 178 Squadron at Amendola on 15 July. Halifaxes were operated throughout, but Liberator VIs were also taken on strength from August 1944. The primary task of this unit was to act as 'pathfinders' for 205 Group.

330 Wing:
142 Squadron. Equipped with Wellington Xs at Cerignola, moving to Amendola on 14 February 1944 and finally to Regina on 3 July. On 5 October 330 Wing was disbanded, the unit returning to the United Kingdom to re-equip with Mosquitoes.
150 Squadron. History similar to 142 Squadron (above). On arrival in the United Kingdom it became a Lancaster unit.

2 (SAAF) Wing:
31 and 34 (SAAF) Squadrons. Joined 205 Group in June 1944. Both equipped with Liberator VIs and operating from Celone.

Appendix II

Bombing, Mining and Supply Operations
Carried Out By No. 205 Group, MASAF
February 1944–May 1945

Date	Target	Aircraft Dispatched	MIA*	Crashed
1/2.2.44	Maribor aircraft factory	30	1	–
7/8.2.44	Padua rail yards	45	–	1
8/9.2.44	Rimini rail yards	14	–	–
	Arezzo rail yards	13	–	–
12/13.2.44	Road transport Campoleone	41	–	–
	Road transport Cisterna	27	–	1
13/14.2.44	Cecchina–Albano highway	14	–	–
	Cecchina–Campoleone highway	27	–	–
14/15.2.44	Cecchina–Campoleone highway	28	–	–
	Cecchina–Albano highway	27	–	–
	Cecchina–Albano–Campoleone highway	9	–	–
15/16.2.44	Grottoferrato–Marino–Albano–Velletri area	12	–	–
	Grottoferrato–Marino area	26	–	–
	Albano–Velletri area	27	–	–
16/17.2.44	Grottoferrato area	24	–	–
	Porto San Stefano	31	–	2
17/18.2.44	Grottoferrato area	11	–	–
	Genzano–Velletri area	26	–	1
	Albano–Genzano area	27	–	–
18/19.2.44	Genzano area	16	–	–[1]
	Grottoferrato area	13	–	–
24/25.2.44	Steyr-Daimler-Puch factory	56	–	4
1/2.3.44	Cecchina–Lanvio road	16	–	–
	Velletri–Lanvio road	16	–	–

* Missing in action.
[1] A 40 Sqn Wellington was flown back by the pilot after the crew had baled out when the aircraft suddenly went out of control.

Date	Target	Aircraft Dispatched	MIA	Crashed
2/3.3.44	Orbetello rail junction and yards	16	–	–
	Mantalto railway	18	–	–
	Porto San Stefano harbour	17	–	–
3/4.3.44	Bihac	32	–	–
7/8.3.44	Porto San Stefano harbour	18	–	–
11/12.3.44	Genoa rail yards	66	–	–
15/16.3.44	Sofia rail yards and town	67	1	10
16/17.3.44	Sofia rail yards	21	–	–
18/19.3.44	Plovdiv rail yards	53	2	1
19/20.3.44	Monfalcone	42	–	–
22/23.3.44	Padua West rail yards	82	–	–
23/24.3.44	Padua North rail yards	49	1	–
24/25.3.44	Sofia rail yards	77	3	1
26/27.3.44	Vincenza rail yards	79	–	–
28/29.3.44	Milan–Lambrate rail yards	78	–	–
29/30.3.44	Sofia rail yards	72	–	1
	Fano/Cesano rail bridges	10	–	–
1/2.4.44	Varese–Macchi aircraft factory	66	–	–
	Piombino harbour	16	–	–
2/3.4.44	Vincenza rail yards	55	–	–
	Leghorn	13	–	–
	Porto San Stefano	12	–	–
3/4.4.44	Manfred Weiss factory Budapest	87	5	–[2]
8.4.44	Niksic	11	–	–
8/9.4.44	Mining Danube	22	12	–
10/11.4.44	Porto San Stefano	25	–	–
	Piombino harbour	25	–	–
11/12.4.44	Varese–Macchi aircraft factory	54	–	–
	Monfalcone shipyards	11	–	–
12/13.4.44	Budapest rail yards	64	1	–
	Mining Danube	34	–	–
14/15.4.44	Piombino harbour	24	–	–
	Porto San Stefano	25	–	–
	Leghorn harbour	24	–	–
	Mining Danube	11	–	2
15/16.4.44	Turnul/Severin rail yards	92	1	2[3]
16/17.4.44	Budapest rail yards	64	2	1
	Leghorn harbour	5	1	–
	Piombino	9	–	–
	Porto San Stefano	8	–	–
17/18.4.44	Plovdiv rail yards	43	1	3
19/20.4.44	Porto San Stefano	24	–	–
	Leghorn harbour	23	–	–
	Piombino	20	–	–
	Genoa harbour	7	–	–
	Plovdiv rail yards	9	–	1

[2] Fw 190 claimed destroyed by a 37 Sqn Wellington crew.
[3] Two Wellingtons collided at base on return, both crews killed.

Date	Target	Aircraft Dispatched	MIA	Crashed
20/21.4.44	Leghorn/Genoa/Porto San Stefano/ Piombino. Most aircraft recalled	66	–	–
	Mestre rail yards – recalled	10	1	–
21/22.4.44	Leghorn/Genoa/Porto San Stefano/ Piombino. Most aircraft recalled	24	1	3
23/24.4.44	Genoa	9	–	–
	Piombino	24	–	–
	Porto San Stefano	24	–	–
	Leghorn	24	–	–
	Parma rail yards	10	–	–
25/26.4.44	Leghorn/Genoa/Porto San Stefano/ Piombino. Most aircraft recalled.	9	–	–
28/29.4.44	Genoa	21	–	–
	Piombino	8	–	–
	Porto San Stefano	6	–	–
29/30.4.44	Genoa	15	–	–
	Spezia	24	–	–
	Leghorn	22	–	–
30.4/1.5.44	Monfalcone shipyards and docks	7	–	–
	Genoa	9	–	–
	Leghorn	6	–	–
	Spezia	14	–	–
1/2.5.44	Genoa	6	–	–
	Leghorn	6	–	–
	Spezia	16	–	–
	Allessandro rail yards	57	1	1
2/3.5.44	Piancenza rail yards	9	–	–
	Genoa	12	–	–
	Leghorn/Spezia	12	–	–
3/4.5.44	Bucharest rail yards	62	1	–
4/5.5.44	Budapest-Rakos rail yards	70	1	1
5/6.5.44	Campina rail yards/Steuva Romana refinery	43	3	–
	Mining Danube	31	–	–
6/7.5.44	Bucharest	80	4	–
	Pitesti rail bridge	3	–	–
7/8.5.44	Bucharest	61	6	–
	Filiasi rail bridge	2	1	–
9/10.5.44	Operation *Joyride* Portes-les-Valences	24	1	–
	Leghorn	8	1	–
	Genoa	26	–	–
	Mining Danube	9	–	–
10/11.5.44	Budapest–Rakos rail yards	55	1	–
11/12.5.44	Porto San Stefano	15	–	
	Portoferrago	24	1	–
12/13.5.44	Porto San Stefano	16	–	–
	Piombino	20	1	1[4]

[4] A 37 Sqn Wellington was attacked five times by a nightfighter, which was driven off and claimed damaged.

Date	Target	Aircraft Dispatched	MIA	Crashed
13/14.5.44	Arezzo rail yards	20	–	–
	Orvieto rail yards	21	–	–
	Furnovo Di Taro rail bridge	6	–	–
	Milan–Lambrate rail yards	8	–	–
14/15.5.44	Ladisana rail bridge	19	–	–
	Tagliamento/Casarsa rail bridge	16	–	–
	Porto Marghera oil refinery	8	–	–
	Avisio rail bridge	16	1	–
16/17.5.44	Piombino	16	–	–
	Portoferraio	21	–	–
	Porto San Stefano	5	–	–
17/18.5.44	Frosinone	12	–	–
18/19.5.44	Frosinone	18	–	–
	Valmontone	18	–	–
	Terracina	30	–	–
21/22.5.44	Portoferraio	22	–	–
	Piombino	15	–	–
22/23.5.44	Valmontone	26	–	–
	Ferrantino	41	–	1
23/24.5.44	Ferrantino	20	2	–[5]
	Valmontone	27	–	–[6]
24/25.5.44	Valmontone	65	1	–
25/26.5.44	Viterbo	57	–	–
26/27.5.44	Viterbo	55	–	–
27/28.5.44	Viterbo	46	–	–
28/29.5.44	Porto San Stefano	52	–	–
	Colle Isarco railway	4	–	–
29/30.5.44	Mining Danube	12	–	–
	Feuersbrunn airfield	38	1	–
30/31.5.44	Subiaco	34	–	–
31.5/1.6.44	Mining Danube	52	–	1
	Iron Gates Canal	38	–	–
1/2.6.44	Szolnok rail yards	50	–	–
	Szolnok rail bridge	9	–	–
2/3.6.44	Guirgiu (Danube)	44	1	–
3/4.6.44	Bridge over river Tiber	50	–	–
4/5.6.44	Terni road junction	48	–	–
5/6.6.44	Viterbo	34	–	–
6/7.6.44	Orvieto road junction	18	–	–
	Viterbo road junction	26	–	–
7/8.6.44	Orvieto road junction	34	1	1
8/9.6.44	Nis rail yards	52	–	–
9/10.6.44	Trieste oil refinery	60	1	–
	Terni road junction	19	–	–
10/11.6.44	Brod Bosanski oil refinery	53	–	–
11/12.6.44	Karlova airfield	50	1	–
12/13.6.44	Almasfuzito oil refinery	57	–	–

[5] Two 70 Sqn Wellingtons are believed to have collided over the target.
[6] Beaufighter shot down in error by Wellington crew. Claimed as Ju 88.

Date	Target	Aircraft Dispatched	MIA	Crashed
13/14.6.44	Munich main railway station	88	4	–
14/15.6.44	Nis East rail yards	41	1	–
16/17.6.44	Timosoara rail yards	41	1	–
	Portoferraio/Portolongone	32	–	–
21/22.6.44	Ventimiglia rail yards	67	–	2
22/23.6.44	Vadoligure–Zinola refinery and rail yards	61	–	–
25/26.6.44	Shell Koolaz refinery Czepel Is.			
	Budapest	104	7	–
26/27.6.44	Aquila oil refinery Trieste	82	–	–
28/29.6.44	Giurgiu oil storage plant	105	5	–
29/30.6.44	Feuersbrunn airfield	78	2	–
1/2.7.44	Mining Danube	76	4	–
2/3.7.44	Mining Danube	10	–	–
	Bucharest–Prahova oil refinery	53	3	–[7]
5/6.7.44	Verona main rail yards	90	–	–
6/7.7.44	Feuersbrunn airfield	61	13	–[8]
8/9.7.44	Brod Bosonski oil refinery	85	–	–
10/11.7.44	Milan–Lambrate rail yards	87	1	–
12/13.7.44	Brescia rail yards	31	–	–
13/14.7.44	Milan–Lambrate rail yards	89	6	–
14/15.7.44	Brod Bosonski rail yards	81	1	–
16/17.7.44	Smederevo oil refinery	90	2	–
19/20.7.44	Fiume Romanio oil refinery	109	–	1
19/20.7.44	Pardubice oil refinery	94	5	1[9]
23/24.7.44	Bucharest–Prahova oil refinery	76	–	–[10]
24/25.7.44	Valence/La Trasorerie airfield	29	–	–
	Supply dropping Balkans	3	–	–
25/26.7.44	Supply dropping Balkans	6	–	–
26/27.7.44	Ploesti Romana Americana oil refinery	82	1	–
	Supply dropping Balkans	6	–	–
27/28.7.44	Bucharest–Prahova oil refinery	90	1	–
30/31.7.44	Mining Danube	53	–	–
3/4.8.44	Portes-les-Valences rail yards	85	–	1
7/8.8.44	Szombathely airfield	74	4	–
	Mining Danube	2	–	–
9/10.8.44	Ploesti Romana Americana oil refinery	81	11	1
10/11.8.44	Kraljevo rail yards	56	–	–
	Mining Danube	13	–	–
12/13.8.44	Hadju Boszormeny landing ground	61	–	–
13/14.8.44	Genoa	59	–	1
	Supply dropping Warsaw	20	3	–[11]

[7] Ju 88 claimed damaged.
[8] Wellington and Fw190 seen to collide over target. Ju 88 claimed shot down by a 40 Sqn Wellington crew.
[9] Bf 110 claimed destroyed and an unidentified fighter damaged.
[10] Ju 88 claimed damaged.
[11] One Liberator captain baled out over the target. The aircraft flew onto Kiev, where the rest of the crew baled out into Russian hands and were later repatriated.

Date	Target	Aircraft Dispatched	MIA	Crashed
14/15.8.44	Marseilles	56	1	–
	Supply dropping Warsaw	15	6	–
	'Mandrel' countermeasures	8	–	–
15/16.8.44	Valence/La Tresorerie airfield	51	–	–
	Supply dropping Warsaw	3	–	–
16/17.8.44	Supply dropping Warsaw	9	4	–
17/18.8.44	Ploesti-Xenia oil refinery	78	3	–
20/21.8.44	St Valentin Hermann Goering Nibelungen Werke	93	5	2
21/22.8.44	Szony oil refinery	81	3	–
22/23.8.44	Miscolo rail yards	64	3	–
25/26.8.44	Bologna main rail yards	76	–	–
	Ravenna rail yards and canal terminus	72	–	–
26/27.8.44	Pesaro	66	–	–
	Mining Danube	7	1	–
28/29.8.44	Pesara	40	–	–
	Mining Danube	10	1	–
29/30.8.44	Mining Danube	7	–	–
31.8/1.9.44	Ferrara rail yards	74	–	–[12]
1/2.9.44	Bologna North rail yards	76	–	–
2/3.9.44	Ferrara rail yards	78	2	–
4/5.9.44	Ravenna rail yards	66	–	–
5/6.9.44	Ferrara rail yards	62	–	–
	Mining Danube	12	–	–
6/7.9.44	Bologna North rail yards	67	1	–
	Mining Danube	18	–	–
9/10.9.44	Ravenna	79	–	–
10/11.9.44	Milan–Lambrate rail yards	71	–	–
	Mining Danube	29	1	–
	Supply dropping Warsaw	11	1	–
12/13.9.44	Bologna East rail yards	90	2	–
13/14.9.44	Athens airfields	98	–	–
14/15.9.44	Athens airfields	89	1	–
17/18.9.44	Brescia West rail yards	93	2	–[13]
18/19.9.44	Rimini	100	–	–
19/20.9.44	Szekesfehervar rail yards	85	–	–
20/21.9.44	Hegyeshalom rail yards	64	4	–
21/22.9.44	Supply dropping Warsaw	5	–	–
	Salonika	73	1	–
22/23.9.44	San Benedetto bridge	69	–	–
26/27.9.44	Borovnica rail viaduct	86	–	–
30.9/1.10.44	San Benedetto bridge	50	–	–
4/5.10.44	San Benedetto bridge	55	1	–
	Mining Danube	22	1	–
	Mining Khalkis	2	–	–
	Supply dropping Yugoslavia	19	–	–

[12] Two Wellingtons collided over the target, but both got back with only slight damage.
[13] A 104 Sqn Wellington returned with the rear turret mising and rear gunner gone, possibly due to a collision.

Appendix II

Date	Target	Aircraft Dispatched	MIA	Crashed
6/7.10.44	Mining Khalkis	2	–	–
9/10.10.44	Athens airfields	22	–	–
10/11.10.44	Verona East rail yards	33	2	–
11/12.10.44	Verona West rail yards	67	3	–
	Supply dropping Yugoslavia	20	–	–
12/13.10.44	Bronzolo rail yards	70	–	–
	Supply dropping North Italy	20	5	1
13/14.10.44	Szekesfehervar rail yards	82	2	–
15/16.10.44	Trieste–Opicina rail yards	65	–	–
	San Benedetto bridge	15	–	–
	Supply dropping Yugoslavia	6	–	–
16/17.10.44	Zagreb East rail yards	77	–	–
	Supply dropping Poland	6	2	–
17/18.10.44	Vincovici rail yards	82	–	–
20/21.10.44	Szombathely airfield	74	5	–
	San Benedetto bridge	15	–	–
21/22.10.44	Maribor rail yards	83	4	–[14]
	Supply dropping Yugoslavia	6	–	–
25/26.10.44	Supply dropping Yugoslavia	26	–	–
29/30.10.44	Supply dropping Yugoslavia	59	–	–
30.10/1.11.44	Supply dropping Yugoslavia	60	–	–
	Podgornica	5	–	–
1.11.44	Supply dropping Yugoslavia	72	–	–
1/2.11.44	Latisana rail bridge	12	–	–
4.11.44	Supply dropping Yugoslavia	92	–	–
4/5.11.44	Supply dropping Yugoslavia	93	–	–
	Sarajevo West rail yards	19	–	–
5.11.44	Supply dropping Yugoslavia	86	–	–
	Sarajevo West rail yards	17	–	–
5/6.11.44	Supply dropping Yugoslavia	89	2	–
6.11.44	Podgornica	72	–	–
7.11.44	Ljes bridge	4	–	–
7/8.11.44	Sarajevo West rail yards	88	1	1
8.11.44	Visegrad bridge	10	–	–
	Novi Pazar	40	–	–
8/9.11.44	Sjenica	38	–	–
10/11.11.44	Latisana bridge	8	–	–
	Supply dropping North Italy	50	1	3
11.11.44	Supply dropping North Italy	9	–	–
12.11.44	Supply dropping North Italy	55	–	–
12/13.11.44	Supply dropping North Italy	15	–	–
	Tagliamento/Cesarsa rail bridge	10	–	–
16/17.11.44	Ficarolo bridge	13	–	–
	Supply dropping North Italy	87	–	2
17.11.44	Novi Pazar–Sjenica roads	16	–	–
17/18.11.44	Udine/Campoformido airfield	39	–	2[15]
	Vincenza airfield	40	–	–

[14] Two aircrew were lost in separate incidents when their aircraft went out of control. In both cases the pilots recovered control and flew their aircraft home.
[15] Both aircraft possibly lost to enemy intruder fighters.

Date	Target	Aircraft Dispatched	MIA	Crashed
18.11.44	Sarajevo West rail yards	43	–	–
18/19.11.44	Roads in Sjenica/Proboj area	19	–	–
	Roads in Novi Pazar/Sjenica area	17	–	–
19.11.44	Visegrad bridge	43	–	–
	Roads in Novi Pazar/Sjenica area	15	–	–
	Roads in Priboj/Sjenica area	18	2	–
19/20.11.44	Podgomica bridge	70	–	–
20. 11.44	Visegrad bridge	27	–	–
	Novi Pazar/Prijepolje	14	–	–
	Visegrad/Prijepolje	17	–	–
	Visegrad/Rogatica	7	–	–
22/23.11.44	Szombathely rail yards	79	6	–
23.11.44	Uzice	33	1	–
	Rogatica	40	–	–
24/25.11.44	Supply dropping Yugoslavia	75	–	–
25.11.44	Supply dropping Yugoslavia	71	–	–
2/3.12.44	Supply dropping Yugoslavia	65	1	1
3.12.44	Bioce bridges	30	–	–
	Podgornica/Klopot	53	–	–
3/4.12.44	Supply dropping Yugoslavia	20	–	–
4.12.44	Supply dropping Yugoslavia	56	–	–
6.12.44	Supply dropping Yugoslavia	80	–	–
11/12.12.44	Supply dropping Yugoslavia	45	–	–
12.12.44	Troop and supply lift to Athens	50	–	–[16]
13.12.44	Troop and supply lift to Athens	83	–	–
15.12.44	Troop and supply lift to Athens	36	–	–
15/16.12.44	Enemy road transport Klopot/Jablan	33	–	–
16.12.44	Enemy road transport Matesevo/Kolasin	52	–	–
	Troop and supply lift to Athens	19	–	–
17.12.44	Enemy road transport Bioce/Matesevo	47	–	–
18.12.44	Enemy road transport Bioce/Matesevo	67	–	–
	Troop and supply lift to Athens	16	–	–
19.12.44	Matesevo bridge	4	–	–
	Enemy road transport Matesevo/Kolasin	37	–	–
19/20.12.44	Sarajevo West rail yards	36	–	–
20.12.44	Enemy road transport Klopot/Mcjkovac	35	–	–
	Mojkovac bridge	5	–	–
	Troop and supply lift to Athens	39	–	–
21.12.44	Enemy road transport Matesevo/Bijelo Polje	28	–	–
	Mojkovac bridge	8	–	–
	Troop and supply lift to Athens	37	–	–
22.12.44	Supply dropping Yugoslavia	47	–	–
25.12.44	Supply dropping Yugoslavia	50	–	–
26/27.12.44	Casarsa rail bridge	43	–	–
	Supply dropping Yugoslavia	41	–	–
27/28.12.44	Supply dropping Yugoslavia	38	–	–
	Piave/Susegana rail bridge	37	–	–

[16] Transport of troops and equipment at the request of the Greek government in order to quell civil unrest in the country following the liberation.

Appendix II

Date	Target	Aircraft Dispatched	MIA	Crashed
28.12.44	Supply dropping Yugoslavia	32	–	–
28/29.12.44	Casarsa rail bridge	37	–	–
29.12.44	Supply dropping Yugoslavia	30	1	–
3/4.1.45	Salcana bridge	56	–	–
	Supply dropping Yugoslavia	34	–	–
4/5.1.45	Latisana rail bridge	53	–	–
	Supply dropping Yugoslavia	17	–	–
5.1.45	Doboj South rail bridge	40	–	–
8.1.45	Supply dropping Yugoslavia	38	1	1
15/16.1.45	Supply dropping Yugoslavia	87	–	–
18.1.45	Supply dropping Yugoslavia	86	–	–
20/21.1.45	Udine rail yards	93	1	–
21.1.45	Supply dropping Yugoslavia	41	–	–
21/22.1.45	Supply dropping Yugoslavia	29	–	–
26.1.45	Supply dropping Yugoslavia	52	1	–
1.2.45	Pola naval ordnance depot	92	–	–
2.2.45	Supply dropping Yugoslavia	74	–	–
3.2.45	Supply dropping Yugoslavia	73	1	–
4.2.45	Supply dropping Yugoslavia	69	–	4
7.2.45	Supply dropping Yugoslavia	55	–	–
8/9/2.45	Verona West rail yards	78	–	–
12/13.2.45	Verona West rail yards	73	–	–
13/14.2.45	Graz Main rail yards	65	–	–
14.2.45	Supply dropping Yugoslavia	64	–	–
15.2.45	Pola naval ordnance depot	72	–	–
16.2.45	Fiume naval base	71	–	–
17.2.45	Trieste dockyard	68	–	–
20.2.45	Udine rail yards	77	–	–
21.2.45	Pola naval ordnance depot	73	1	–
22/23.2.45	Padua North-East rail yards	69	–	–
23/24.2.45	Verona West rail yards	68	–	–
24/25.2.45	Brescia east rail yards	74	–	–
25/26.2.45	Supply dropping Yugoslavia	63	–	–
27/28.2.45	Verona West rail yards	81	–	–
1.3.45	Arsa coal wharves	51	–	–
2/3.3.45	Verona East rail yards	77	1	–
3/4.3.45	Mining Venice	8	–	–
	Mining Pola	5	–	–
	Porto Marghera oil storage complex	28	–	–
	Pola naval ordnance depot	38	–	–
4/5.3.45	Casarsa rail yards	51	–	–
5/6.3.45	Graz rail yards	63	2	–
7/8.3.45	Genoa rail yards	37	–	–
	Udine rail yards	38	1	–
9/10.3.45	Verona–Parona rail bridge	62	–	–
11/12.3.45	Verona East rail yards	72	–	–
12/13.3.45	Padua North-East rail yards	69	–	–
13/14.3.45	Treviso North-East rail yards	69	–	–
15.3.45	Supply dropping Yugoslavia	60	–	–
16.3.45	Monfalcone naval base	61	–	–

Date	Target	Aircraft Dispatched	MIA	Crashed
18/19.3.45	Vincenza rail yards	73	–	–
19/20.3.45	Bruck rail yards	78	1	–
20/21.3.45	Pragersko rail yards	73	–	–
21/22.3.45	Novska rail yards	78	–	–
22/23.3.45	Villach North rail yards	75	1	–
23/24.3.45	St Veit East rail yards	51	–	–
24/25.3.45	Dobova rail yards	51	–	–
25/26.3.45	Villach North rail yards	50	1	–
31/1.4.45	Graz rail yards	87	1	–
1.4.45	Arsa coal wharves	56	–	–
2/3.4.45	Trento rail yards	82	–	–
3/4.4.45	Novska rail yards	63	–	–
4/5.4.45	Brescia West rail yards	79	–	2
5.4.45	Monfalcone shipyards	48	–	–
8/9.4.45	Trento rail yards	57	–	–
9/10.4.45	Army Co-operation Santerno river	95	–	–
10/11.4.45	Innsbruck Railway Station and rail yards	56	–	–
11/12.4.45	Army Co-operation Lake Bastia	86	–	–
12/13.4.45	Army Co-operation Argenta	57	–	–
13/14.4.45	Army Co-operation Portomaggiore	71	–	–
15/16.4.45	Villach North rail yards	90	1	–
16/17.4.45	Caselecchio	87	–	–
17/18.4.45	Portomaggiore	50	–	–
19/20.4.45	Malalbergo	71	–	–
20/21.4.45	Verona–Perona bridge	57	–	–
23/24.4.45	Verona–Perona bridge	57	–	–
25/26.4.45	Freilassing rail yards	92	–	–
7.5.45	Supply to Rivolto landing ground	22	–	–

Leaflet operations totalled 128 sorties between 1 February 1944 and 8 May 1945. Two aircraft failed to return, a Wellington on 2/3 July 1944 and a Liberator on 21/22 September 1944. Two further aircraft crashed on return; a Wellington on 24/25 May 1944 (two crew killed) and a Liberator on 12/13 September 1944 (crew safe).

Summary
In the fifteen months from February 1944 to May1945, there were 431 possible days/nights for operations – 205 Group flew on 332 of them. 416 operations were carried out with the loss of 215 aircraft missing and 35 which crashed near their bases. It is estimated that well over1,400 airmen were lost.

Appendix III

Operations of Maurice Lihou,

Sergeant Pilot, 633080

37 Squadron

Date	Target	Comment	Bomb Load	A/C	Missing	Crashed
2/3.3.44	Orbetello	2nd pilot	9×500	16	0	0
11/12.3.44	Genoa	2nd pilot	Flares	66	0	0
15/16.3.44	Sofia	2nd pilot	9×500	67	1	10
22/23.3.44	Padua	Captain	9×500	82	0	0
24/25.3.44	Sofia	Landed Crotone	6×500	77	3	1
26/27.3.44	Vicenza		1×4000	55	0	0
28/29.3.44	Milan		9×500	78	0	0
1/2.4.44	Piombino		9×500	16	0	0
2/3.4.44	Vicenza		9×500	55	0	0
3/4.4.44	Budapest		6×500	87	5	0
12/13.4.44	Danube	Minelaying	2×1000	34	0	0
14/15.4.44	Leghorn		9×500	24	0	0
16/17.4.44	Budapest		9×500	64	2	1
19/20.4.44	San Stefano		9×500	24	0	0
23/24.4.44	San Stefano		1×4000	24	0	0
2/3.5.44	Genoa		9×500	6	0	0
3/4.5.44	Bucharest		3×500&2×250	62	1	4
5/6.5.44	Campina		3×500&2×250	43	3	0
7/8.5.44	Bucharest		3×500&2×250	61	6	0
22/23.5.44	Ferentino		9×500	41	1	0
24/25.5.44	Valmontone	Lightning strike	–	65	1	0
26/26.5.44	Viterbo		9×500	55	0	0
29/30.5.44	Feuersbrunn		12×250	38	1	0
31.5/1.6.44	Danube	Minelaying	2×1000	52	1	0
1/2.6.44	Szolnok	Burst hydraulics	–	50	0	0
3/4.6.44	Ostia Bridge		6×500	50	0	0

Date	Target	Comment	Bomb Load	A/C	Missing	Crashed
6/7.6.44	Viterbo		9×500	34	0	0
7/8.6.44	Orvieto		1×4000	18	0	0
9/10.6.44	Trieste		1×4000	60	1	0
11/12.6.44	Kalova	Lost	–	50	1	0
13/14.6.44	Munich	Wessling bombed	6×500	88	4	0
16/17.6.44	Portoferraio	Combined op	1×4000	32	0	0
21/22.6.44	Ventimiglia		6×500	67	2	0
25/26.6.44	Budapest		6×500	104	7	0
29/30.6.44	Feuersbrunn		2×250	78	2	0
1/2.7.44	Danube	Minelaying	2× 1600	76	4	0
6/7.7.44	Feuersbrunn		6×500	61	13	0
8/9.7.44	Brod		9×500	85	0	0
10/11.7.44	Milan		9×500	87	1	0

40 Squadron

Date	Target	Comment	Bomb Load	A/C	Missing	Crashed
14.2.45	Tuzla	Engine failure	–	64	0	0
16.2.45	Fiume	9×500&3×250	Mixed	71	0	0
17.2.45	Trieste	9×500&3×250	Mixed	68	0	0
20.2.45	Udine	9×500&3×250	Mixed	77	0	0
21.2.45	Pola	9×500&3×250	Mixed	73	1	0
24/25.2.45	Brescia	9×500&3×250	Mixed	74	0	0
25/26.2.45	Icarus	Supply drop	–	63	0	0
27/28.2.45	Verona		2×2000	81	0	0
11/12.3.45	Verona	Engine failure	–	72	0	0
12/13.3.45	Padua	9×500&3×250	Mixed	69	0	0
13/14.3.45	Treviso	Last raid*	1×4000	69	0	0

* This was also the last raid by Wellingtons in the European Theatre of War.

INDEX

The index is arranged alphabetically except for entries under the author's name, which are in chronological order. Page numbers in *italics* refer to illustrations.